Films and Feelings

Films and Feelings

RAYMOND DURGNAT

THE M. I. T. PRESS

Massachusetts Institute of Technology
Cambridge, Massachusetts

First published in mcmlxvii
by Faber and Faber Limited
24 Russell Square London WC1
Printed in Great Britain by
Latimer Trend & Co Ltd Plymouth

Library of Congress Catalog Card Number: 67–20174

Acknowledgements

The chapters on Cinema Style are based on a Postgraduate research thesis prepared under the auspices of the Department of Film at the Slade School of Fine Art, University College, London, under Thorold Dickinson.

They were first published in *Films and Filming* from December 1964 to April 1965. The chapter on 'Auteurs and Dream Factories' also appeared in *Projektio*, 1966, No. 2. 'Architecture In, and Of, The Movies' appeared in *The Architectural Review* for March 1965, and 'The Cinema's Art Gallery' in *The Burlington Magazine* for February 1967.

'Inside Norman Bates' first appeared in *Films and Filming* for March 1962 and in *Sexus Eros Kino*, published by Carl Schunemann Verlag in Germany in 1964. 'A Great Defect' appeared in *Films and Filming* for October 1963. 'The Wedding of Poetry and Pulp' appeared in *Midi-Minuit Fantastique* for February 1967. Revisions and expansions have been made for their publication in volume form.

My warmest thanks are due to Thorold Dickinson for making so much of his wide experience of every aspect of movies available to me during our discussions; but the analyses, observations and opinions expressed are entirely the author's own. I should also like to thank Sir William Coldstream, Benedict Nicholson, J. M. Richards and Peter Baker, for leaving me the reprint rights of material prepared in the first place for them. Special thanks also are due to Robin Bean of *Films and Filming*, John Kobal and Michel Caen for their help in procuring illustrations.

ACKNOWLEDGEMENTS

The still from *The Big Sleep* is by courtesy of Warner Brothers; that from *The Man with the Golden Arm* by courtesy of United Artists; that from *This Island Earth* by courtesy of Universal-International-Rank.

Contents

Illustrations

Plates between pages 48 *and* 49

Introduction

Beyond what interest it may possess as a collection of different cinematic topics, this text is offered also as a basis for re-exploring an art-form which seems to pose certain aesthetic problems more insistently than other media have done.

Apart from the aesthetic questions, approached in the opening chapters on cinema style, a second source of confusion lies in the sharpness with which, for various historical and economic reasons, the medium generates conflicts between its function as an 'art form' and its function as an entertainment 'dream factory'.

These conflicts in turn have helped to confuse other problems with which the sincere screen artist is faced. Film criticism tends to assume a sophisticated spectator. But in James Agate's words, 'The film critic wants a picture to be so good that it will stand up to educated taste, whereas the aim of the film producer is to produce something which cannot be defeated by lack of taste.' To what extent does criticism habitually dismiss as 'bad' art films which are 'coarse-grained'—but authentic and rewarding— art—and so falsify its view of the medium?

All these confusions are further compounded by the controversies and tensions existing within the schools of aesthetic opinion. The possibilities of misunderstanding are exemplified, but by no means exhausted, by the following contrast.

Denys Thompson urges a schoolmasters' conference that 'the full weight of the grammar school ethos must be directed against the enticements of the mass media' (in which the popular cinema is obviously included) while Carl Foreman remarks, 'I must say that one of the things we suffer from most is the spate of snob critics with no equipment other than the flip approach and the total lack of knowledge. By now one would have thought that the game of "let's hit Hollywood" had become a bore, but the trouble is that almost anyone can play it, and still pass for an intellectual.'

There thus seemed room for a book which, instead of restricting itself to one particular province of the cinema, and, resisting the temptation to argue out a reconciliatory aesthetic (which could hardly be done in the space, since what we lack is sufficient sphere of experience common to the various approaches), would instead try to indicate just such a sphere of experience out of which an aesthetic could subsequently be developed. And this is what we attempt to do here; to find not only some 'lowest common denominators', but also some 'highest common factors' of taste, and to do so, less by theory, than by exploring specific films.

It will be noticed that while 'sociological' and 'Freudian' undertones are explored, they are not offered as supplanting what is conventionally meant by 'personal' and 'conscious' spheres of meaning.

Thus our first part (Chaps. 1–7) constitutes, not a map, but a series of signposts, related to the question of film style, and to a rephrasing of that sempiternal distinction between 'content' and 'style' which, given a special sharpness by the film's aesthetic mixtures, has so long bedevilled film criticism.

Our second part (Chaps. 8–12) endeavours to reveal the close connection between the content of cinema entertainment and certain sociological facets. It has long been accepted that one of the interests of works of art is their expression, and/or criticism, of a *zeitgeist*. Here we look at one aspect of the popular cinema, the star system, and show how, alongside its obvious 'escapism', it also expresses the realities from which it escapes.

The third part considers some distinctions between the 'academic' aesthetic (more accurately: assumptions easily made by critics with a university background when they turn to the cinema), and idioms which popular films adopt to contact relatively uneducated audiences.

Many 'academic' critics, while meeting with a generous fair-mindedness different opinion emanating from their own cultural 'strata', seem to fear, when invited to adjust some ideas so as to include rather than to dismiss the often rougher but no less generous responses of the 'uneducated' public, that they are being asked to abjure the special responsiveness which is in itself a cultural achievement, and which has about it just a little of 'spilled religion' (not forgetting 'displaced snobbery'), and to surrender to the mob and to the moguls.

Though for obvious reasons the bias of tone in this volume is in the direction of justifying the 'popular' aesthetic as against certain assumptions in 'high culture', these justifications are not intended to carry any wider implications, and still less are they intended to question the meaningfulness of distinctions between 'good' and 'bad'. Clearly, the suggestion is that some common types of evaluation may need to be revised, but this dissent over specific judgements and principles is in no way an attack on standards as such.

It is surprisingly easy so to deploy certain exegetical techniques as to make extremely simple and dreary works of art sound interesting, but I've 'played the game' here by not writing in an enthusiastic or involved way about any film which I didn't find involving me in a genuine 'artistic' experience. This isn't to claim that *Johnny Guitar* (for example) is a masterpiece; my point here is that it typifies the interesting dramatic and moral points, and 'resonance', of a competently made film.

Nor am I saying that every 'point' made in the course of these analyses has been consciously noted by the average, or indeed by any, spectator. In this respect I have followed current critical practice, of assuming that 'a work of art may communicate before it is understood', that it may communicate even when it is misunderstood. A discussion of the assumption is a subject for a book in itself, but I should perhaps say the assumption seems to me incorrect in so far as it is taken to mean that all works of art communicate before being understood, or that such communication is a substitute for understanding. Here I have tried to make explicit (understood) only those points which seem to me relevant to, part of, communication, which contribute to the general resonance, richness and shock of a film. It's probably inevitable that exegeses will be coloured by the personality of the critic, and I am secretly rather relieved about my inability to be an objective interpretation machine. The accounts and summaries offered here are my own, not those of Mr. and Mrs. Bloggs, whose responses, though possibly very different from, are no less significant than, these. However, I have tried to offer interpretations which are as fair and as true to each film's text and 'home culture' as I could contrive, in the hope that they would be better than nothing. The study of the 'range of responses' which are compatible with a 'correct' reading of a film would be extremely interesting, but it's first necessary to have established some common 'sphere of experience'.

Part One

PUTTING ON THE STYLE

1 · The Mongrel Muse

The great difficulty in talking about cinema style is that the cinema is a *potpourri* of art forms, sharing elements in common with each, but weaving them into a pattern of its own.

In that it centres on actors, on the human form, it comes closest to the theatre. In its origin, too, it is associated with theatrical forms (the 'music hall' act). But it is 'deficient' theatre, for the show lacks the actor's presence. Instead of one person physically, constantly, present here and nowhere else in the world, we have only a Polyfoto presence, a pack of images, changing in shape and size—half-way to abstraction.

The cinema can compensate in other ways for its shortcomings in this. It can call on all the resources of photography. It can dispense with the human person altogether (the documentary) or merge him with the landscape (the Western). Its sense of place, in flexibility and realism far beyond theatrical possibility, confers on it something of the novel's narrative fluidity.

But compared with the novel its way with words, and therefore with ideas, is clumsy. The talkie's words take second place to the visual presentation of reality. Film visuals can show a 'lame old black cat sitting on a worn grey mat'. Or a 'playful tabby stretched out on a mat with a pattern of roses on it'. But they can't say, simply, 'the cat sat on the mat'. They can show a beautiful statue in sun, then in rain, then in snow, but they can't say simply, 'A thing of beauty is a joy for ever.' Their powers of abstraction are limited. They can't match the writer's swift, deft way with metaphors. Film is a reasonably good medium for persuading, but it's a very clumsy one for arguing. And by means of words, which present objective reality through ideas, the novelist can mix visual reality and ideas in a rich, intimate way. Here the cinema is infinitely poorer.

Yet its literary poverty is compensated by its visual richness. It is a visual art, like painting. In the words of Marcel Carné, 'One must compose images as the old masters did their canvases, with the same preoccupation with effect and expression. Cinema images have the same needs.' The film critic will often need to use the vocabulary of the visual arts rather than of literary criticism.

In sensitivity of line, tone, form and other plastic qualities the ciné-camera is, however, vastly inferior to the painter's brush. The very best cartoons, like Hector Hoppin's and Anthony Gross's *Joie de Vivre* (1934) may have something of the artist's freedom of line, but the cartoon isn't after all the mainstream of cinema.

The photographic cinema can compensate for its deficiences here by its theatrical-narrative interest. And by the visual possibilities opened to it by its being a *succession* of images, in *movement*. Here it has its own possibilities of plastic, formal nuance and organization.

Indeed, it relates here to music and the visual arts at the same time. The visual art of architecture has been described as 'frozen music'—meaning that just as architecture is shapes and structures and tensions standing static in space, music is musical shapes and structures and tensions in time. It's true that there is a certain *time* element in architecture (you walk past a façade, or through an arch), just as there is a 'space' element moving in music (you are conscious of things happening 'simultaneously', in counterpoint). But these are secondary—'time' in architecture is reversible (few buildings are based, like symphonies, on a beginning, a middle and an end). And 'space' in music is a result, rather than a determinant, of form. Only the film is shapes and structures and tensions both in space (the image) *and* in time. Only the film synchronizes, interweaves, visual and musical shapes (picture and soundtrack). Norman MacLaren's *Begone Dull Care* (1949) represents the 'missing link' between painting and music. It shows us visual colours and patterns flashing, dancing, quivering in counterpoint to the Oscar Peterson Quartet.

Thus the cinema combines elements from the various arts into its own synthesis. It can also co-opt the various forms as a whole. The film adds words to pictures to music. As Resnais's camera roams over the surface of Picasso's *Guernica*, 1949 (breaking it down into a *sequence* of smaller images, that is, converting space into time), the commentator intones, first, statistics, then, a poem of Paul Eluard's

—thus making a new synthesis of two art forms. Of course, the film will not have the emotional impact of painting *added to* the poem—for so long as the spectator is attending to both, he cannot pay full attention, or respond with his full power, to either.

Elements from different media may be blended in many different ways. One of the most moving moments of Jean Renoir's *Partie de Campagne* (1936) has the camera tracking along a river stippled by raindrops, while a girl sings a wordless song. In Resnais's *Hiroshima Mon Amour* (1959) the camera tracks down streets and corridors while Riva's voice overlaid summarizes her thoughts—and Resnais experimented, matching different reading speeds to different tracking speeds, before finding the combination of speeds which was emotionally just 'right'.

The cinema is not the only 'art of mixed arts'. The opera is notoriously a *beau monstre*, a (sometimes rather absurd) blend of music and theatre. The theatre itself is a mixture of acting, lighting and text. 'Total theatre' is a blend of absolutely everything, taking even cinematic sequences under its wing. The cinema is another such synthesis of the arts.

Ever since the cinema began, aestheticians have sought to define 'pure' cinema, the 'essence' of cinema. In vain. The cinema's only 'purity' is the way in which it combines diverse elements into its own 'impure' whole. Its 'essence' is that it makes them interact, that it integrates other art forms, that it exists 'between' and 'across' their boundaries. It is cruder and inferior to every other art form on that art form's 'home ground'. But it repairs its deficiencies, and acquires its own dignity, by being a mixture.

The film medium depends on a blend of different media, and various films blend them in different proportions. A few films depend principally on criteria analogous to those one would bring to a short story or a novel. Thus for example Joseph L. Mankiewicz's *A Letter to Three Wives* (1948) is to a great extent a 'text' film. The films of Eisenstein require more 'painterly' critical descriptions than those of, say, Howard Hawks. Many films—Garbo's—can only be considered as 'star' performances, and one responds as one would to a 'star' performance in the theatre. The eloquence of Marcel Marceau, of Charles Chaplin, and less obviously Emil Jannings, lies in acting so stylized, so rhythmic, as to be nearer 'mime' than 'realistic' acting. Is Luis Bunuel's and Salvador Dali's *Un Chien Andalou* (1928) a Surrealist 'poem' (because of its 'symbolic meanings') or is it a Surrealist 'painting' (because it is a set of pictures?). An 'abstract' film like Norman MacLaren's *Begone Dull Care* accepts only those criteria that apply to abstract painting, linked with others that apply to music.

Yet each of these films is a mixture of the arts. Each of these films is 'pure' film.

Because there are so many varieties of film it is easy for the best-intentioned spectator to mistake a film's language. In *Strike* (1923) Eisenstein shows the Tsarist cavalry cutting down strikers with drawn sabres. To enhance the effect he intersperses the sequence with shots of a bull being slaughtered and hacked up in an abattoir. Some spectators find that the shots of the bull intensify the horror, while others, on the contrary, find that they distract from it. The difference seems to lie in the way the spectators' minds work. Some spectators get passionately concerned with the strikers and the cavalry. This action is completely distinct in their mind from the bull, which only interrupts, and so decreases, the tension. Others, presumably those who look at film *style* as such rather than identifying with the people *in* the film, are quicker to make the 'intellectual' connection: the bull=the crowd, the proletariat = cattle, people= lumps of meat. Many filmgoers today find that such metaphors in Russian silent films weaken rather than strengthen, especially when, unused to the thought and conventions of the time, we mistake a metaphor for a change of scene. Pudovkin means us to understand that 'the prisoner's joy is expressed by the breaking of the ice'. Instead we may assume a change of scene and get completely confused as to who's where. 'He was in his cell, now he seems to be standing by the riverside, has he been let out? or is this a dream? or are we with someone else altogether?' By the time we work it out, the film's gone as cold as a fish on the slab.

Similarly a spectator used to looking for detailed psychology, realistic acting, location settings, and so on, may be quite at sea with films whose subtleties are entirely visual ones. Most film critics (outside Italy) have a literary background, and the fact that films, like novels, tell stories, reinforces their tendency to consider the 'core' of film as being somehow 'literary'. Their indebtedness to a (waning) fashion *in* literary criticism usually leads to the further assumption that the 'core' of literature is 'psychological insights'—exact definition and motives, and so on. To these displaced persons a film's visual qualities are only 'style'. The documentarists' influence on film criticism completes the long-dominant emphasis on literary qualities, psychological realism, and social consciousness.

On the other hand, it was also apparent that the dominating creative 'charge' of many films was the director's, rather than the writer's or the actor's. So here was a paradox: the *quality* of a film depended less on the writers and actors, who one might have expected to contribute the literary-psychological interest, than on a man whose province was that of 'visuals' and 'style'. 'Visual' directors like Eisenstein, Murnau and Dreyer retained their prestige as 'geniuses' less, one feels, because these critics really understood or thrilled to their films, than before they were protected by an aura of 'prestige'. The critics of, for example, *Sight and Sound* whom, for all their individual differences, it is reasonable to consider as a team with a common attitude, typify a fading English critical orthodoxy, with all its confusions and contradictions—summarizable as: 'literary content' and 'style' are either indistinguishable or the same thing but the first is emphatically more important than the second.

This part attempts to offer some new ideas, to revive some very old ones which fell into disuse when the 'literary content' school acquired their stranglehold on film criticism, and to revitalize principles to which it consents in theory but obscures in practice. Space, unfortunately, forbids us from examining each point from as many angles as one would like to. It offers only a series of signposts, rather than a map.

Let us first look at the implications of the antithesis of 'content' and 'style'. Among film critics 'content' is equated with 'literary content', that is, anything in a film which a novelist could fairly easily put into words if he were writing 'the book of the film'. And 'style' becomes, virtually, anything which isn't 'content'.

In the other arts the uses of the word 'style' are rather different. In painting 'literary content' is obviously of minor importance, while much great music is absolutely devoid of all 'literary content' whatsoever. By this definition abstract paintings and symphonies would be 'pure' style, altogether devoid of meaning—and importance? Clearly then there must be a sense in which 'style=content'.

The opening definition of 'style' in *The Concise O.E.D.* is: 'Manner of writing, speaking or doing . . . as opposed to the matter to be expressed or thing done.' In other words, an artist's 'style' is his answer to the problems with which he is faced in the course of creating his work of art. On the one hand, he has a certain intention, a certain 'vision' or 'drive', an experience to communicate (even if he isn't himself too sure in his conscious mind of exactly what it is). Similarly, the film director has a scene in a script, or a certain plot point to make. This scene is built around this point, so he thinks of it, for a while, as what the scene 'contains', his 'content'. But his sense of craftsmanship, certain practical exigencies, the need for a slick, easy flow of ideas across the screen, etc., confront him with various practical problems. Should he make the actor walk into shot? or should he pan the camera to pick up the actor? There may be no particular reason for his choice, except, in the case of a dull director, habit or convention, or, in the case of an original director, some intuitive, inexplicable preference. It just feels right to him—more smooth, more elegant, more lively than other possibilities. That choice is his 'personal' style. The writer, the actor, the cameraman, the director, will each have such a personal style of his own—favourite, intuitive, unexamined ways of doing things. Often he will be quite unaware that other solutions would have been possible. The director, as *integrator* of everybody's work, has more 'stylistic' problems than anyone else; hence his 'style' usually flavours the film.

Now let us look at 'style' in a medium other than the cinema. Two actors will declaim Shakespeare's words ('content') in altogether different ways ('style'). One makes Hamlet a warrior-hero who can't make up his mind. The other makes him a neurotic intellectual who can't steel himself to action. The 'literary content' is exactly the same but the 'theatrical content' (gesture, voice) is altogether different. So different that it transforms the meaning of the text. Here, the style is just as much a part of the content as the 'content'. In fact much of what film critics call 'literary content' is in fact 'theatrical content', depending less on the text than on acting and staging, and, to this extent, the ordinary fiction film is nearer the theatre than literature.

Of course, not all features of 'style' make much difference to the 'content'. It may make no difference whatsoever whether an actor lifts his left eyebrow before or after he waggles his right finger-tip. This is a change of 'content' too, but only a minor one.

From this definition, the question whether style is more important than content is a misleading one. Style is simply those pieces of content which arise out of the way the artist makes his basic points. These may (as often in painting and poetry) be only a pretext, a wire on which to 'thread the beads'. If style is 'manner of doing', then we can say that the way a thing is done is often a way of doing a different thing. To say 'sorry' *superciliously* is doing a different thing from saying 'sorry' courteously or servilely, etc. Certain tones of voice make 'sorry' mean: 'Look where you're going, you clumsy imbecile.' 'It ain't what you do it's the way that you do it.' 'Le style, c'est l'homme.'

Let us look at one or two screen examples. Here are two frame-stills from Dreyer's *La Passion de Jeanne d'Arc*, 1928 (Plates 1 and 2). In a sense, they both have the same 'content'—Joan (our identification-figure) is being bullied. In general composition, both shots have marked similarities. But they also have many differences. In each case her tormentors have different faces and characters, so that the kind of threat is very different. The spatial relationships are an important part of the human relationships. Thus, in the second shot the perpendicular inquisitor towers gaunt, cold, dry as a cliff. The other shot conveys a sense of boiling wrath, of directed attack. Joan's different postures (the turn and tension of her neck) express different feelings. The content is in the style.

Suppose a director has filmed four takes of the same scene which shows an argument between two equally sympathetic characters. Take (1) shows the scene as a series of 'reverse angles' (alternating full-face close-ups). Take (2) is a continuous two-shot of two profiles. Take (3) shows B's full face, but the back of A's head prominent on the screen. Take (4) is an 'over-shoulder' of A, with B's head not very obtrusively present over to one side of the screen. In (1) we will feel each person's responses intensely during *his* close-up, and the other's responses will be temporarily soft-pedalled, even forgotten; until we return to him with a little 'shock'. Our identifications alternate. In (2) we see and feel both responses simultaneously. Our reaction to A's words is continuously modified by B's reaction, which may be sceptical or pitying. We feel a smoother, softer, mixture of feelings. In (3) with the back of A's head, almost in the middle of the frame, we will be very conscious of his constant 'obstruction'; he is a real force, but an enigmatic one. In (4) we may almost be unaware of him and be aware mainly of A's feelings—although the vague presence of B makes for a more complicated composition and 'feel' than a mere close-up.

Are these differences of style, or of content? Both. And the differences are not a matter of *information provided* about the characters so much as of *the spectator's participation* in their feelings.

The distinction between '*literary* content' and 'visual style' is particularly misguided because even in the work of literature much of the 'content' comes from the 'style'. Suppose we call someone 'slow but thorough' we feel this is, on the whole, a compliment. His slowness is a trifling disadvantage, the last word acts as a summing-up, an assertion of his value. But if we call him 'thorough but slow' there is an implication of criticism. The ideas and the words are exactly the same—but to change their order is like inserting some invisible words. One order says: 'We can rely on him.' The other: 'He should pull his socks up.' More often, literary 'style' is a matter of choosing different words—different ideas, different content. My friends are 'unfaltering', my enemies are 'obstinate'. I show 'intensity of purpose', you are a 'fanatic'. Our friends are 'original', our rivals 'eccentric'. Writers show such concern over points of 'style' (e.g. *le mot juste*) because of their concern over points of 'content'.

Such nuances of order, sound (especially in poetry), vocabulary, and so on, don't just *colour* the 'content' of a passage. They *constitute* its content. The passage may be badly written, but of interest as a description of an interesting event—traffic accident, a battle or a riot. But this event is not its 'literary content'. It's only the *subject*. Another passage may describe an apparently boring event, but bring to it a wealth of ideas and insights. And in this case we may speak of the author's 'style' as enlivening a banal 'content'. But this wealth of ideas and insights isn't 'mere' style—it is 'content'. And, here, to ask whether style or content is more important is like asking whether water is more important than $H_2 0$. The words are different, the things's the same, which phrase one uses depends on one's context and emphasis. It is not the importance of their subjects, but the richness of their 'content-style' which distinguishes good artists from mediocre ones.

Another quite common and useful sense of the word 'style' is to refer to the whole mass of details which go into a film, but which happen to be confusing and difficult to describe in words. Thus a *specific* reaction—horror, joy, etc.—tends to be called 'content' because it is easy to define, it offers a nice, solid idea to lean on. On the other hand, an actor's postures, gestures, smiles, the quality of his glance, the tension of his facial muscles, the director's spatial relationships, the tones of grey caught by the cameraman, all these may be very eloquent and forceful in communicating experience (and so are 'content'). But because it is difficult to analyse or explain their exact meaning in words they tend to be referred to, vaguely, as 'style'. But here again 'content' and 'style' are indissoluble. In fact, here, the 'content'—horror, joy—is a spectator's deduction from what the screen actually contains. This is why spectators so often disagree on what a film's content is. The screen contains the style, but not the *content*, which is the spectator's deduction, and not contained on the *screen* at all!

If we speak of an artist's 'style' as being as individual as his face or his finger-prints, it is because he tends to bring similar insights and details to every subject which he treats. Dreyer's style is the visual expression of certain attitudes, interests and feelings which arise in him whether his subject is *La Passion de Jeanne d'Arc*, *Vampyr* (1932) or the naughty carry-ons of *The Parson's Widow* (1921). In this sense, 'content- style' is the quintessence of an artist—although often his choice of subject also is determined by his personality. Thus personal 'style' is a matter, not of mere visual mannerisms, but of plot, characterization, and so on. For example, King Vidor's heroines are tomboys expertly weilding shotguns in *Duel in the Sun* (1946), *Beyond the Forest* (1949) and *Ruby Gentry* (1952), and there are reminiscent traits of forceful independence in the heroines of *The Big Parade* (1925), *The Fountainhead* (1947), *Man Without a Star* (1955) and *Solomon and Sheba* (1959). His heroines' *style* is an important part of King Vidor's vision of the world. (Always when we speak of an artist's 'personal style' we might as well speak of his 'recurrent content'.)

In a sense, the total content of a film is made up of a vast array of details. But the meaning of each detail is heavily influenced by the context. For example, Karel Reisz writes '. . . the discreet distance which Ophuls' camera keeps from his players reflects a lack of identification', and Andrew Sarris '. . . Bunuel's . . . camera has always viewed his characters from a middle distance, too close for cosmic groupings and too far away for self-identification. Normally, this would make his films cold and his point of view detached. . . .'

These are fair enough as critical approximations, but it would certainly be wrong to conclude that identification is weak without a high proportion of close-ups. Silent films used far fewer close-ups than films of the 40's, and cinemascope Westerns use fewer again, but this has little effect on identification, compared with the main determinant, which is the spectator's affinities of emotion, experience and moral sympathy with the screen characters (their 'resonance' with him). Further, artists who don't know where the spectators' sympathies lie, how to make them chop and change from one character to another, how to create the anxious tensions and suspense of 'split sympathy', won't stay out of the bankruptcy court very long.

Where a film has a very popular star, the spectators so keep their eyes glued on him that even when he's in long-shot *physically*, he's in close-up *psychologically*. This is not to say that camera distance has no importance; only that it is only one of many elements of style-and-content working simultaneously. I'd suggest that the only partial identification made by most spectators when seeing a Bunuel film for the first time is mainly due to the fact that his characters are very complex individuals, and presented with a certain mystery. Seeing *El* (1953) for the first time, my principal emotion was one of fascination, of passionate curiosity; but at a second viewing, when the film's main pattern had been understood, a much stronger identification with the characters was possible. In Ophuls (and here space forces one to schematize) a purpose of the long-shots is to show the characters in their décor (close-ups tend to 'abolish' décor). His characters are 'glimpsed' amid their richly period setting, there is a quality of *nostalgia*. But the significance of 'style' can never be defined exactly, any more than the meaning of a line of poetry can be defined exactly, not only because any work of art worth having arouses a complex chord of emotions, but because different spectators' minds work in different ways (as we saw in the case of *Strike*).

One or two further examples may make our point clearer. When the camera tracks forward swiftly (as in, say, a musical number) the spectator often feels a mild exhilaration, as if he in his seat were gliding effortlessly through the action. There is a general sense of well-being, of dynamic excitement. But in Truffaut's *Jules et Jim* (1961) the helicopter skims swiftly over a hilly landscape—and a hill rearing up before us suddenly reveals a sheer drop on the other side. Here any 'exhilaration' is modified by the turbulence of the landscape, and killed by the 'sudden drop'. In the same way, the film is about the turbulence and unsteadiness of human relationships (Jeanne Moreau's song: 'chaqu'vn pour soi et hop parti—c'est le tourbillon de la vie'). In the same film, there is a sense of chaos, of confusion, when, seen from the helicopter, the train carrying one of the *ménage-à-trois* steams out of the country station. The last scenes of Joshua Logan's *Picnic* (1954) have a similar theme—a train seen from a helicopter, carrying William Holden away from Kim Novak. But the whole tone is different. Not only is the landscape different (level), but the dramatic context is different—this time the lovers are determined not to be separated for long. There is no sense of chaos—our helicopter shot is, so to speak, a 'fate's eye view', a map revealing that their paths will cross. It is the exact opposite of the 'similar' effect in *Jules et Jim*.

Within the general framework of a two-shot many different 'spatial relationships' are possible. In *The Magnificent Ambersons* (1942) Welles expertly puts his characters in tough, angular, separated compositions, creating an effect of loneliness-by-antagonistic-wills. In Renoir's *La Règle du Jeu* (1939), more fluent and informal arrangements leave plenty of space for the characters to move around, to change their minds, to remain individuals while being members of free and easy groupings.

Suppose a film ends with the camera tracking back from the lovers embracing alone on the beach. This may mean 'how tiny and unprotected they are' or 'how frail and futile their love' or 'the whole wide world is theirs' or 'this is the moment of destiny' (for plan views can suggest a 'God's-eye-view') or 'Good-bye, good-bye', depending on which emotions are floating about in the spectator's mind as a result of the rest of the film. Hence style is essentially a matter of intuition. There is no possibility whatsoever of an 'objective', 'scientific' analysis of film style—or of 'film' content. It is worse than useless to attempt to watch a film with one's intellect alone, trying to explain its effect in terms of one or two points of style. Few films yield any worthwhile meaning unless watched with a genuine interest in the range of feelings and meanings it suggests. To any work of art one must bring one's own experience if one is to take from it its experience. Indeed, professional film makers have a point when they accuse film 'highbrows' of an almost fetishistic attention to whichever aspect of style happens to be in intellectual fashion. In the 20's it was *Caligari* décor, from *Potemkin* (1925) on it was montage and it was dubious whether cinema art could survive the hideous barbarism of the spoken word, in the 40's it was camera angles and location photography, and today it's camera movements.

The reputation (rather than direct influence) of *Cahiers du Cinema* and of its late doyen, André Bazin, has recently been goading British critics to a new interest in style and theory. Yet a certain 'fetishism' often cramps Bazin's intelligence. For example, writing about William Wyler's *The Little Foxes* (1941) and *The Best Years of Our Lives* (1947) Bazin calls their deep focus more 'democratic' than shallow-focus because it enables the director to have more important characters on the screen simultaneously, thus permitting the spectator to choose whichever character he will look at and identify with. Yet in these films Wyler had effectively determined which characters the spectators would be interested in, by the moral and emotional traits with which he endowed them, and which he balances one against the other with just as much care and control as do such shallow-focus films as *Johnny Guitar* or *This Island Earth*, as we shall show later. Within the limits of their tendencies to moral schematism, tendencies from which Wyler is not exempt, American directors can calculate audience sympathies to the nth decimal place, with a finesse which, given the cultural diversity of their audience, is a far from inconsiderable 'classicism'. The spectator is no freer, no more 'democratic', in Wyler's film than in the others.

Conversely, Welles uses deep focus in his *Citizen Kane* to present an extremely 'egocentric' universe, Kane's. There's no reason why Leni Reifenstahl, Hitler's cinéaste-laureate, shouldn't have used the 'hierarchical' possibilities implicit in deep focus to Fascist effect (the Leader in big close-up with 'the people' reduced to little faces peering hopefully up from far away, and so on. In practice of course the points made by the visuals would counterpoint rather than repeat those made by narrative or dialogue or audience assumption—e.g. one would enhance the Fuhrer's real grandeur by showing him far away and small).

Often the best way for a director to sensitively nuance every aspect of his medium is to forget about 'style' altogether and immerse his conscious mind in his feelings and ideas; just as the thoughtful spectator will often arrive at the most sensitive understanding of a film by giving the artists the benefit of any reasonable doubt, and, within the spirit of the word 'reasonable', assuming that every aspect of the film is the way it is as the result, not of mere 'mechanics', but of an 'intuitive intention'. (This generous responsiveness also exposes the 'twee', bad, 'stylist' more surely than bluff indifference to nuance.)

'Style'—or rather, *nuance*—is conventionally associated with the creation of a personal, a subjective, a 'non-objective' world—a world that is *this* artist's (or *this* character's, or both). And in the next chapter we shall try and consider, in view of this, the cinema's reputation as a particularly 'realistic', 'objective' medium.

2 · Ying Realism, Yang Fantasy

Cecil M. Hepworth tells a delightful story about early days. He was giving a film show to a church literary society, and half-way through the reel realized he'd forgotten to remove a striptease sequence from his last show. At the last minute he had an inspiration, and introduced the item as 'Salome Dancing Before Herod'. The vicar was delighted and in his closing remarks said he had no idea the 'cheeney-martograph' had been invented so long.

This story neatly enshrines a point regularly overlooked by the theoreticians for whom the cinema's 'essence' is realism. Just because the moving photograph satisfies our sense of reality, it is an ideal medium for making fantasy seem real. And cinemagoing is notoriously as near dreaming (images rising up in darkness . . .) as looking at everyday life.

Even the completely realistic film includes impossibilities of many kinds. The camera's quick changes of viewpoint within the scene, the cut, the flashback and cross-cutting all outrage simple 'literalism'. So does the tilted screen for which Carol Reed's *The Third Man* (1949) is famed (although this 'expressionistic' device had been used more selectively in Duvivier's *Un Carnet de Bal* in 1938 and James Whale's *Bride of Frankenstein* in 1935). Background music is an outrage against realism, but, when creatively used, can have an effect as powerful as the visual images. In *The Third Man* and François Truffaut's *Tirez sur le Pianiste* (1960) zither and piano add their own colour to the atmosphere created by the visuals—expressing life's, fate's, bitter, mocking indifference to the characters. And Sir William Alwyn testifies to the contribution made by the most conventional background music, 'I can't tell you what *Henry V* was like until the music was put to it. Though I say it, I wouldn't have believed it possible that the music could make so much difference. I used to go and see run-throughs of the bits I had to put music to, and really I could hardly keep awake for five minutes.'[1]

Quite unliteral is the use of overlaid commentary (in any newsreel), and of *today's* voice over *yesterday's* actions (as in many flashback sequences). Splitscreen is common enough in musicals (Donen's) but doesn't break the spell in serious dramas. Thus in Robert Wise's *Two For the Seesaw* (1962) Robert Mitchum and Shirley MacLaine, telephoning from different apartments, are shown side by side on the screen. Alf Sjoberg's 1951 version of Strindberg's play shows Miss Julie as a young woman in the foreground remembering, while Miss Julie as a child enters from the background. Thus time, space and personal identity are all outraged, with no flaw in 'real' emotion!

When we are confronted with films like Josef Von Sternberg's *The Blue Angel* (1930) and Eisenstein's *Ivan the Terrible* (1945) the term 'realism' scarcely serves to describe our feelings. We know we are in a 'hallucinated', a dreamlike, universe, that the clothes, the décor, are not just 'realistic', they embody emotions just as emphatically as the characters do. Everything on the screen is as rhetorical as the verbal poetry of Olivier's *Henry V* (1945).

So while the old-fashioned film criticism is still permeated with the assumption that the cinema is at its 'best' when it records 'real life', the cinema in fact accommodates fantasies and fairytales of every kind and style—cartoons like Disney's *Bambi* (1942) satirical allegories like *Two Men and a Wardrobe* (1958), elaborate nowheres as in Welles' *The Trial* (1962) and in *L'Année Dernière à Marienbad* (1961), crazy comedies like *Million Dollar Legs* (1932), expressionist films like *Waxworks* (1924), metaphysical struggles as in Murnau's *Faust* (1926) and Cocteau's *Orphée* (1950), fairytales like the Powell-Berger-Whelan *The Thief of Baghdad* (1940), science-fiction like *This Island Earth* (1955), surrealistic serials like Feuillade's *Les Vampires* (1915) and Franju's *Judex* (1964), and fantasies of libidinous emotion like the endless variations on *Dracula* and *Frankenstein*.

[1] The theoreticians' dislike of background music is a leftover from their campaign against sound films (as well as a reaction against Hollywood cliché). In fact, silent films were never shown in silence, and the lone pianist was found only in the tinier fleapits. Every self-respecting suburban hall had its own orchestra, often of substantial size; and some cinemas even had special sound-effects machines. The crudest Hollywood soundtrack is simply this orchestra on the film instead of in the pit. But the film society habit of reverently watching silent films in reverent silence is an artistic barbarism.

G. W. Pabst, celebrated for his 'realism', reacted vehemently when questioned. 'Realistic? me? . . . From my very first films, I chose realistic themes with the intention of being resolutely a stylist. . . .' And on neo-realism, '*Sotto di Sole di Roma* is a great film, but because Castellani has *style*. Renoir and Carné are great directors for the same reason. Realism must be a trampoline from which one bounces higher, and it can have no value in itself. It is a matter of going beyond reality. Realism is a means, not an end. . . .'

An end to what? To showing, surely, something deeper than the surface of life, whether it be the subjective experiences of the characters in the story, or a clarification of social processes, or the artist's feelings about these things. All these things are invisible to the camera-eye; which can't see the inside of a man's mind, or a historical process, or a sociological generalization, or a theological or philosophical belief, or the artist's own responses. These 'invisible' realities can, must, be reached through diverse methods, or by different methods in various combinations: the 'sample moment' of *cinéma-vérité*, expressionism, or studio trickwork, or dialogue, or music. . . .

Even if we consider the visual surface of life, we find different approaches and styles equally valid. This is reflected in *literary* style (and content!). Thomas Hardy describes landscapes, rooms, faces with an almost pedantic visual exactness (often surpassing Robbe-Grillet). His novels are conceived in visual 'scenes', and he shows the most developed visual and filmic eye in English literature. Whole chapters of his novels are shooting-scripts, complete with establishing long-shot, tracking-shots, etc. He writes, 'A passer-by might have seen . . .' and goes on to put himself in the place of the camera. Colette also has an acute visual eye, but, whatever the scene, selects a category of detail quite different from Hardy's: furnishings, make-up, *feminine* detail. At the other extreme, a writer like Dr. Johnson has no visual eye whatsoever; he is almost 'blind'; he describes everything in sonorous, abstract phrases, which have their own (very great) beauty.

Suppose all three writers were describing the same person in the same room. Each would select his own types of detail. One might not even realize that Colette and Dr. Johnson were working from the same model. Which of these three is the 'realist'? All of them.

Much of the confusion has arisen from the 'abduction' of the word 'realism' by left-wing critics, to mean 'a realistic picture of the individual in society—i.e. 'social realism'. Similarly, in painting, the antithesis 'realism-or-artificiality' has little or no meaning in relation to, say, Titian or Turner. They are both 'realistic', or unrealistic, but each displays his own rich, rewarding subjectivity. In a real sense, Rembrandt's 'mythological' subjects are just as 'realistic' as his 'realistic' ones.

Some aestheticians still deny that the cinema can still be an art, because the camera *mechanically* reproduces whatever is put in front of it. Pudovkin summarizes the certainly true, but incomplete, defence with which film theoreticians have been content ever since. 'There exists between real events and their reproduction on the screen a fundamental difference, and it is this difference which makes film an art.' This difference is that of *selectivity*. The cameraman does not merely reproduce, he interprets reality, by his selection of certain details, angles, and so on. Then there are creative possibilities of choice of lens and lighting, and all sorts of manipulations on the cutting-bench.

In fact, except in the case of a minor genre, documentary, much of the creative effort takes place *in front of* the camera. It's the face and the performance of the actor, the sets and lighting which between them carry most of a film's meaning. The camera doesn't record 'reality' at all. It records a fictional 'construction' which is already a work of art, or rather, designed to become so on film. To the 'primary' elements (what the camera sees) there are added the 'secondary' elements (derived from the possibilities of photography) and 'tertiary' elements (from manipulating the strip of film). These three elements can't be separated, but at least the distinction reminds us that the film is a work of art even before it's in the camera. The director and art director can *build a painting* and photograph that—the décor of *The Cabinet of Dr. Caligari* (1919) is a work of art which (like architecture) was built to accommodate movement in three dimensions, but (like a painting) appears in the flat on the screen. With its painted décor and daubed-on faces, Weine's *The Cabinet of Dr. Caligari* is half-way to being a cartoon.

In one scene, the somnambulist Cesare (Conrad Veidt) carries the heroine (Lil Dagover) away along a painted path. The perspective of the path is subtly foreshortened, so that Cesare scuttles from foreground to horizon in three strides flat, giving an effect of nightmare speed. Here the effect is gained by the 'primary' elements. On the other hand, Orson Welles often uses low-angle close-ups with wide-angle lens, so that his characters tower over the camera gigantically. When they step away from the camera, they diminish in size so rapidly that in two steps they seem to have covered about twenty yards. Here the same effect of 'giant stride' is obtained by 'secondary' elements (camera lens). German silent films often isolate the central character by a spotlight (primary effect) where Griffiths would use a mask or iris-in (secondary eflect) and where a modern film would cut from three-shot to close-up (tertiary effect).

Traditionally, film criticism has overstressed tertiary and secondary elements and forgotten that the director does the bulk of his creative work in setting up what the camera sees, in his *staging*. It's a matter of the *pictorial* and the *theatrical* element of the cinema.

Let us take another example. A rule of thumb in film appreciation is that scenes of fast and exciting movement, like railway trains rushing along or gay dances, need plenty of fast cutting. Certainly, they can be handled in this style (as in Jean Mitry's *Pacific 231*, 1949), but they can also be presented just as effectively by deliberately slow cutting. In *La Bête Humaine* (1938), Jean Renoir builds a train journey into a sequence of great visual tension by using a few long takes of countryside seen from the train. Hedgerows, bridges, viaducts, stations, tunnels, horizons, flash past the camera in a flowing series of contrasts. And in the climactic dance of *French Can-Can* (1955), Renoir's cutting is not particularly fast. The dazzle and frenzy is created by the way in which the dancers' clothes and movements are played off against one another 'inside' the shot. It's a matter of *staging*; fast cutting would ruin the effects. The movement is located *within* the image and virtually demands a fixed, consistent camera-viewpoint.

In an essay typical of the *Sight and Sound* line, Tony Richardson tried to draw a distinction between those directors who were *artists* and those who were merely *metteurs-en-scène* (as artists he excluded German expressionists, Dreyer, Ophuls, Visconti and Kazan). But we propose here to use the term *mise-en-scène* in a different way; to refer to the creative arrangements of things *within* the screen. Some directors manage to get a particularly intense performance from their actors. Others direct for cutting. We wish to draw attention here to the *mise-en-scène*—strong, eloquent arrangements within the image (or series of images).

This *mise-en-scène* has two aspects, often allied. There is the 'theatrical' element—the dramatic scenes are staged (for the camera), the characters arranged in space, with their exits, entrances, movements, gestures and so on. (Matters of casting and acting, equally important, are 'theatrical' without being *mise-en-scène*, which we may define as 'staging for the camera'.) And there is the 'pictorial' element (pictorial composition, 'painterly' qualities, and so on).

It is obvious that the 'theatrical' and the 'pictorial' must often overlap, and often provide two different names for the same effect. In fact during the First World War Max Reinhardt's stage productions paid as much attention to the *pictorial* organization of the stage as did the silent German films of the 'golden age' (many of which were influenced by his work). Similarly it's reasonable to attach some little importance to the 'theatrical' element of certain paintings —say, Géricault's *The Raft of the Medusa.* Indeed Tintoretto and Gainsborough used to work out their paintings with the aid of a model theatre, testing the effects of light and shade with models, cut-outs and candles.

The traditional prejudice against the 'pictorial' element of films is typified by two remarks in Paul Rotha's *The Film Till Now.* Of Dreyer, 'The damning fault of *La Passion de Jeanne d'Arc* was . . . the beauty of the visuals, which were so pleasing in themselves that they were detrimental to the expression of the theme. . . .' And, 'Sternberg seems lodged in this gully of pictorial values . . .' to which Rotha's disciple, Richard Griffith, adds, 'Sternberg's . . . strange, compulsive preoccupation with pictorial composition . . . action and even continuity were progressively drained away in favour of an ordered flow of a pattern of images, often lovely in themselves, sometimes floridly vulgar, but always empty of real dramatic meaning.'

Our viewpoint here is that this 'gully of pictorial values' is actually one of the principal elements of film art, and that unless the critic accepts, and keys his sensibility to, pictorial values, he will be unable to pay more than lip-service to the real richness of such directors as Eisenstein, Sternberg, Dreyer, Pabst, Murnau, Ophuls and many others. It is no accident that Eisenstein evolved away from his 'cutting' style to the slow, elaborate pictoriality of *Ivan the Terrible* which, stylistically, is very near Dreyer and Sternberg.

A sensitive response to *mise-en-scène* means paying just as much attention to make-up, lighting, décor, costumes, gesture, and other 'technical', 'stylistic' details of a film as to dialogue and plot—noticing them not for their own sakes, but for their emotional meaning, their psychological impact. The mask which Jack Pierce created for Boris Karloff in James Whale's *Frankenstein* (1931) is no more 'childish' an effect than the make-up daubed on Werner Krauss in *The Cabinet of Dr. Caligari*, it is just as much a *vision* of the personage. And Christopher Lee's sensitive mime as the Monster in Terence Fisher's films is an aesthetic effect of the same idiom as Conrad Veidt's lean, spidery Cesare.

The Pierce-Karloff vision of the Frankenstein Monster is prefigured in the weird being dreamed up by Goya for *The Chinchillas* (Plate 3). Many horror films, like Goya's etchings, offer a *demential* insight into the disorders of human nature and society. And, for all their implausible situations and comic-strip dialogue, they may have a visual flair which makes them, creatively, the equal of well-written dramas with only mediocre visuals.

The costumier's art mingles with the art director's. Any criticism of *Ivan the Terrible* must pay as much attention to costume as to dialogue. Dress may establish character in ways about which the script remains silent. In Richard Fleischer's *The Big Gamble* (1960) Irish adventurer Stephen Boyd brings his new French bride (Juliette Greco) back to his puritanical family. She wears a black leather coat, a tightly moulded red dress, and a white flower in her buttonhole. The coat suggests she's knocked toughly around the world. The tight red dress suggests promiscuity (as when in Victor Fleming's *Gone With the Wind* (1939) Rhett, thinking Scarlett has slept with Ashley, makes her go to Melanie's party wearing a red dress). And the white flower says she is pure at heart. The dramatic modulations of atmosphere possible through wardrobe are neatly described by Cecilia Ager, describing Garbo's in Cukor's *Camille* (1937):

'. . . the colours of her costume change from white, in the carefree beginning, to grey when the forces of tragedy gather momentum, until, at last, sable black, with all its dark meaning, appears. First, in an all-black velvet dress and large black hat that she wears for her journey to the country. Then, when it seems that she is to be happy, white again, in cannily picturesque lawn dresses with only a black cloak to remind you her fate is sealed; black again after her renunciation—shimmering black net with sequins, but black. For her death, so that you are not too miserable, and may find solace in something, a white gown ecclesiastical in feeling with its monk's cowl, sending you to religion, there to take courage to bear it. Adrian has never been more touching, not, fortuitously, more decorative.

Garbo's *coiffure* also acts; the frivolous curled bangs that cover her forehead in the beginning are gradually lifted until at the end the whole serenity of her brow is revealed; there is something spiritual about this process too.'

Thus there exists a whole sensuous 'layer' of film meaning with which film criticism has scarcely begun to deal. Michael Caen underlines the importance of colour and clothes in Terence Fisher's *Dracula* (1958) and its sequel. 'What more can be said of Jack Asher's forests in *Brides of Dracula* except that they are more Gothic than ever Bram Stoker dreamed them? or of the glasses and decanters in which liquors shimmer in all colours from crimson to *creme-de-menthe*, except that they contribute to the sheerly decorative richness a note of that baroque which is precisely the key to the Victorian era? Fisher as no other knows how to use soft blues to lyricize the sepulchral atmosphere of these haunted crypts. . . . As part of a spectrum so hypersensitized, black takes on a new, its full, power. It ceases to be that meaningless tonal value rendered by panchromatic stock . . . it takes on life, substance (the shiny black of satin is played off against matt velvet), it acquires the value of an ethical symbol . . . it inserts itself like a wedge into a colour world where the mauve gowns and turquoise *déshabillés* stress the vulnerability of the women selected as victims. . . .'

A black-and-white analogy occurs in Franju's *Les Yeux Sans Visages* (1960) about a megalomaniac surgeon who cuts off girls' faces. In its pattern of surfaces, it is an *epidermal* film. There are elaborate contrasts of clothing—satin, leather, rubber and towelling. The camera dwells on the rainy 'surface' of the sky (Franju notoriously keeps his whole unit, expensively, waiting for the weather to be dramatically exact), on black branches dancing in car headlights, or reflected black-on-black, in the sleek 'skin' of a Citroen Déésse. The furnishings form part of the same visual complex—blacked-over mirrors, carpets, portraits, the patterned leading of windows. Franju's film evokes the Surrealist remark that, 'Fear, the incongruous, and the fascinations of luxury are emotional factors to which we never appeal in vain', and Baudelaire's, 'The furnishings seem to be dreaming, endowed with some somnambulistic consciousness, like that of plants. . . .' Franju's, like Minnelli's films, like *L'Année Dernière à Marienbad*, are *décor* films.

Connected with film 'pictoriality' is a sense of bodily physique and sensations. King Vidor's films are frequently eloquent in their physical movement and tension: Bette Davis's dying crawl at the climax of *Beyond the Forest*, echoing her earlier greedy writhing on the fur-coat she covets; the jagged, fierce, forked-lightning-fast movements of Kirk Douglas in the extraordinary dance-banjo-and-gunplay sequence of *Man Without a Star*; the rhythms of digging in *Our Daily Bread*, the death-crawls and dying embraces of *Duel in the Sun* and *Ruby Gentry*. Against the slow narrative rhythms of Arthur Penn's *The Left-Handed Gun* the fiercely *choreographed* gunduels have a quite explosive impact. *The Olympiad* (1936) is one of the great 'physical' films of all time. In Leni Reifenstahl, even Nazism, alas, can claim its genius.

Films abound in sensuous, even sensual, experience. Von Stroheim's are particularly rich in such moments, whether of luxury or revulsion—close-ups of black blobs of caviare, of fur slippers, of corpses dragged through wet mud, of violets held near a glinting cavalry boot, verbal references to the smell of new-mown hay, or Von Stroheim as the seducer in *Foolish Wives* (1921) dabbing perfume behind his ears and on his eyebrows. Throughout *The L-Shaped Room* (1962) Bryan Forbes' camera dwells on such little nastiness as a cake of soap studded with bedbugs, flat beer jigging in a glass on a piano-top, and (nauseous in close-up) a mess of cat-food. This is the world 'sensed' through the physical responses of a depressed and pregnant woman.

Dreyer described the film as related more nearly to architecture than to any other art. It may seem astonishing that he should compare so *static* and so *fluid* an art. But the film entails, like architecture, the creation of a visual world through which people move. Sometimes the two coincide, as in the opening sequence of *L'Année Dernière à Marienbad*.

We have come a long way from the 'literary' conception of a film as 'explaining' or 'analysing' people's psychology. The film's job is not so much to provide 'information' about the characters' minds as to communicate their 'experience', whether intellectual, emotional, physical, or a blend of all three. The *temps-mort* in which Renoir's films are so rich, which Becker schematized, and which Antonioni's camp-followers abused, is, more quietly, a constituent part of many purely commercial films. The pleasures and miseries of 'getting up in the morning' are evoked, vividly, at length, and quite independently of the plot, in such films as Jerry Lewis's *The Ladies' Man* and Daniel Mann's *Butterfield 8* (luxuriously), and (drably) in de Sica's *Umberto*

D, Gilles Grangier's *Gas-Oil* and Sidney Gilliatt's *Only Two Can Play*.

Quite apart from 'literary' values, the average audience is interested in 'how things are done'—and many feature films take in their stride little moments of documentary interest. Rossellini's *The White Ship* shows how wounded men are transferred from a ship at sea to an ambulance aeroplane, and not simply as a symbol of the pure Christian charity with which the Fascist forces cared for their injured crusaders: the procedure is in itself matter for art. Wyler's *Ben Hur* shows how sea-battles were fought in Roman times. King Vidor's *Hallelujah* celebrates among other things, the simple efficiency with which cotton is baled in the deep South. A tragedy of Flaherty's career was its steady decline from the eloquent *practicality* of *Nanook of the North* (1922) to the middlebrow *schmalz* of *Louisiana Story* (1948).

This emphasis on styling and staging enables us to refute those aestheticians who deny that the film is an art because the director can't do everything himself and is at the mercy of collaborators and of accident. Even Peter Ustinov falls for this nonsense, when he says, 'The script is no blueprint. And in the practical world of the cinema, if a director decides to use a certain cameraman and that man is not available, then he will already get a slightly different result from the cameraman he actually uses. He is not entirely in control. The man who is most in control is the man who is looking through the camera and who sees the shot at it is being made . . . and you as a director have to rely on him . . . it is really remote control . . . films are full of accidents. . . .'

But this argument also proves that music, ballet and the theatre are not art forms. Composers like Bach and Beethoven now have no control over what conductors and performers do to their music; and it is because the player's interpretation really does alter the meaning of the piece that we give him the status of a 'creative artist'. Who is 'in control'? The composer? or the conductor? or the soloist, who actually plays the music? None. Equally, a ballet may be a compromise between different creative interpretations: the choreographer's, the conductor's, the dancer's (and two 'stars' may have very different ideas). And who is 'the' creator of a play? The author? The producer? The star actor? In the practical world of the theatre, isn't the casting just as much at the mercy of 'accident' as choice of a cameraman?

Peter Ustinov's argument leads him to the peculiar position that a play is a work of art when it's read by the author, but not when it's being performed on the stage by a company!

The fact is that the film is only one of many media in which art takes in its stride the effects of collaboration and of accident, which in any case may help as well as hinder. Such novelists as Dickens and Hardy didn't write in a vacuum; they wrote *for* their readers, and in a very real sense they 'collaborated' with them. The desire to *communicate* is itself an acceptance of *collaboration.* Even self-expression requires compromise with accident—composers have to settle for what's playable on what musical instruments exist. The whole development of thought in a poem is constantly being affected by the need for rhyme or rhythmic patterns.

But let us return to film practicalities. Gérard Gozlan described how André Bazin once rhapsodized over Wyler's very personal handling of a scene in *The Little Foxes.* Wyler, who was present, embarrassedly explained that he filmed the scene the way he did, not for Bazin's deep philosophical reason, but to hide the fact that Herbert Marshall had a wooden leg. Similarly a director may have to choose a particular camera-angle because his glamorous leading lady turned up this morning with a pimple on her left cheek.

But André Bazin's remark isn't so foolish. Given a 'pimple' or a 'wooden leg', different stylists will find different solutions. One changes the camera-angle; another introduces a last-minute panning shot; another will retain the original set-up, but throw heavy shadows to conceal the offending detail; another will interpose a pot of flowers or a table-cloth to conceal the trouble spot from the camera. The director has ample opportunity to maintain his style in the face of 'accident'. And it's no exaggeration to say that such stylists as Dreyer and Bresson would imperturbably maintain their characteristic style even if the entire cast suddenly turned up with pimples *and* wooden legs.

Of elaborate critical interpretations, Fritz Lang made a very fair comment. 'I always laughed when people came to see me and explained what it was that I was trying to do in my pictures. And then I happened to think in the following way. My profession makes me like a psychoanalyst. Unconsciously, when you write a story you have to psychoanalyse the characters. Then I have to make myself clear why the characters act the way they do so that I can explain it to the actors. Maybe the critic is a psychoanalyst too. Perhaps he finds I do certain things of which I am not conscious.'

We return to one of our definitions of the word 'style'. Personal style is the content which the artist contributes, intuitively, to every subject with which he deals. Inevitably, it is frequently the deepest, the determinant part of the content.

3 · Sensation, Shape and Shade

Although there is no clear line of demarcation between the 'theatrical' and the 'pictorial' elements of the cinema, we have described *mise-en-scène* as the way the action is *staged* and the way the images are *composed.* If we go on now to make a few comparisons between cinema and theatre on one hand, and cinema and painting on the other, it is simply a way of exploring, or emphasizing, particular 'wavelengths' of the cinema's spectrum. We don't intend to press the analogies too far, nor to set up any profound philosophical similarities.

Among the many ways in which British film critics can be grouped and regrouped, there is a distinct chasm between those who *contrast* 'literary content' and 'style' and those who respond to the 'theatre' elements—notably, of course, the personality of the actor, which finds its extreme in the star system.

The second group of critics are of course far nearer the habits of the general public than the first. All critics are aware of the unique quality of a few 'grand' stars—Garbo, Bette Davis, and so on. But outside this little group, 'intellectual' criticism currently pays relatively little attention to the central importance, in the film's content, of the actor's personality, and the way in which, by lighting, and all the features of his own style, the director can modify that personality. This neglect is a comparatively recent development—the English magazine *Close-Up* (1927–31), and its French contemporary *La Revue Du Cinema* are very responsive to personality.

Unlike the 'legitimate' stage, the cinema can accommodate complete amateurs (to whose authenticity or spontaneity the director can contribute the necessary artistic control) and it can accommodate actors who can't act in any real sense but have an emotional vibrancy of some sort (like Alan Ladd, Joan Crawford or Clara Bow). But if the popular cinema can manage without actors, it couldn't manage without personalities; 'documentary' is condemned to be an ancillary genre. Many of the screen's favourite personalities graduated from the 'illegitimate' stage—music-hall, revue and cabaret. The appeal of many film stars compares with that of music-hall personalities who, like Harry Lauder, or Vesta Tilley, display, not 'acting talent', but a warm and resonant personality-role. As Jean Renoir remarked, 'As for actors, the best training-ground for them used to be the café-concert. Which doesn't exist any longer, but it's in the cabaret, in night-club numbers, that you can find your future stars.'

The general public is very quick to recognize these qualities, once, at least, they have found their 'role'. As early as 1915, a brief glimpse of an extra looking with sad adoration at Lillian Gish in *The Birth of a Nation* (1915) brought torrents of enthusiastic letters from all over the States. Alas, the extra had been paid off, and Griffith never managed to trace him. George Raft recounts how 'Mae West was in one of my early pictures . . . and she had one line in the picture which knocked me right in the box . . . she comes on and checks her rag, saying, "Check it!" Just that. . . . From then on, she became a definite personality and the public wanted to see more of her. . . .'

The 'acting' required is qualities as simple and subtle as those which made music-hall stars of Jack Warner, Gracie Fields or Will Hay. The light, crisp, exhilarating dancing of Fred Astaire isn't just a *tour de force* to be admired for its cleverness; it creates a *physical* well-being amongst the audience. Even when he's not dancing, his very walk is so light and sweet and easy it's a pleasure to see him walk across a room. And when this slender figure begins to dance it's as if mild Kent Clark had turned into a pint-size Superman with anti-gravity. . . . A brief pen-portrait by Michel Mourlet nicely registers the kind of quasi-physical nuance which registers so powerfully with screen audiences, 'Charlton Heston is an axiom. By himself alone he constitutes a tragedy, and his presence in any film whatsoever suffices to create beauty. The contained violence expressed by the sombre phosphoresence of his eyes, his eagle's profile, the haughty arch of his eyebrows, his prominent cheekbones, the bitter and hard curve of his mouth, the fabulous power of his torso; this is what he possesses and what not even the worst director can degrade.' Richard Roud seemed to feel the idea of the relevance of physique rather unpleasant ('nutty and crypto-Fascist'), but it's not a new idea.

In the words of Sarah Bernhardt, 'There is a fitness of things intellectual and a fitness of things physical, and the latter should receive as much attention as the former.' And Ellen Terry was accustomed to say, 'It is no use an actress using her nervous energy battling with her physical attributes. She had much better find a way of applying them as allies.' Indeed, one of the most eloquent aspects of Welles' *Touch of Evil* (1957) is the contrast of personalities between Welles' fat, gross, crooked cop, who has run both physically and morally to seed, and Charlton Heston's incorruptible Mexican. The latter character is built on the internal tensions between his 'liberal' part and the actor's 'Bronze Age' personality.

In the same way, many of a film's meanings lie in physical gestures and parallels. Whenever the Belmondo character in Godard's *A Bout de Souffle* (1960) is uncertain of himself, he rubs his lips with his thumb; and as she watches him lie dying, through her treachery, Jean Seberg 'catches' his gesture. Riccardo Freda's staging of *The Spectre* (1963) is influenced by Barbara Steele's lean, expressive hands—as she and her lover caress, her hands rove round his face and neck, restless, aggressive. Freda proceeds to invent, or to stress, actions which make us watch her hands—screwing up paper, opening a snuffbox (which then oozes blood), wrestling with a heavy coffin-lid, tugging her lover's corpse upstairs, shaving her paralysed husband (with murder in her heart), then 'flagellating' her lover's face, with the same razor, in an action which is itself a variation on 'shaving'. In E. A. Dupont's *Variété* (1925) henpecked husband Emil Jannings powders, pats and dries the baby; later he rubs down his youthful mistress (Lya da Putti) after her trapeze performance. Here the meaning lies less in the nuances of movement than in the action itself—a kind of doting fatherliness, shading into a weak motherliness.

Altogether the cinema is freer of literature than even the theatre. The camera's darting, analytical eye is made to stress such gestures and can dispense with speech altogether. In Visconti's words, 'The cinema which interests me is an anthropomorphic cinema. Of all the different aspects of a director's work, that which excites me most is what I do with the players. Experience has taught me that the weight, the presence of a man is the only thing that really counts on the screen. . . . I could make a film in front of a blank wall if I was sure of finding the real human elements of the character placed in front of this bare décor. . . .'

The fact that the cinema *can* use the amateur, the man-in-the-street, and an almost-deadpan acting style, is sometimes used to suggest that it *ought* to use these styles in preference to others. But, in fact, it accommodates artificial styles equally well, whether the expressionistic style of Emil Jannings, the stylized mime of Charlie Chaplin, or the 'Lyceum' performance of Bette Davis.

One can distinguish the following principal styles of film acting.

(1) The 'semaphore' style—the stylized gestures and signals used in early silent films.

(2) The 'pantomime' style of Mack Sennett. Chaplin refined and sensitized this and brought it near the 'poetic mime' of Marcel Marceau.

(3) The 'expressionism' of Emil Jannings and the German silent cinema's 'Golden Age' (1919–25). Later German films compromised between this and a more 'realistic' style.

(4) The 'Kulyeshov' style of early Eisenstein and Pudovkin. Brief shots of 'fixed' expressions. (Kulyeshov made the experiment of intercutting the same shot of Mosjoukine, absolutely expressionless, with a soup-plate, a woman and a corpse, and spectators complimented him on Mosjoukine's lyrical expression of hunger, love and grief.)

(5) The 'later silent' style—including pretty well anything which audiences of that time accepted as 'realistic'. Some actors have dated more than others: Louise Brooks in Hawks' *A Girl in Every Port* (1927) is quite as 'modern' as Kim Novak; of Hawks and Kim, more later. Mosjoukine in L'Herbier's *Le Feu Mathias Pascal* (1923) ranges from heavy 'expressionist' poses to Chaplin slapstick.

(6) The mainstream sound style is a modification of this silent style. Again, there is great variety within the range. The 40's and 50's specialized in glum, deadpan faces (Ladd and Lake, Audie Murphy, Kim Novak), succeeded by another kind of realism, the 'Method', a conscious, perhaps, somewhat cerebral, reaction against this lack of feeling, towards a deeper, more revealing and spontaneous, kind of self-awareness.

(7) The heavy 'monumental' style in highly pictorial films, like Eisenstein's *Ivan the Terrible* or Dreyer's *La Passion de Jeanne d'Arc*.

(8) In contrast, the swift, fluid, responsiveness of Renoir's 30's films. Visconti's *Ossessione* (1942) is a Renoir-ian film, and, as such, the first 'manifesto' of the great wave of Italian neo-realism.

(9) Visconti's *La Terra Trema* (1948) is a brilliant blend of the last

two styles. Antonioni's first feature, *Cronaca di un Amore* (1950), also has an extraordinary deliberate sense of bodily posture.

(10) The English 'documentary' style of 'understatement', so fashionable during the war. It's, not falsity, but artificiality, is revealed by the comparison with:

(11) *Cinéma-vérité*—which isn't a style at all.

Different styles can be combined in the same film. Thus Marlene's Lola-Lola in *The Blue Angel* hasn't dated at all; here is a laconic, 'underplayed' performance; Jannings' is more expressionist and dated, especially at the climax, when it is liable to seem ludicrous unless one makes the effort to adapt to it. And Mosjoukine switches style very smoothly from one scene to another in *Le Feu Mathias Pascal.*

With Eisenstein and Dreyer, we feel, not that the actor dominates the image, but that the actor is part of a visual composition—that he has practically been hammered and planed into shape. The 'theatrical' is subordinated to the pictorial. These directors often work on their actors by liberal use of make-up, or, by scrubbing their faces clear of make-up and etching every wrinkle, *carving* every feature, with a sculptural sense of light and shadow. They work on their actors in another way too. To play Joan of Arc, Dreyer took a young woman, Falconetti, whose smile was dazzling and modern enough for the toothpaste advertisements on which she featured, and talked to her, worked on her, in his stuttering French, until her mind transformed her features from within. He wasn't above a little physical—not torture, exactly, but lack of consideration, keeping her kneeling lengthily on stone floors—but his whole effort was devoted to locking on to her features, sculpting them into, feelings which hitherto had been dormant within her, or merely passing moods. He superimposed his portrait of her *on* her face.

Dreyer's visual flair is very strong, very simple, very strange. The 'low angle' in Welles makes the character seem proud, as he looks down at others. The 'low angle' in Dreyer makes Falconetti humble (often because from this angle even her *level gaze* seems to be looking imploringly upwards). He photographs Falconetti from a low angle, so as to increase the slight downward curve of her very vigorous mouth, giving her an air of tragic dejection—he uses perspective to change the shape and 'meaning' of her features. He lets on to the faces a white light which seems to grind them down, to scrape them clean, to impart to them the permanence of stone. He photographs a face as if he were photographing a piece of sculpture. Maybe he can't chip and chisel away at his actors' bodies to get the shape and pose he wants, so he arranges their clothes—flowing monks' robes, which he can 'compose' quite freely, some into sharp, mean crooks and cranks, others into billowing explosions of their wrath.

One group of directors, like Eisenstein and Dreyer, tend to think of each screen 'picture' as a little composition of its own, so deliberate and strong that one becomes aware of each image, organized as a whole, following and replacing its predecessor, with a little impact. The pictures are *joined* by their 'collision', which sets a kind of solid, hard-edged mood, much as brushstrokes set mood in painting. And these directors often strengthen the 'impact'—one shot will be, for example, a strong diagonal, the next a scatter of round forms, the third a bold horizontal-vertical, and so on. These directors, as if by temperament, incline to ask from their actors strong, deliberate movements. Others, again, like Renoir and Rossellini, are pretty nonchalant, even sloppy, about compositions, leaving them 'loose' so as not to cramp the actors' spontaneity and quasi-improvisation. They ask the spectator to concentrate on the flow of postures, gestures, movements, streaming steadily through the shots. Each image as a whole becomes 'invisible', for the movement flows smoothly through the images. And these directors tend to prefer lighter, more fluid styles of acting. Renoir's sensitivity to his actors' bodies and gestures is as fine, in its very different way, as Dreyer's.

Renoir's exceptional awareness of posture and gesture reveals a visual concentration of a deliberate, disciplined kind. In Renoir's words, 'I began to realize that the gesture of a laundress, of a woman combing her hair before a mirror, of a streethawker near a car, had an incomparable plastic eloquence. I made a sort of study of French gestures through the paintings of my father, and those of his generation.'

No better example could be set for any aspiring film director—to learn to *see*, through paintings, through life. Far from being a 'dissipated' talent, Renoir in his greatest films has contrived to 'load every rift with ore'.

Between the extremes of Dreyer and Renoir come men like Pabst, Antonioni, attentive both to compositions and postures, finding some sort of compromise between the two.

For Dreyer, the face is a *landscape*. (Plate 4.) Following Pierre Bargellini's brilliant study of the 'cinematic' aspects of Giotto, we

1, 2. The two inquisitors: *La Passion de Jeanne d'Arc* (see p. 25)

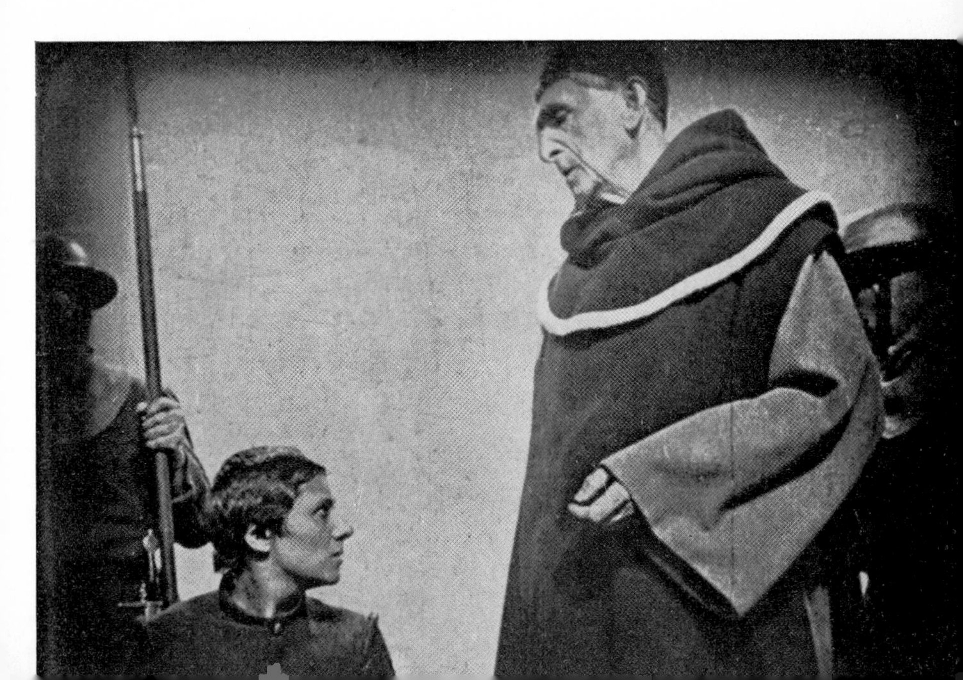

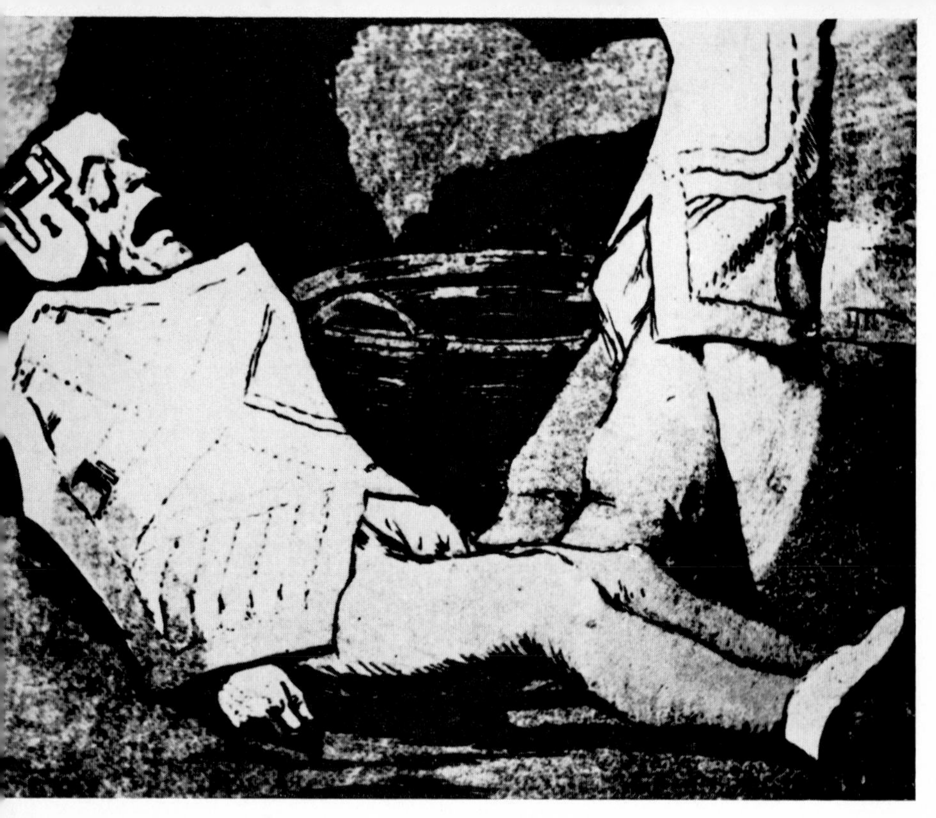

3. 'The sleep of reason brings forth monsters . . .' *The Chincillas*, from Goya's *Los Capriocios*, 1797 (see p. 37)

4. Face as landscape: *La Passion de Jeanne d'Arc* (see p. 48)

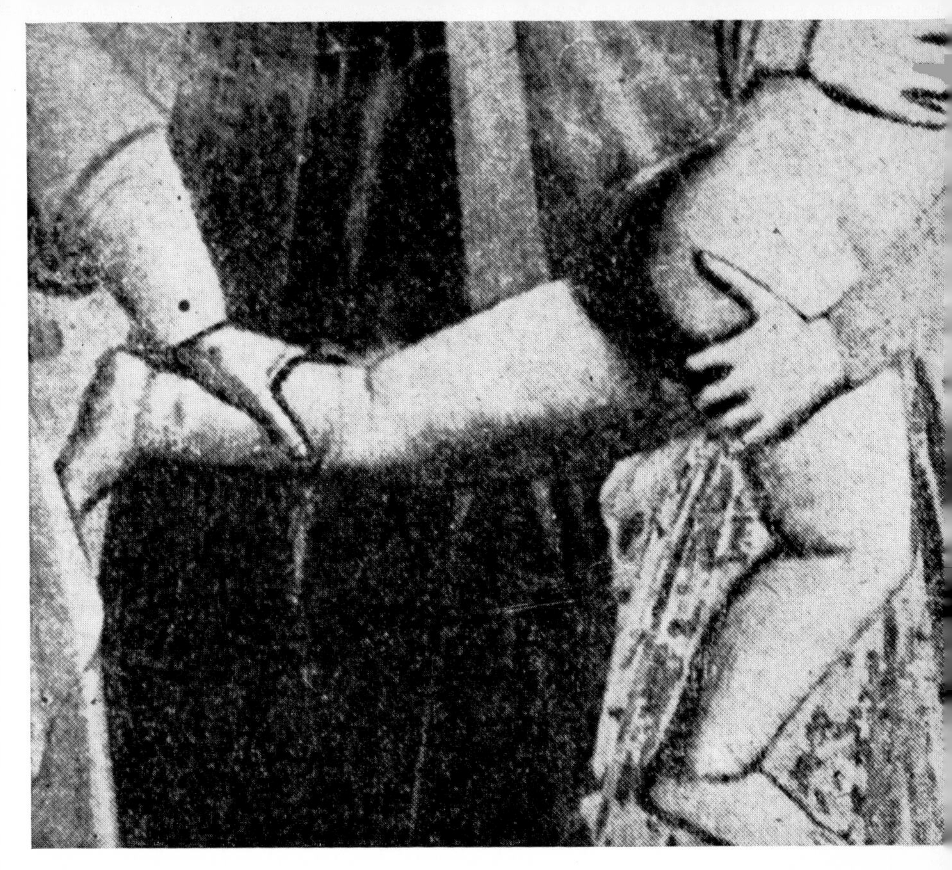

5, 6. Two close-ups: from Luciano Emmer's *Il Dramma di Cristo* and from *La Passion de Jeanne d'Arc* (see p. 49)

7, 8. Movement and informality: *Nana* and *La Passion de Jeanne d'Arc* (see p. 51)

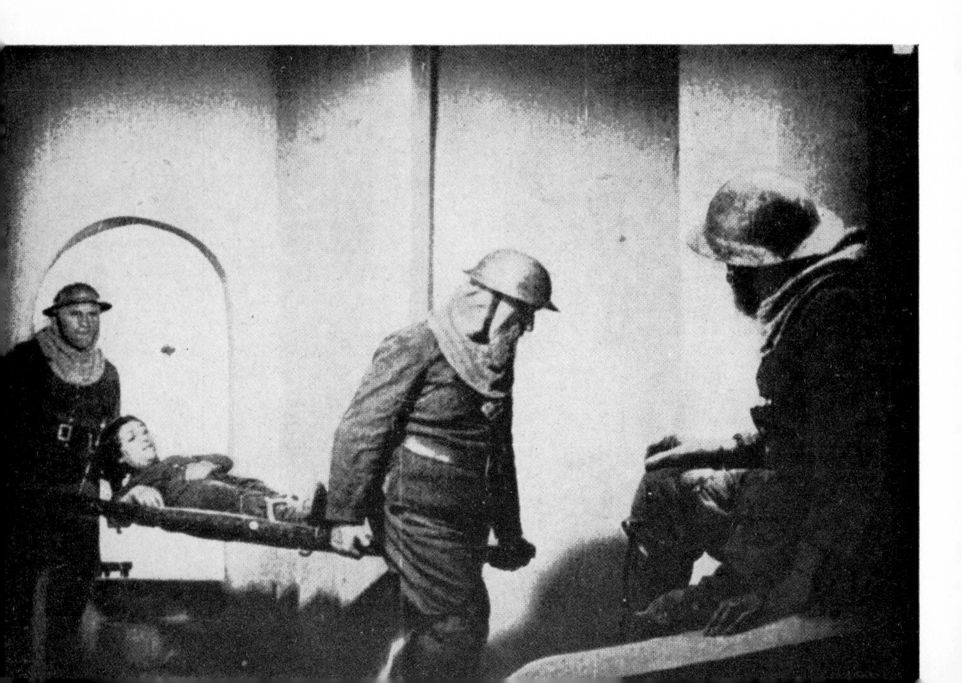

9, 10. Studies in depth: *Day of Wrath* and *Vampyr* (see p. 51)

11, 12. Choreography and space: *La Passion de Jeanne d'Arc* (see p. 51)

13, 14. Two compositions: *Alexander Nevski* (see p. 51)

15. Echoes. *Ivan the Terrible* (see p. 53)

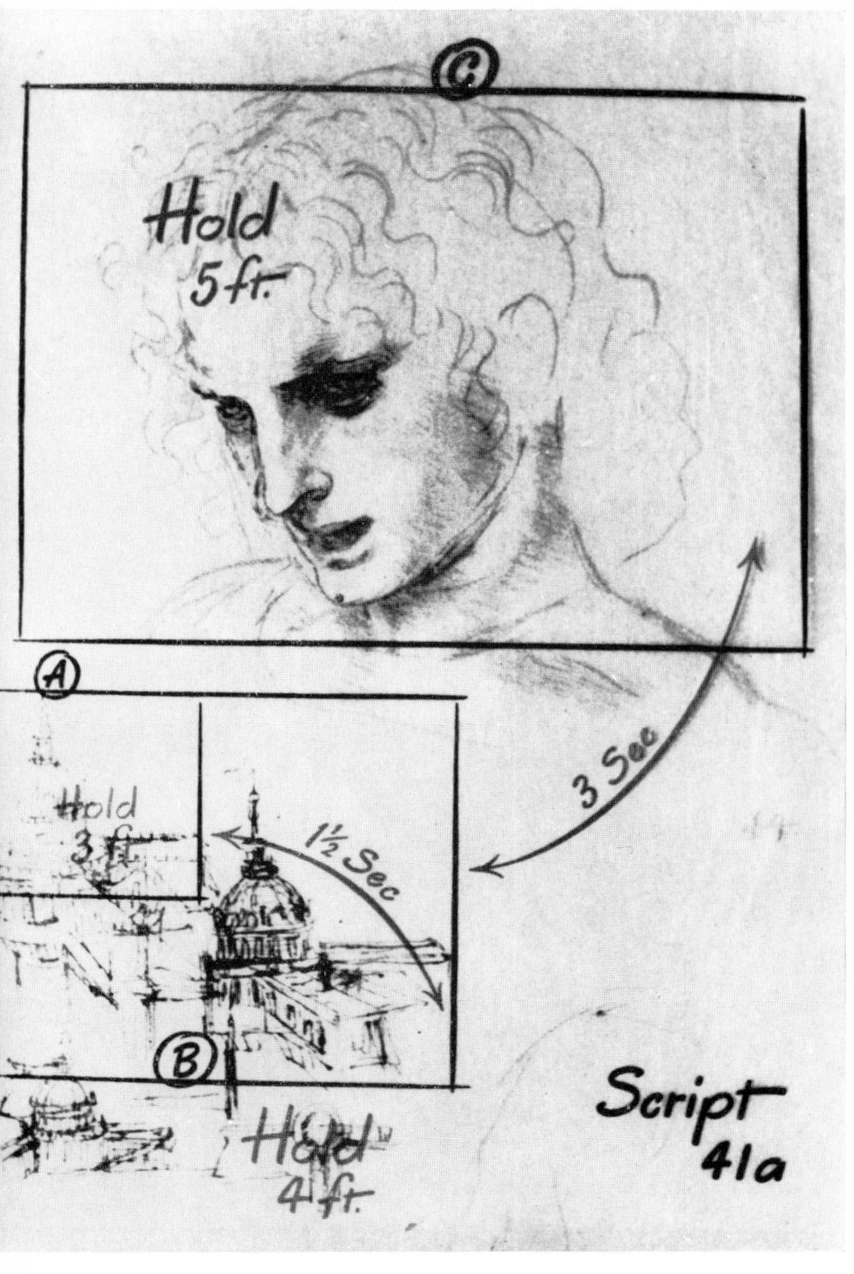

16. Space into time. A production sketch from *The Drawings of Leonardo da Vinci* (see pp. 115, 118)

17, 18. Echoes: *La Passion de Jeanne d'Arc* and *Tabu* (see p. 52)

19, 20. Structures of light: *Ivan the Terrible* and *Tabu* (see p. 53)

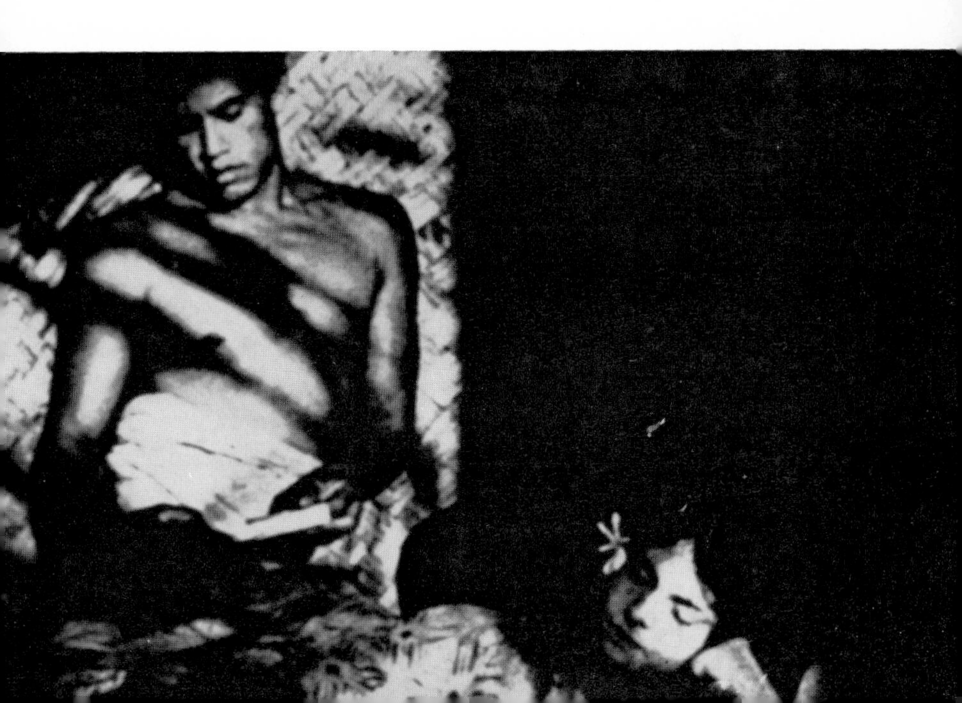

21, 22. A continuity. *Fury* and *Metropolis* (see p. 93)

23, 24. Bodies and poses: Emil Jannings in *The Last Laugh* (see p. 91) and Jennifer Jones, Robert Sully, Gladys Cooper in *Love Letters* (see p. 169)

25, 26. Personalities: Barbara Steele in *Danse Macabre* (see p. 147) and Kim Novak and Frank Sinatra in Otto Preminger's *The Man With the Golden Arm* (see pp. 84, 139, 166)

27, 28. Guns and buddies. Lauren Bacall and Humphrey Bogart in Howard Hawks's *The Big Sleep* (see pp. 74, 83, 142) and Jean-Claude Brialy (left) and Gerard Blain (*right*) in *Les Cousins* (see p. 202)

29, 30. Two deserts. Orphée and Heurtebise in slow-motion in 'la zone'; and Metaluna. (*Orphée*, see pp. 103, 239; *This Island Earth*, see p. 256)

can compare such a Dreyer close-up with a 'close-up from Giotto, where the modelling of flesh and physique is similar. Posture is controlled as carefully as in any painting. At the other extreme, Renoir is nearer Degas. Renoir's being an art of movement, most stills betray it, though some (Plate 7) suggest the wealth of 'behaviour' that can crowd the screen.

If Renoir leaves visual space so that his actors are free, it is because, for him, human nature is flowing and free. Whereas Dreyerian space, so carefully patterned and sculpted, expresses his *protestant* sense of human nature as tight, tense, *locked.*

Of course, the fact that a director or cameraman has a consciously 'visual' style does not mean that his style is of interest. There are bad (banal) visual styles, just as there are bad scripts, bad dialogue. Laurence Olivier tried desperately hard to give *Hamlet* (1948) a worthy visual style, but, as Renoir remarked of its barn-sized sets and deep focus compositions, 'You feel dizzy when you look down from a great height? So what? What has that to do with Shakespeare?' The style *confuses* the issue. Similarly, Alexander Korda's *Rembrandt* (1936), conscientiously uses Rembrandt-era furnishings and sets and reminiscent faces, but the only lively thing in the film, apart from Laughton's stylish performance as Charles Laughton (never as Rembrandt!) is the highly individual face and style of his wife, Elsa Lanchester, who is almost the Barbara Steele of the early 30's. There is only the crudest resemblance between the massive visuals of Eisenstein's *Time in the Sun* (1932) and all those peasant-faces-against-the-clouds-shots in Emilio Fernandez's *The Pearl* (1946). Only schizophrenics go through the day feeling 'noble and pure' all the time, and visuals which keep insisting on this are just as fake.

Among the visual academicians we must include Aleksander Ford (cf. *Young Chopin* (1952)), Blassetti, despite one or two nice shots in *1860* (1933) and *Fabiola* (1948), and Arne Sucksdorff, especially the pseudo-*cinéma-vérité* of *Rhythm of a City* (1947). Nor can visual analysis settle for primitive rules of thumb like 'diagonals for urgency, visuals for repose, low-key shadows for drama, high-key shine for comedy'. After all, Autant-Lara, Wilder, and Kubrick all use very gloomy lighting for their comedies—witness *La Traversée de Paris*, *The Apartment* and *Dr. Strangelove*.

Here we can only make a few *ad hoc* points. Far from aiming at being even an introduction to a 'theory' of film visuals, they are meant only as examples, to illustrate the wealth and subtlety possible when directors, instead of merely 'illustrating' a script, *think* in graphic terms.

There is no need for each image to be a 'careful' composition or to be a lyrical expression of one particular feeling. The muscle of art is subtle contrast, so subtle that the spectator doesn't notice it as such. For example, one of the best ways of making the spectator conscious of fast or vigorous movement is by discreetly juxtaposing the movement with something very solid and static. In Pabst's *Kameradschaft* (1931) the miner's lorries, as they move off to the rescue of their French comrades, contrast with the heavy, immobile buildings and gates of the mine, or the lines of women and children silent along the roadside. Throughout the climax of Pabst's *Der Dreigroschenoper* (1931), when London's starving proletariat ruin the Coronation by mobbing the Queen, the crowds stream and bustle along past such 'static' features as a bend in the road. Similarly, in Eisenstein's *October* (1927), the scattering of a crowd under machine-gun fire is underlined by a very static visual feature—the immobile space of the square as they thin out.

A second point is that there can be no 'grand style' without emotional intimacy. The academicians like Fernandez always try for a 'grand', 'heroic', 'cosmic' style, all beautiful clouds, crags and skylines. But such effects are meaningless when there isn't also a sense of human joy and pain, of the ordinary, everyday scale. Dreyer's style is highly organized, formal, monumental, anything you like. But his characters are not really 'on a pedestal'. His eye is very sharp, piercing, in a sense, informal. The sense of 'face as landscape' is a kind of intimacy. This frame still is as 'intimatist' as anything in Humphrey Jennings' admirable documentary of World War Two *Fires Were Started* (1943) (Plate 8).

Analysts of composition in paintings love to cover the canvas with what looks like an underground map of lines and circles, and this is very sensible, for the canvas is a static design over which the eye moves to and fro, analysing and reanalysing the picture into its various patterns of colour, chiaroscuro, perspective, mass, balance, symbolism, etc. Screen visuals are usually rather simpler (for the equivalent to the canvas is the sequence, a series of 'details'). Further, the composition of a screen image depends on the narrative interest. The spectator usually has a definite centre of focus—the hero's face, the central event—and any compositional effect must be noticeable in relation to his 'centre of focus' rather than to the image as a whole.

Screen visuals usually make their point by one or two contrasts rather than by an intricate organization. A favourite device is to set off a strong architectural feature—a colonnade, a jetty, a bridge—at a diagonal to the line between the faces of two dramatically important characters. Or characters' bodies, arms, glances and positions in space may comprise a clutter of sharp, tense diagonals. The angles between two walls, or between walls and ceilings, may be brought into play. This still from *La Passion de Jeanne d' Arc* (Plate 12) contains a set of tense, painful angles—the pike, Joan's head (against her body) the two men who carry her, the 'heavy', 'unsettled' diagonal of the roof. The pyramidal form of the men carrying Joan creates a sense of weight, of struggle.

Similar 'lines' may be set up by the play of spotlights through darkness, by colour, by shift of dramatic centre, and so on.

Or a composition may derive its beauty from a simplicity of outline on a flat plane. (Plate 10.) Or from *hints* of depth (Plate 9)—how beautifully the visual suggestion reinforces the psychological uneasiness.

Pabst and Ophuls are specialists in multi-plane compositions. The central action is glimpsed through a foreground 'screen' of hats, flowers, bottles on a shelf, minor characters or furnishings, and beyond the main action we become aware of a 'background' plane—dancers, lookers-on, a door into another room, or perhaps a mirror reflecting the main action from another angle. Contrasts of spotlight and shadow can be used to direct the eye and prevent the picture being a clutter; while the abundance of environment gives a very powerful sense of atmosphere. Pabst's *Der Dreigroschenoper* and Ophuls' *Madame De* are particularly rich in such effects. Both directors specialize in using light and smoke to make one aware of the air around the characters.

A beautiful recessive pattern of movements is shown in this frame-still from the riot sequence in *La Passion de Jeanne d'Arc* (Plate 11).

The first still from Eisenstein's *Alexander Nevski* (Plate 13) is a masterly combination of bold outlines, simple form and complex detail. Its near-symmetry would be stodgy were it not for the projecting beam which gives it such life, leaping out from the tower like a cry. Yet every visual feature echoes the same basic shape—the cowls, the crosses, the tower, the helmets, are all variations on the one theme of virile upthrust, which is in grim contrast to the hanging man. A simpler, but equally subtle, 'theme and variation' is offered by the shot of the three Teutonic helmets. (Plate 14) Each helmet is a brutal face. First our attention is drawn by the watchful eyes in the largest helmet on the right. Then we see the more closed helmet, second in size, on the left. And finally, ramming the message home, we see the even more metallic face between them, like reinforcements lying in 'ambush'. The degrees of 'closedness' form a climax.

In a very different key, Renoir's *French Can-Can* offers another form of theme and variations. One after the other, three young friends of Nina (Françoise Arnoul) present themselves for an audition as can-can dancers. The first, a laundress, shows a brave spirit, but can't dance very well. The second, a frail, pale, long-faced girl, with lanky limbs and a thin lock of bouncing hair, is apparently a gymnastic expert, for she does high kicks in an almost laughable mechanical style—we feel like laughing until, as she gathers confidence, she relaxes and shows an exuberance which really is impressive. After her comes our third candidate, a haughty, physically opulent milady who cannot raise a leg without wobbling violently. And this succession of 'twists' is further diversified-and-unified as Nina, a trim redhead, dances expertly beside her friends to encourage them. All this is taken by Renoir at a cracking pace, as if to stress the contrasts. Quite apart from the *characterological* interest of each different girl, there is a magnificent variety of emotion—nervousness, disappointment, and so on. Though this little sequence exists in time, and as a narrative, it is constructed on the same principle of 'theme and variations' as the shots from *Alexander Nevski.*

Another form of 'variation' is exemplified by the still from *Ivan the Terrible* (Plate 15)—where the gap in the wall 'echoes' Ivan's shape, and the winding crowd the hang of his sleeve. The care behind the image is revealed by the way in which the 'twist' in the line of the crowd re-echoes in the 'twist' of Ivan's staff and to his sleeve and shoulder.

The next two stills, one from Murnau's *Tabu* (Plate 16), the other from *La Passion de Jeanne d'Arc* (Plate 17) show how otherwise very different visuals may have certain marked features in common—in this case, a vigorous organization of diagnosis and zigzags.

Often the composition is a matter of lights and darks. In the still from *Tabu* (Plate 19) the left and right hand sides are 'mirrors' to each other. Just as there is a triangle of darkness on the left, there is a triangle of light on the right. The image from *Ivan the Terrible* (Plate 18) is a *pointilliste* 'spatter' of lights and darks. (If one half-closes one's eyes, the chiaroscuro can be seen more clearly.) The shot from *Tabu* is more than a merely formal pattern: the contrast between the flesh of the man's torso, as he lies awake, and the girl's face, lost in the darkness of sleep, between flesh (on the left) and darkness (on the right), is part of the emotional impact.

A film may be built on a contrast of textures—whether of fabrics and objects as in *Les Yeux Sans Visages*—or of *photographic* textures. There is a beautiful run of colour contrasts during the credits of George Sidney's *Pal Joey*, where we cut from a 'hot', glittering shot of neon lights at night, to a 'cool', silver, metallic train, and then to the soft, creamy pastel white of a ferryboat. Somehow, this is more than mere technical 'dandyism'—it seems to be saying something about the blend of gloss and melancholy in American life. Freda's *The Terror of Dr. Hichcock* has an extraordinary funeral sequence. Black-clad mourners in black umbrellas walk under a silvery glitter of sunlit rain; they pass bright flowers; the grain of the coffin is warmly visible in the sun. The living wood. . . . As the procession passes a row of silhouetted, green-tinged cypresses, a shaft of sunlight pours down on them and for a split second is broken up by the camera lens into all the colours of the rainbow. 'Artificial' as it is—the human eye wouldn't see it—the effect 'fits', because it lifts to the level of paroxysm the tragic irony of sunlight at a young woman's funeral.

Although the photographic image has no 'line' (being only patches of light-and-dark) robes, swirling water or other objects may be used to create a 'calligraphic' effect. The folds and swirl of robes in Cocteau's *La Belle et la Bête* have a nervous linearity reminiscent of Cocteau's drawings—and not really very far from the calligraphy of robes in 'The Three Graces' by another tormented soul, Botticelli.

Film lighting is a primary factor in creating atmosphere—though very much at the mercy of a good print. For *Le Sang d'Un Poète* Cocteau asked Perinal for 'a debauched sort of lighting', but the film's quality of four-in-the-morning-blues is due to many factors. There is the stealthy, slithery, strained postures of the poet, whether he is crouching horrified over the lips bubbling in the palm of his hand, or sidling along the enigmatic corridor. The light, without quite *sculpting* his muscles, picks out their movement, caressively. There is the contract between his bare flesh and the drab, seedy wall.

A lucky accident helped the film's atmosphere. '. . . the sweepers were told to clear up the studio, just as we had started on our last shots. But as I was about to protest, my cameraman (Perinal) asked me to do nothing of the kind; he had just realized what beautiful images he would be able to take through the dust raised by the sweepers in the light of the arc lamps.'

All Cocteau's films are extremely sensual, and to consider them as a collection of merely literary symbols is to miss half of their power. The symbols themselves are sensual—snow, blood, opium, poisons, rubber gloves and suits, women in white fur against white snow, negroes with shining muscles, champagne served in a house with peeling walls, *les enfants terribles* sucking away at prawns in bed, bodies struggling and straining against the wind, or oozing along in reverse- or slow-motion, giving an effect of laborious sickliness. One can *feel* the lips bubbling under water in the poet's hand. And what could be more physical than the idea of mirrors which turn to water when you hurl yourself into them?

As Death (Maria Casarès) in his *Orphée* dons and removes her crackling rubber gloves, we are not far from the fetishistic sensations which upset Emanuelle Riva while she was making *Le Huitième Jour* for Marcel Hanoun. She testifies: 'The erotic scenes are intended to shock. . . . He found the putting on of rubber gloves particularly exciting, and made a great deal of the crackling noise they made and the vaguely sensuous idea of a second skin. . . . I had really a very unpleasant time making it.' When Orphée (Jean Marais), finding the mirror remaining glass, impenetrable, sinks down wearily against it, we hear his flesh squeak against the glass. 'Oh that this too too squeaky flesh might melt. . . .' Such sharp little details of physical realism give a hallucinatory power to the film's world.

The film director can sensitively orchestrate light. He can model, give or remove depth and contour, vary or contradict the shapes and surfaces of his décor. In café or ballroom scenes, the light is a prime source of atmosphere, weaving light and smoke into nets of chiaroscuro. By light, says Sternberg, 'air can be made to glow. Just as I spray trees with aluminium to give life to the dull green, just as one filters the sky to reduce its whiteness . . . the skin should reflect and not blot light, and the lights are to be used to caress, not to wipe out, what they strike. . . .' A character's 'walk . . . or movement through space should be made into an encounter with light . . . lifeless surfaces should be relentlessly treated to take light, and over-brilliant and flaring surfaces must be reduced to their order. . . .' It is plain that one has not fully felt a Sternberg film, whether in the 'dirty' key of *The Blue Angel*, or the 'glittering' key of *The Devil is a Woman*, or the mysterious gradations of *The Saga of Anatahan*, until one can share something of this painterly *sensuality* about light. The same is true of Murnau, of Leni, of many of the German directors of the silent era.

Particularly with colour-and-Cinemascope, it is possible to speak of 'décor' directors—one thinks of Minnelli's *The Bells are Ringing* and *Two Weeks in Another Town*, of Cottafavi's *Hercules Conquers Atlantis* and Bava's *Hercules at the Centre of the Earth*, and Kurt Maetzig's *First Spaceship on Venus*, at which we shall glance again later. At the other extreme, the harmony of cloths and furnishings in Renoir's *French Can-Can* isn't unlike Minnelli's films in its 'Mozartian' colour. But Minnelli seems to have difficulty in escaping from the academicism of a certain 'colour elegance', even if most of his films have admirable scenes. Décor directors are usually also costume directors—as exemplified by the 'echo' of robe and wall in *Ivan the Terrible*, where the cloak becomes part of an overall architectural structure.

Camera movements constitute an integral part of the cinema's visual repertoire. In Autant-Lara's *Le Diable au Corps* Gerard Philippe's first love-scene with Micheline Presle is climaxed by the camera tracking past a chequered bedshead to two hands clasping over the light-switch and each other. But later, as the heroine lies dying, in the same bed, giving birth to her lover's son, the camera repeats the movement—this time, though, her hand closes over her husband's, while she cries her lover's name. And her husband takes it as the name she has chosen for their child. . . . Without the repetition of the camera position and movement, we would feel much less sharply the irony of deception and misunderstanding, the immortal moment denied and reasserted. . . .

The same 'elegaic' use of camera movements is found in Ophuls, but developed to the pitch of paroxysm. As James Mason remarked,

'I think I know the reason why,
Producers tend to make him cry,
Inevitably they demand
Some stationary set-ups, and
A shot that does not call for tracks

Is agony for poor dear Max,
Who, separated from his dolly,
Is wrapped in deepest melancholy.
Once, when they took away his crane,
I thought he'd never smile again. . . .'

The camera's movements through elaborate Ophulsesque décor carries an astonishing lyricism. Whenever camera movements depart from 'natural' lines of sight or of movement, the spectator becomes vaguely conscious of a certain uneasiness, or of exhilaration. Thus when in Clair's *Le Quatorze Juillet* the camera moves along the outside of a house from window to window, one has a mixture of feelings—of cheeky wit (we are 'Peeping Tom'ing in this Godlike way); of melancholy (we are *outside* the house); of intimacy (our partial exclusion emphasizes the privilege of catching them in secrecy); there is the absurdity of all these characters so near to each other, and so self-engrossed; and the curious feeling of superiority in our magic gliding through mid-air. Similarly, long trackings can create a kind of gathering excitement, as the landscape streams past us. Particular tensions are possible when the camera moves at oblique angle towards a 'point of intersection' with a moving centre of interest (a dancer, a rider, a train).

By his camera movements, Ophuls gives both visual life and emotional dynamism to the stuffy, hierarchicalized, static décor—and society—of Vienna 1900. His camera moves past screens, flunkeys, fans, candles, whispered conversations, much as a Henry James sentence winds its way through innumerable reservations, concessions and hesitations to its final rather tentative assertion. Ophuls' films are full of symbols of movement—staircases, spiral staircases, immensely long corridors, the can-can in *Le Plaiser*, coaches, the lovers waltzing in *Madame De. . . .* In *Lola Montès*, even the ship waltzed under the stars, and when Lola and Liszt live together, it is in two coaches, travelling.

Until Ophuls, technicians' lore had it that one must never, never bring a pan back to its starting point. But again and again Ophuls' camera performs *la ronde*. It moves as his plots move. *La Ronde* begins and ends with the same prostitute, for Viennese love is a merry-go-round which spins industriously and none too merrily. The plot of *Madame De . . .* is based on the jewels which keep *returning*. *Lola Montès* is a film of circles—the circus ring round which the ringmaster moves incessantly, Lola on a carousel. . . . Ophuls' way of telling stories in flashbacks is another form of 'circularity'—we are constantly returning to the past, and then returning to the present. Thus past and future are mingled—just as in *La Ronde* Anton Walbrook leads Simone Simon from 'now' to 'six months later', when, ironically, she will betray the soldier who betrayed her then. Ophuls' fondness for episodes is another form of his fondness for flashbacks—both suggest that human encounters are shapeless, indecisive, in a sense, pointless, leading to nothing in the future.

To over-simplify, perhaps, Ophuls' camera movements suggest a mellow 'fatalism'. Everything ends where it begins. The world is a maze of ironies, of impermanence, of nostalgias. If Ophuls' camera moves, it is *à la recherche du temps perdu.* But it isn't possible to separate the camera movements from the décor through which it moves, and which it shows to us, or the dramatic context in which it occurs. It has lately become fashionable to attribute to camera movements effects which are really due to décor and lighting. John Guillermin's (interesting, and cleverly styled) *Waltz of the Toreadors* has a track-through-a-dissolve-to-the-same-ballroom-years-before which Ophuls would have been pleased to have thought of. But the total effect is weaker because the lighting and staging haven't the Ophuls music.

Similarly, movement *within* the frame may be 'carried' from one scene to another. The rhythms of Fellini's *La Dolce Vita,* are beautifully controlled in their very slowness. Quite exquisite is the way in which the curve of Anita's 'cardinal' hat, as it falls in the wind from the dome of St. Peter's, is continued by the movement of a saxophone in the next shot. I described Franju's *Les Yeux Sans Visage* as a metronome-and-protractor film, and King Vidor literally used a metronome to regulate the action climaxes in both *The Big Parade* and *Our Daily Bread.* 'I was in the realm of my favourite obsession, experimenting with the possibilities of 'silent music'. . . . When we filmed the march through Belleau Wood . . . I used the . . . metronome and a drummer with a bass drum . . . so that all in a range of several hundred yards could hear. I instructed the men that each step must be taken on a drum beat, each turn of the head, lift of a rifle, pull of a trigger, in short, every physical move must occur on the beat of a drum. . . . When the picture opened, I requested Sid Grauman to have the orchestra stop their musical accompaniment at the beginning of the sequence, and keep silent until its finish. . . .' Again in *Our*

Daily Bread, 'The picks came down on the counts of one and three, the shovels scooped dirt on count two and tossed it on four. . . .' Similarly, Greta Garbo's movements during the scene in Rouben Mamoulian's *Queen Christina* where she 'remembers' the furniture were timed to a metronome.

A film may be built on its sense of space, like *Entr'acte* (which is regularly credited to René Clair, although Clair acted mainly as a technical assistant to the dadaist painter, Frances Picabia). The film (whose title means 'Intermission') formed part of a dada ballet called *Relâche* ('No Performance Today'). Picabia's problem was to translate the ballet's flow of jokes into terms of screen action and movement.

The film was originally shown on a very large screen, giving a 'Cinerama' effect. It falls into two parts, the first rather static and full of arbitrary dada in-jokes. In the second a narrative crystallizes, and we have the celebrated sequence of a funeral procession rushing along at the double after a runaway hearse (which is drawn by a camel).

But amidst all the comment of the baffling *non sequiturs* of its 'literary content', only Bardèche and Brasillach point out that the 'continuity' of the first part is its play with sensations of space and balance—to link it with the surrounding ballet. The rooftop setting, and panning shots round the horizon, the tilt up a 'column' of windows, the theme of people *taking aim* from rooftops (with shot-guns or cannons, sometimes into the audience), the coconut bouncing on the jet of water, all are intended to create in the audience a kind of spatial uneasiness, indeed, giddiness. Interwoven with these are dislocations of movement—two men floating over a cannon, the unexpected angles on a ballerina, the visual echo between a worm's-eye-view of her knickered thighs and a pair of boxing gloves nudging each other, a slow chess game proceeding on the rooftops, which begin spinning crazily. The film becomes much more satisfying and 'logical' if one more or less forgets the 'literary content' of the symbols, concentrates on the visual-spatial sensations and jokes offered by objects and settings, and finds most of their 'poetic' meanings in these physical relationships.

In films like these the film's mixed-art status is confirmed. During the shooting of *The Big Parade* 'one British veteran wanted to know if he were performing in "some bloody ballet". I did not say so at the time, but that is exactly what it was—a bloody ballet, a ballet of death.' Equally, 'I decided to treat . . . building this ditch in a manner I imagined a choreographer would use in plotting out the movements of a ballet. . . .'

Griffith was a master of counterpointing shapes-in-motion. There is far more than narrative interest to the celebrated 'cross-cutting' in his chases. The final 'movement' of *Intolerance* (1918), where preparations for a hanging proceed while a car races a railway train with news of a pardon, is built up out of story ingredients which can't possibly carry conviction today. But the sheer sense of movement does. Griffith contrasts the steady, sweeping, winding curve of the train with the car's bullet-like movement on a twisting, switchback-like road—meanwhile the three prison officials bob up the little staircase to the scaffold with a petty, jagged, insistent movement, like the meticulous ticking of a watch. The surging train, the yo-yoing car, the brisk little movements in the condemned cell, all form a choreographic 'whirlpool' of movements. The descent of Cyrus' army on the Babylonians has some astonishing play with crowd movements. Choreography rules even the intimate scenes—as the Three Uplifters advance to seize the young mother's baby, all their grasping arms and hands move like the tentacles of an octopus. As the Huguenot girl is slaughtered by a Catholic mercenary, Griffith asks us to *feel* the contrast between the soldier's spiky uniform and sharp brutal movements, and the girl's slow slide in her flowing nightshirt to the floor as she dies. Griffith broke down the 'semaphore' acting code of his time (outstretched arms for 'go', clasped hands for 'please', jumping up and down for joy, and so on) and gave it a choreographic organization. His sense of organizing movement is at least as great an innovation as his narrative developments. It inspired Lang's *Metropolis* (1926), and seems to me a more important feature of Eisenstein's silent films than his application of theories about 'intellectual' montage.

Such devices, in their mechanical forms, have become an integral part of film technique, but are capable of more imaginative application—whether the tempo is *lento ponderoso* (as in Lang's *The Woman in the Window*, Franju's *La Tete Contre Les Murs*), or allegretto (Chaplin's little comedies abound in the sprite orchestration of chases in every direction and dimension of space and shape of obstacle), or whether in the sustained, symphonic structures of Alexander Dovzhenko. A cut in Jules Dassin's *Thieves Highway* serves to indicate other contrasts. A shot of a heavy fruit-truck careering off a road is followed by a shot of the oranges showering all over the screen. The cut brings into play contrasts of shape, form, pattern, direction of movement, sensed texture. . . . There is a fascinating effect in Kurosawa's *The Seven Samurai.* As they answer an alarm, we see, in quick, sharp succession, four shots, each showing one Samurai running, from right to left. But in each shot, the Samurai is further to the right of the screen than his predecessor was. Each is, so to speak, 'falling back'. In short—they're all running as fast as they can, straining at the limit of their strength, can't run at the superhuman speed they feel they need.

Our survey of visual effects has necessarily been summary and impressionistic, but will have served its purpose if it shows how extensively content is created out of details of style, and what sort of 'pictorial content' can work effectively on the cinema screen.

4 · Auteurs and Dream Factories

Questions of style bring us to the so-called *auteur* theory and the debates about it that sprawl through French, British and American film magazines. Our concern is not to discuss these controversies in all their aspects, but to concentrate on those which concern the issue of style and personal vision.

At the same time, it may be helpful to enlarge the field of reference a little, so as to see how, behind the specific disagreements, many assumptions have been operating which have confused what only seems a 'purely' aesthetic disagreement.

The *auteur* theory is the assumption that most films can be interpreted in terms of their director's artistic personality just as intensively as a novel can be interpreted in terms of its authors'. It is obviously true of, for example, Dreyer and Bresson, so that much discussion has centred on the question of how far, if at all, such an approach is relevant or adequate to Hollywood directors.

We may perhaps usefully contrast *limited* and *extended* applications of *auteur* theory. A limited theory was central to the tenets of what one may call the '30's school' of British criticism, running from Paul Rotha and John Grierson through to Richard Winnington, Roger Manvell and the *Penguin Film Review* (1946–49). Their *auteurs* were such artists as Griffith, Eisenstein, Pudovkin, Flaherty, Disney, Capra, Carné, Welles, Sturges, Huston, Lean and so on. But side by side with this appreciation of the artist, these critics generally had a special interest in a film's reflection of social reality, and a special antipathy to Hollywood 'glamour' (which was tolerated, or not, but generally felt to be antithetical to seriousness, with the occasional exception, as for Garbo). Thus the documentary movement was felt to be extremely meritorious, because it showed docks and post offices and all the exterior paraphernalia of 'social realism', whereas Sternberg's films with Marlene Dietrich were felt to be more or less meretricious (distinction between these and the Garbos was assumed rather than explained). The critics were very sympathetic to the *auteur* struggling to be individualistic and honest within the restraints of the Hollywood system (which indeed attained a peak of rigidity in the early 40's). Their lively awareness of the negative aspects of the Hollywood system constituted a powerful check to *auteur* theory. Another check came from their advocacy of the documentary *movement* and *its* themes and qualities. It was assumed that a director might make one or two good films, or come up with the brilliant fluke, then yield to pressures, or stray after false gods, and be lost to serious film-making. Even the films of obvious *auteurs* would be related to general aesthetic directives or social issues with little exegesis and less close linking with their creators' artistic personalities. All this constituted a *limited* form of *auteur* theory.

A new spirit appeared when a group of Oxford undergraduates, notably Gavin Lambert, Karel Reisz and Lindsay Anderson, founded their magazine *Sequence* (1948–52) which, without reacting against the older critics, moved a little way towards a less earnest tone, and to more probing exegeses, after the model of the undergraduate English essay. Lindsay Anderson's enthusiasm for John Ford's *She Wore a Yellow Ribbon* (1949) and Gavin Lambert's for Jean Cocteau signalled an increase in interest in what *Sequence* called 'the poetic vision', as against the documentary and realist virtues, which were in no way decried. Nonetheless Richard Winnington, who had initially encouraged these young critics, repudiated them, just before his death, for having regressed to a precious aestheticism.

Gavin Lambert, aided by the *Sequence* team, had by then become editor of *Sight and Sound* and of its sister-journal, *The Monthly Film Bulletin*, which had fallen into a dismal academicism. Lambert and Ken Tynan, who contributed excellent appreciations of gangster films and Tom and Jerry cartoons, looked like continuing the tradition of appreciative criticism that had been so positive a factor of *Sequence*. But Lambert and Tynan left, and the magazine began a period of slow stagnation, all the more marked by contrast with the convulsive transformations of French criticism. It maintained a sufficiently authoritative tone to be accepted both here and abroad as 'the' organ of English intellectual opinion, which is why we pay attention to it here.

The range of *auteurs* was scarcely widened from that which they had inherited from the '30's school'. Indeed, by the late 50's, John Grierson reproached the magazine for having neglected the discovery of new talent (it promptly discovered Richard Quine, and then left Hollywood at that for the next few years).

While the old-established *auteurs* were treated with consistent respect, and an uncritical adulation for Ford prefigured the excesses of extended *auteur* theory, there was a group of directors who were held to have had their time as *auteurs*, but to have lapsed into the Hollywood ruck. These included Fritz Lang, King Vidor and Alfred Hitchcock (*auteurs* for some of their pre-war films), Frank Capra (for his 'socially conscious' comedies of the 30's), Minnelli (for his flirtations with populism and for his musicals). *Red River* (1948) was the last Hawks film to have an enthusiastic review. Nicholas Ray, Robert Wise, Jules Dassin and Joseph Losey earned short-lived reputations for early films (*They Live by Night*, *The Set-Up*, *The Naked City* and *The Dividing Line*) which were in accepted traditions, but were dismissed when they grouped for new idioms and attitudes. Veterans like Raoul Walsh and Allan Dwan were as unnoticed as a relative newcomer like Otto Preminger, and none of the new directors to emerge in the 50's provoked enthusiasm comparable to the old *auteurs*. Thus Richard Brooks, Sam Fuller, Elia Kazan, Frank Tashlin and Budd Boetticher were scarcely distinguished from the Hollywood 'ruck'.

Interest in 'social realism' itself underwent a change. In theory, at least, a special importance was attached to 'social consciousness', whether documentary or neo-realistic in type, or inclining more to the 'poetic vision', like Ford's *The Grapes of Wrath* (1940). A tense cynicism and questioning was accepted, but only within certain limits of tone and topic. Thus Preston Sturges' edgy comedies were securely within the pale, whereas Billy Wilder's aroused a faint distaste. The 'Raymond Chandler' mood was welcomed for its lyrical astringency, but there seemed an increasing deprecation or resentment of those films which brought this astringent, questioning mood into relation with specific social issues, or with the American social climate as a whole, notably Fritz Lang's *The Big Heat* (1953). The idyllic, 'Ford' Western was still enjoyed, but not the new bitter tone of Sam Fuller's *Run of the Arrow* (1957) or Anthony Mann's *Man of the West* (1958). Now Richard Winnington's denunciation, which at the time had seemed excessive, began to justify itself as a shrewd insight. Films such as Richard Brooks' *The Blackboard Jungle* (1955) or Nicholas Ray's *Rebel Without a Cause* (1955) were damned with faint praise. Lindsay Anderson denounced Elia Kazan's *On the Waterfront* (1954) as 'implicitly, if unconsciously, Fascist . . . hopeless, savagely ironic . . . fundamentally contemptuous . . . without either grace, joy or love', but his vehemence was, in a way, more worthy a response than the supercilious shrug which greeted many equally 'concerned' American films. Unusually gracious was P.H.'s description of Nunnally Johnson's *The Man in the Grey Flannel Suit* (1955) as 'uneasily fascinating'.

But whether such films were condemned, tolerated, or adduced as evidence of symptoms of moral decay, their *auteurs* were credited with little ability to think about, or make any interesting comment on, either their topics in particular, or human nature in general. They were spiritually depersonalized, they were merely 'Hollywood', and the word 'Hollywood' was used with a quiet, but firm, dismissiveness. Hollywood had slickness, yes, but intelligence, never. The only exegesis of such films was destructive; Penelope Houston attempted to prove that Stanley Kramer's *On the Beach* (1959) made fallout glamorous.

Gradually, this derisive approach extended even to obvious *auteurs*. The first Bergman film to be shown here, *Sawdust and Tinsel* (1953), was dismissed as a neurotic throwback to the tricks of Germanic expressionism. Even after Bergman's increasing celebrity had modified this attitude, Peter John Dyer saw in *The Virgin Spring* (1960) only 'consulting-room horrors . . . exhibitionism . . . at its most pathological'. The same article dismissed Visconti too; his *Rocco and His Brothers* (1960) was 'the boldest example of fraudulent conversion since *Ossessione*'. It displayed 'self-indulgence' (a trait which this school of criticism was quick to notice, perhaps because it bears so close a resemblance to self-expression), and Eric Rhode, writing about Visconti's *La Terra Trema*, concurred in this 'hypochondriac' approach to the *auteur*: 'There is something wrong somewhere' (context implies: with Visconti's emotional health) 'when a nobleman makes a film entirely about Sicilian fishermen' (presumably we should each keep to our own class?). To the first Bunuel film to reach this country for several years, *La Mort En Ce Jardin* (1956), Dyer conceded 'a workable script' and some interesting ingredients, but concluded: 'What is missing is the barest competence in direction.'

Whatever one's opinion of these films may be (mine is that only the last three are anywhere near 'masterpieces') it was difficult not to be startled by the contrast between the brutal, summary tone adopted by the English magazine, and the thoughtful and complex exegeses characteristic of the wide range of continental approaches. The *Sight and Sound* team seemed unreflectively to identify the most concerned and vital American directors with an 'unhealthy' American climate, while castigating distinguished European artists for an equally unhealthy individualism. In England, only 'Free Cinema' (intimately connected with the magazine itself) earned more than token appreciation.

What seemed an attitude of complacent contempt set the tone for the bitterness with which *Sight and Sound* was attacked by the younger English critics, notably the 'new wave' of undergraduates who were associated first with the Liberal magazine *Oxford Opinion* and later with *Movie*, and who were generally felt to be English proponents of *auteur* approach.[1]

The main dispute was not whether a film had to be by an *auteur* in order to merit critical opinion, but, which directors were the *auteurs*. The younger critics accepted most of the orthodox 'elect', and the dispute centred largely on the status of directors whom *Sight and Sound* had consigned to the Hollywood 'ruck'. The *Movie* critics accorded particularly high places in their canon to the post-war films of Hitchcock, Hawks, Preminger and Ray. In America, Andrew Sarris, the most thorough Anglo-Saxon exponent of *auteur* theory, went on to postulate as *auteurs* some fifty Hollywood directors, thus, if not actually denying, at least sharply diminishing, the significance of traditional criticisms of the Hollywood system.

In this respect *Movie* and Sarris concurred with the 'second generation' (*ca* 1954–58) of critics of *Cahiers du Cinema*. These critics, dubbed the 'Hitchcocko-Hawksiens', included such *Nouvelle Vague* directors-to-be as François Truffaut, Jean-Luc Godard, Claude Chabrol, Jacques Rivette, and Eric Rohmer. Thus, by the time the controversy came to England, they were possessed of immense prestige, for their stylistic and thematic innovations as for their international success.

The supposed indebtedness of the younger British critics to *Cahiers du Cinema* gave rise to many a merry jest, though I doubt

[1] Not at all as rigid as that of *Cahiers* in theory, though most of their writing centred round *auteurs*.

whether *Cahiers* was much more to them than a signpost to some directors, and, otherwise, a flag to rally round. There was certainly little emulation of its approach or thought. *Movie* offered, instead of *Cahiers*' characteristically 'philosophic' approach to style (of which more later), something between 'exegesis' and 'functional analysis'. Its critics often restricted themselves to clarifying the relationship of stylistic details to the whole, and they generally refrained from judging the quality of the view of life in the films of their favourites. Ian Cameron wrote, coat-trailingly, 'To judge a film on anything other than its style is to set up the critics' own views on matters outside the cinema against those of its maker. This is gross impertinence.' This, surely excessive, limitation on the scope of criticism becomes more understandable when one bears in mind the cavalier dismissals which had become the rule in *Sight and Sound*. The younger critics, while capable of summary writing-off, wrote at length only about the films they had enjoyed.

There can be little doubt that this critical line, however controversial in detail, had the excellent result of extending critical interest and respect to the films of many interesting directors, who for decades had been relegated to the outer darkness. For as we have seen *Sight and Sound* had become rather more rigorous in its disdain of Hollywood than the 30's school had been. And incapable of extended *appreciative* exegesis, restricting itself to, not interpreting, but 'evaluating', a film in a rather piecemeal way (the acting was 'sensitive', the direction was 'imaginative', the film a 'poetic vision' and so on). Indeed *Movie* and *Film* both showed that many criticisms were virtually paraphrases of criticisms by *other* members of the team of *other* films—identical phrases recurred, no 'specific' points were made. The equivalent French magazines had never adopted such a 'negativity'.[1] From 1928 to 1931, and again from 1945 to 1950, *La Revue du Cinema*, under the editorship of Jean-George Auriol, was devoting major reviews to such films as Dassin's *Brute Force* (1947), Charles Vidor's *Gilda* (1946) and William Dieterle's *Love Letters* (1945).[2] There was nothing specifically new, youthful or 'rebellious'

[1] Not, at least, on aesthetic grounds. *L'Ecran Francais*, while dominated by French Stalinists, had embarked on a systematic denigration of Hollywood films, but the movies there were political, rather than 'supercilious'. The *Sight and Sound* attitude was of course helped by a confluence of two attitudes: a general sympathy for the left, and the cultured English disdain for vulgar Americana.

[2] During its earlier period, it had an English equivalent in *Close-Up*, which however, was much less interested in American films.

about *Cahiers'* responsiveness towards American films. Indeed, the majority of French magazines were also exploring Hollywood extensively. *Positif* (founded 1952), with its Marxist and Surrealist tendencies, soon asserted its predilection for, notably, Robert Wise, Richard Brooks, John Huston and Frank Tashlin. And Henri Agel, doyen of the Roman Catholic school of film criticism, had also been paying serious attention to such refreshingly unexpected films as Hawks' *Monkey Business* and King Vidor's *Duel in the Sun.*

Indeed, it is possible to regard the *Cahiers* version of the extended *auteur* theory as a 'dogmatized' degradation of this general tradition. To understand it one must refer briefly to the figure of *Cahiers'* 'senior wrangler' André Bazin.

Bazin was a left-wing Catholic, completely unpuritanical, broad-minded and generous in his attitudes to the cinema. With his passionate responsiveness to the cinema as an authentic 'humanism', as an essentially 'impure' art, went a sensitivity to the cinema as a culture whose nuances and sensitivities could be as non-literary, as specifically cinematic, as those of music are specifically musical. He had two particular interests which were to be over-developed by younger writers. There was his concern with the philosophical implications of stylistic nuance, implications which he expressed in terms bordering on the metaphysical. This was partly a natural result of his Catholicism, partly because he often wrote as if style expressed mainly the *auteur's* attitude to the character's experiences (whereas I would argue that it more often expresses nuances in those experiences). Schematically rather than accurately, one may say that Bazin identified himself with the director, and the director with a very kindly God, who was blowing a kind of spiritual life into his subject-matter, much as God breathes life into Adam. A very kindly God, but also a rather vague one. For Bazin, in his very kindness, often dissolved the specific personal or social issues of a film into a spiritual generalization, rather after this pattern: 'Of course, *Bicycle Thieves* is, in a superficial sense, 'about' *this* workman in *this* society. But this predicament is only an image for something *deeper*: the *universal, human* predicament. . . .'

The, not so much flaws, as limitations, of such an approach must be evident. Soon, no film is felt to be 'about' its subject-matter. Its specificity, concreteness and consequently its richness of detail, dissolve into a sort of spiritual soup, which itself makes nonsense of all the differences between one culture and another, one person and another, one film and another. Without some sort of specificity *through* which any 'universality' can be attained, as a sort of none-too-important 'bonus', 'art' sinks back into something like religious-generalization-in-individualistic-metaphor. And much of Bazin's criticism is quite different from exegesis. It is about the relationship of an *auteur*-God to his creation. Bazin's 'collected works' read like one long stream of theological rumination, all the more amiable, perhaps, for centring on man rather than God. They sometimes read like tentative prologomena to *Honest to God*, and, however full of solipsisms, have, not only their own cinematographic interest, but a quite theological tension and flow.

Bazin certainly makes the point that in the films of a genuine *auteur* every detail can be taken as 'meant', and is neither accidental nor 'pure form'; and also that style 'is' content.

But some of Bazin's successors in *Cahiers* made of his approach a Procrustean bed. They sometimes denied that an *auteur*'s films could validly be related to anything other than its creator's attitudes. Once they accepted a director as an *auteur* (and only directors were *auteurs*), then he could no more be deposed, or fall below himself, than God. The *auteur* had a quality of 'efficacious grace' that enabled him to score repeated triumphs, down to the minutest detail, over the Hollywood system. If an *auteur*'s film was dramatically trite and boring, they shifted their interest to its 'allegorical' level. Or they felt that the *auteur* had, if not deliberately chosen, at least seized upon, so 'empty' a subject, so as to give *carte blanche* to his nuance-laden style, through which the critic could apprehend, by camera movement or other subtle means of stimulating reflection, the 'spiritual generality' of which the film was an illustration. Or, again: only so 'banal' a subject could enable style to be its own subject-matter; so that a trite film could be talked about in a jargon verging on that used of abstract painting (surprisingly, it never did more than verge on it, perhaps because the critics' real interest was philosophical). They occasionally argued that poor technical quality (e.g. of back-projection) showed a director was interested only in the 'deep' (allegorical, philosophical) aspects of his plot. Or he might be speaking to those connoisseurs who knew how to 'decode' the inner meanings of his films.

In itself, none of these principles is far-fetched or absurd. They are used every day in criticisms of the other arts. The much-ridiculed idea of *auteurs* speaking through an esoteric symbolism is relevant in the case of certain films, notably, of course, those which the *Cahiers* critics themselves went on to make. The idea of offering 'special' meanings to one's *amis inconnus* is common in all the arts, and quite compatible with the idea of the work of art communicating before it is understood. The idea of 'meaning through style' is very fruitful in the case of, for example, Max Ophuls or Joseph von Sternberg. This essay has advocated virtually this approach to the films of Bresson and Dreyer, by suggesting that the spectator understands them best when he 'plays the game' of assuming that every detail in a film is 'meant'.

But the application of these principles was often disquieting. What might seem that most sympathetic of critical aberrations, the 'delirium of interpretation', soon revealed itself as not at all generous. For it was used to rule out the film's differences from the critic's own sensibility. Thus Ophuls, Hitchcock and Bunuel were all mashed together as crypto-neo-Platonic-Catholics-despite-themselves. And Bazin's own 'generous' indifference to social significance hardened among his followers into something like resentment of it, with the implication that this aspect of a film could be only 'obvious' or 'banal', a 'party line', as it were. Thus a concentration on 'the philosophy of style' too often went with quick evasions or dismissals of a film's literary or dramatic components. A cabbalistic subtlety was attributed to films which showed no other sign of deep thought, or even of being more than entertainments of moderate competence. Since the 'esoteric' meanings weren't very profound either, there seemed neither a *prima facie* case, nor a reward, for all this complicated decoding. Indeed, many of the directors celebrated had made it amply clear that they were very rarely in complete control of their films, that they made many potboilers for 'alimentary' reasons, that compromises, concessions, unwanted scripts and stars, were forced upon them.

One willingly grants 'total meaning' to Bresson and Dreyer because they give ample evidence, internal and external to their films, of having achieved their extraordinary degree of control. But it isn't a dogmatic assumption made before every film, nor an assertion that every artist has equal control over his own experience, his medium, and his creative circumstances.

The attribution of 'secret meanings' to otherwise unremarkable craftsmen looked suspiciously like (*a*) a way of treating films as *objéts trouvés*, rather than as part of a communicating situation (so distorting them), and (*b*) a way of enjoying the Hollywood film while giving it an apparent, but basically distortive, congruence to 'high culture' ideas about authors and creative personalities.

For all this, it would be misleading to overlook the more 'moderate' positions always characteristic of the best writing in *Cahiers*. It would be most inaccurate to equate French criticism as a whole with *Cahiers*, or *Cahiers* as a whole with all that was most extreme and limited in *Cahiers*. Unfortunately, this last was taken virtually for granted throughout the *auteur* controversy in Britain, largely as a result of *Sight and Sound*'s own, defensive reflex. Sarcastic as its own dismissals of Bergman, Visconti, Losey, Ray *et al.* had been, the magazine felt wronged when attacked itself, in exactly similar terms, by the rising generation, and replied in terms which seemed to aim less at a genuine understanding of the issues at stake than at a crushing polemical victory. Thus Penelope Houston and Richard Roud both chose to identify French criticism as a whole with the extreme trend in *Cahiers*. They seized on its repudiation of social significance, and on its acceptance of style as its own subject-matter, so as to contrast their own 'humanism' with the 'non-humanist aestheticism' which Roud presented as *The French Line*.

Penelope Houston even went on to equate the younger English critics with something like a 'hoodlum' view of life. 'To the generation which has grown up during the last few years, art is seen as something for kicks; films which stab at the nerves and emotions; jazz and the excitements surrounding it. . . . Violence on the screen is accepted as a stimulant. . . .' Not surprisingly, the younger critics disliked being called kicks-crazy when all they were asking for was for more directors to be treated with critical respect and for more attention to be paid to subtleties of style.

The *Sight and Sound* team proposed two solutions to the 'style *v.* content' issue. Miss Houston settled matters peremptorily: 'Cinema is about human relationships, not about spatial relationships.' But this rules out the possibility, surely obvious, since the cinema is a visual medium, that spatial relationships might themselves be metaphors for human relationships. Richard Roud's conclusion seemed more conciliatory. 'We would gain . . . by adopting . . . the firm belief that form is at least as important as content.' But the persisting separation of form and content which 'as important as' implies, reveals its consequences when Roud, commenting on the spatial relationships in *L'Avventura*, sees its visual qualities as only 'an additional, non-representative element for our pleasure; a formal choreography of movements which accompanies the films, providing a non-conceptual figure in the carpet'. Yet this formulation itself falls into precisely that 'non-humanist aestheticism' so derided in *Cahiers*: 'A film's style is not about human relationships, but about its style.'

To criticize this non-response to the eloquent visuals of *L'Avventura* is in no way to deny the possibilities of visual abstraction in films, nor of a possible layer in *L'Avventura* itself, of aesthetic interest for its own sake (a layer to which I would myself attach little 'cultural' importance). But what is curious is the difficulty in seeing that the spatial relationships might be connected with the story.

Also worth remarking is the hardening attitude towards the *auteur*. The 30's school awareness of the Hollywood 'system' went with a certain sympathy for the artist who was trapped within it; *Sight and Sound* made little or no attempt to distinguish, in the current films of Hitchcock, Lang, Losey, Hawks, and so on, anything that wasn't 'system'. The extended *auteur* theory, on the other hand, makes little or no allowance for the 'imposed' aspects of a film. It is content to 'decode' meanings and experiences from cryptic hints, imaginary or real, and, in so doing, to accept, for the full emotional picture of an experience or attitude, a rather cerebral 'notation'. No distinction is made, or felt, or respected, between the 'sign' for an experience from the 'symbol' for it. But before we look at some consequences of this non-distinction, its origins can perhaps be clarified.

The *Sight and Sound* critics were heirs to an upper-middle-class climate of cultural habit and opinion exemplified, at its best, by the novels of E. M. Forster, at its most mediocre, by the complacent pessimism of the remarks on the popular cinema by Palinurus in *The Unquiet Grave*, and, at its least pleasant, by disdainful assumptions of superiority over, and censorious defensiveness towards, the 'popular'. They brought to the task of film criticism a philosophical infrastructure which, felt rather than stated, and certainly never examined, included such axioms as that the civilized few must protect the humanism of a minority art-culture against an unthinking and vaguely unpleasant world, which was exemplified by, variously, 'the moguls', the 'mass media', the 'undiscriminating public' or an undefined, *sensed* 'ruck' of inferiority. Further, since art is a 'sensitive individualism', then if a film isn't by an artist with an obviously sensitive feel for the moods and nuances of human relationships, then it is probably an insensitive, impersonal film; i.e. it is a product of the 'ruck', unthinking, a specious substitute, and therefore unpleasant.

Now, these nuances are sensed only when expressed by literary and dramatic elements (because in Britain literature and the theatre are facets of general culture, whereas the appreciation of the visual arts is more specialized), and furthermore the critic can recognize quality and sensitivity 'intuitively'. He brings no ideological nor intellectual dogma to a film, he 'senses' whether it is true or not to his own experience of life. If there isn't this immediate 'recognition' effect, the film is probably untrue, therefore unthinking, therefore cheap and contemptible, like Kazan's, Bergman's, or Visconti's; it has *nothing* to offer.

Indeed, under the pressure of these assumptions, the stress on 'social consciousness' steadily receded throughout the 50's. Mere 'social realism' took second place to 'sensitive nuance', lack of which relegated, for example, John Frankenheimer's *The Young Savages* (1961), to the untrue-unthinking-contemptible category.[1]

However, this whole tradition had begun to lose hold on the younger critics. For them, the 'sensitive nuances' of relationships were only parts of human relationships, which were primarily determined by strong, basic drives and attitudes. Marxism, psychoanalysis, sociology, the war, the new social mobility, a general cultural requestioning, had shifted attention from 'nuances' to 'fundamentals'. Thus the 'sensitive nuance', though still a factor, had ceased to be the *touchstone* for a film's quality. From this view, E. M. Forster's novel *A Passage to India*, without in any way disputing its positive qualities, is uncongenial, in so far as it tends to present racial tensions, sexuality, national cultures, religious prejudices, and so on, in terms of 'nuances', rather than as strong, driving, insistent urges, and so we never get a clear, 'dynamic' view of their play and interplay. On the other hand, Nicholas Ray's film *Rebel Without a Cause* may be 'stylized', it may fall into rhetoric, it may be rather less sensitive in its study of mood and nuance than E. M. Forster's

[1] Hence in the mid-50's *Definition*'s young critics, taking their inspiration from the post-Suez New Left, attempted to reverse this trend, reproaching *Sight and Sound* for making vaguely progressive noises while rejecting all ideological interests. For this criticism Miss Houston denounced them as 'cultural gauleiters'. Lindsay Anderson, whose discovery of Ford in *Sequence* days had contributed to the eclipse of 'social consciousness', had, by the late 50's, become a champion of the New Left, and, enjoying prestige in both camps, was spared both their broadsides. He has now decided that he was a 'romantic' all along.

novel. But it is likely to be more congenial to those who see life in terms of 'basic' drives and their intricate relationships. For its (relative) lack of sensitivity, its rhetoric, its concessions to melodrama, are compensated for by the central place which it allots to basic tensions and their interaction: the relationships of mother, father and son (Freud), its complacent evasions (middle-class culture), the insidious blend of toughness and conformism in peer-group morality, which the hero gradually renounces as he comes to equate virility with tenderness (to the heroine) and moral responsibility (he adopts a paternal role to another teenager). Thus he is freed from the state of alienation and nihilism whose cultural origins are mediated through such lyricized symbols as the planetarium, the ruined house and so on.

This contrast between the limitations of E. M. Forster's novel and the structure of Ray's film is meant only to stress that the film has a quite direct and valid appeal to a new common kind of sensibility. But it is also arguable that the 'resonance' of these basic clichés makes Ray's a more sensitive and disturbing film than a study which, though more 'sensitive' ('truthful to conscious experience'), in a Forsterian way, has little or nothing to say on this more 'dynamic' level.[1]

The assumption that the critic is one of the cultured few who must defend his sensitivity against mass crudity has also undergone alteration. The younger critics have grown up with the mass media—films, comics, records and so on. They are used to picking their way through them, and for them the 'superficial' film is in no way a 'specious' substitute for an 'authentic' work of art; it is a 'fun' film that one sees once and enjoys, more or less: 'superficial' doesn't imply 'contemptible'. There are films to which one returns again and again, but no Manichean polarity as between the 'elect' and the 'philistine'. Nor is a film that criticizes society felt to be *ipso facto* more 'salutary' or true or brave than a film that accepts it.

There seems also to be a difference between the very quick and total dismissals characteristic of the 'sensitive nuance' school, and the perhaps more cerebral, but also more thoughtful and adaptable, responses of the younger critics. For the absence of 'dogma' on which

[1]There is a further twist to this in so far as people think in terms of psychoanalysis, sociology, etc., a film can refer to such 'dynamics' quite briefly and concentrate, again, on nuances (as Antonioni does in *L'Avventura*). My own feeling is that this procedure is often a pretext for a thoughtless and boring lack of thought; not always, of course. Either way it doesn't affect my point, that there is another kind of 'awareness', of 'dynamics'.

the 'sensitive nuance' school prides itself is not without its narrow-mindedness. After all, one may be very sensitive to the sorts of nuance that are relevant to the feeling-tones of upper-middle-class English liberalism (and its currently favourite 'exoticisms', notably, American sophisticated comedy of the 30's, Kurosawa, Ford Westerns, Satyajit Ray's India, Raymond Chandler); and yet be very insensitive to anything uncongenial to those feeling-tones. A film which is immediately 'plausible' to one's sensibility may be far less accurate in its picture of alien sensibilities, and far less rich in insights, than a film which one learns, almost against one's will, to trust. To take only one example: Lindsay Anderson attacked Kazan's *On the Waterfront* for its 'Fascism', using as his implicit standard of comparison either the attitudes of London dockers towards trade-union solidarity or nebulous notions that working-class solidarity must be the same all over the world. Yet Daniel Bell's account of the *specific* labour disputes on which Kazan's film is based convincingly vindicates it against most of Anderson's criticisms.

The issue is not so much one of the critic's knowledge of the world, as of the extent to which he is willing to try to lend himself to a film, on its own terms, *before* he decides whether to accept or reject it as a whole or in part. The younger critics have the advantage in that, adapted as they are to a time of cultural fluidity and change, they often find more relevance to their own problems in American or foreign films than they do in English tradition. In the same way, Belmondo in Godard's *A Bout de Souffle* turns, not as his father might have done to his age, to the novels of Gide, but to a photograph of Humphrey Bogart (who is of course an 'intellectual's' star). This very flexibility tends to go with a more 'cerebral' approach, an acceptance of 'sign' for 'symbol', of 'idea' for 'experience'. One may regret, as I do, that so many young critics reacted against a too-arrogant attitude towards the artist's vision of life into a refusal to criticize it, an opposite, if more amiable, excess. Yet for critics to think of themselves as artists' friends and accomplices is surely more responsive and constructive, a better beginning for eventual evaluation, than the assumption that a critic can judge works of art 'off the cuff', from some stratospheric impartiality of his own.[1] The difference, in the end,

[1] In the event of course the brutal tone had to be at least partly abandoned in the face, not only of European critical attitudes, and of the younger criticism here, but of the extent to which the English 'literary' and intelligent public became interested in films.

is less between 'humanists' and 'aesthetes', than between reviewers who feel it their job to taste and judge, and critics who try to understand and explore.

At any rate, it is not so much the French influence as the importance traditionally attached to a 'personal vision' in art, that has provoked the younger generation to feel particularly concerned to show that, for example, Hawks and Preminger are each valuable for their qualities of personal vision and style. But I should like here to question the centrality of this issue, and to reassert an attitude more like that of *La Revue du Cinema*.

The *Concise O.E.D.* gives us another definition of the word 'style'. It signifies also the 'collective characteristics of the writing or direc-

The subsequent course of *Sight and Sound* was erratic. There were a few ventures into criticism in which philosophical terms were used freely, and sometimes incoherently, in an effort to sound as profound as Bazin was thought to be. The tone (exemplified by Rhode's feeling that Visconti must be mentally sick to be interested in the proletariat) lacked Bazin's generosity, and continued what was worst in the old, hostile complacency. At the same time, Pauline Kael was 'imported' from America to 'debunk' various sorts of intellectualizing about movies (one of her articles is cited later).

These destructive rearguard actions were followed by a general elevation of Hawks, Ray, Mann, Losey and others to the realms of critical goodwill, an elevation not extended to those *auteurs* who hadn't been forcefully pushed into the limelight by the younger generation. The influence of younger or French critics was never acknowledged.

There was a notable change in the attitude to 'pulp' movies. This the magazine's pseudonymous columnist, Arkadin (reputedly John Russell Taylor) asked, 'Why don't we take horror films more seriously—well, not seriously seriously,' as if unaware that the rest of the world had been taking them seriously for some years. Since then the floodgates have opened and for the last two years the magazine has been dabbling in an ostentatiously hedonistic acceptance of, for example, Don Sharp's *The Face of Fu Manchu.* One of the excellences which T.M. advances as evidence of this being 'a *really good film*' (my italics) is that 'when a sinister hand coils round the edge of her door, Karin Dor doesn't just scream, she very commendably slams the door on it'. John Russell Taylor is also staggered by such creativity: 'when the young heroine is threatened by a sinister oriental hand sliding round her living-room door with a missive, she wastes no time in helpless wails, but smartly slams the door on it. . . .'

It's hard to believe that people of these critics' culture and intelligence could really have been so impressed by such 'innovations' (which aren't), if they weren't forcing themselves to 'be jolly'. Yet the whole point of appreciating a good film which happens to be couched in the idiom of a pulp thriller is that you don't lower your normal standards an inch, you're no more indulgent to Bond than you would have been to Liberace or Rin-Tin-Tin. The partial *volte-face* from critical 'superiority' to uncritical acquiescence is more than an example of the general aesthetic upsets generated by the current confluence of 'high culture' and popular art. The nervous strivings to keep up with 'festival opinion' on one hand and high camp on the other are the vacillations of a stiffly classbound 'liberalism' in a cosmopolitan world.

tion or artistic expression or way of presenting things or decorative methods proper to a person or school or period or subject; manner exhibiting these characteristics'. In other words, a director's vision or style may be of great interest and sincerity even when it is shared by a great many directors—just as in architecture one speaks of collective styles—Norman, Early English, decorated perpendicular, Tudor, Queen Anne, and so forth. Similarly, in literature there are 'groups' of artists (just as there are groups of critics!) who have many opinions and mannerisms in common—the 'Metaphysicals', the 'neo-classicists', and so on. These writers can both be contrasted for their differences and compared for their similarities, the latter being no less significant than the former. For the purpose of art is not exclusively or even particularly to express the unique individual, but also to express feelings, attitudes and values of any kind, whether individual or communal. Indeed, the unique individual is often prized as an artist because he crystallizes, with unique strength and clarity, many of the tensions in a 'communal' climate. A film may be of considerable cultural significance even if it is quite anonymous—just as medieval religious paintings, stained-glass windows, certain poems (Beowulf) or buildings (the Taj Mahal) reveal little or nothing about any individual *auteur*. Most folk art is, by definition, anonymous, but none the less poignant and significant. A cathedral may be altered down the centuries, by one generation after another (certainly with no one mind in control!) but still be of artistic importance. In fact the very notions of 'culture' and of the 'spirit of an age' are arrived at by taking as significant those elements which artists have in common. *Kiss Me Deadly* isn't important because it tells us anything about an individual called Robert Aldrich. Aldrich is important because *Kiss Me Deadly* reveals something about America, and about us all.

The fact that a director has an 'individual' style doesn't of itself make his films interesting (except for those connoisseurs who collect odd styles like some people collect quaintly-shaped inkpots). To take literary parallels, Enid Blyton, Marie Corelli, Dean Farrer and Amanda McKittrick Ross all have 'individual' visions and styles, and are undoubtedly *auteurs*, but this doesn't make them great creative artists, or even readable, except for the relaxing giggle.

It is not denigrating the importance of personal idioms, nor of individualism as such, to say that there is also merit and significance in the 'collective' aspects of Hollywood style. It is fast, bold, terse, flexible and clear. Its sharp cuts and bold reverse angles express a philosophy of life as fact confronting fact, face confronting face, in a series of collisions and challenges, a philosophy of dynamic action-reaction, viewing life as a sequence of decisions tending to some purpose. It has the limitations, but it has also the meanings and merits, of any 'classicism'.

Another peculiarity of the *auteur* approach is that, in practice, if not in theory, all the *auteurs* seem to be directors, and little interest is taken in the many important creative personalities who are producers. One thinks of Mark Hellinger, and of David O. Selznick, who virtually directed some of his films 'through' his director, reputedly bombarding him with fifty-page telegrams telling him exactly how a given scene ought to be played. Selznick is an *auteur*, in that *Portrait of Jennie* is 1 per cent Dieterle and 99 per cent Selznick. Other *auteur* producers include John Houseman, Stanley Kramer and Hal Wallis. Several screenwriters are *auteurs*—Philip Yordan in Hollywood, Bryan Forbes in Britain, Carl Mayer in Germany, Jacques Prévert in France. As Renoir remarked, '. . . anyone that says that *Les Enfants du Paradis* is Carné's film is crazy. It's Jacques Prévert's. Prévert was the dominant personality. Not that Carné is not a good director—but I think he was born to be a good director of great writers.' Renoir continues, 'Sometimes it can even be the actor who dominates—take the Mary Pickford films, for example.' The mere fact that the public follows stars proves that a star is an *auteur*. So are 'undirectable' actors like George Arliss and Charles Laughton, certain personalities (Louise Brooks, Robert Mitchum), and, particularly, comedians like Jerry Lewis and Laurel and Hardy.

It isn't unknown for excellent parts of an *auteurs* film to be directed by someone else. Thus the chariot race of Wyler's *Ben Hur* and the land race of Anthony Mann's *Cimarron* were both handled by Andrew Marton, the exteriors of Corman's *The Terror* by Monte Hellman. *Gone With the Wind* has a consistent visual style through all its changes of director because it was master-minded by Selznick and storyboarded by William Cameron Menzies. Nominally an art director, Menzies created the visuals of many British and American films. His own directorial efforts suffer from a poor story sense and slightly stilted acting, but he is certainly an *auteur*, and many directors have enjoyed the praise for effects which were actually Menzies'.

Many films bear the marks of several *auteurs*. *Le Crime de Monsieur Lange* is 100 per cent Prévert, and 100 per cent Renoir—total

200 per cent. *Duel in the Sun* is 80 per cent Selznick and 80 per cent Vidor—total 160 per cent. But a good film is always a subtle balance of creative energies and ascendancies, especially in Hollywood where until recently the *auteur* was at bay against the production line system imposed by such studio chiefs as Louis B. Mayer and Harry Cohn (who, though the 'villains of the piece', also, occasionally, had first-rate ideas).

Some brilliant films have been made by directors who, for one reason or another, have not emerged as consistent *auteurs*. One thinks of, for example, Joseph H. Lewis's *Gun Crazy*, E. E. Reinert's *Quai de Grenelle*, or Norman Panama and Melvin Frank's *L'll Abner*. And who is the *auteur* of such weird and brilliant one-shots as *The 5,000 Fingers of Dr. T* (director, Roy Rowland), *Gilda* (director, Charles Vidor), *This Island Earth* (director, Joseph M. Newman)? In these cases the fullest list of credits offers little clue. As Renoir said, 'A good film is a miracle . . .' that is, a series of happy accidents.

Inevitably, a mediocre or bad film by a 'great' director will be of more interest to connoisseurs than a mediocre or even a good film by a mediocre director. Renoir's *Le Déjeuner sur L'Herbe* might have been the work of two men, containing as it does one beautiful sequence (the disturbed picnic) in a context whose dithering results (one hopes) from a wrong theory pushed to the limit. Any artist's inspiration results from a conflict, that is, a precarious balance, of attitudes and emotions, and there's nothing illogical in, for example, my own feeling that King Vidor's *North-West Passage* and *H. M. Pulham Esq.* are as nauseating as such films as *Hallelujah* and *Ruby Gentry* are inspiring. However moved we may be by the archaic charm and careful thought in the veteran Allan Dwan's *The Enchanted Island* it's no use pretending that *The Most Dangerous Man Alive*, by the same producer and director (Benedict Bogeaus—Allan Dwan) is anything but a stinkeroo. Conversely, Benedek's subsequent decline casts no reflection on his achievement in *The Wild One*. Often, film *auteurs*, like novelists and poets, die before their death—like Tay Garnett, Stanley Donen, Edward Dmytryk, Robert Siodmak.

A special form of *auteur* is the *anti-auteur*—the man who delights in adopting different themes and styles for each of his films—for example, Fred Zinnemann in America, René Clément in France and Alberto Lattuada in Italy. Ford has had two distinct styles—his 'open-air' style (*Stagecoach*) and his 'expressionistic' style (*The In-*

former), (it's a pity, maybe, that even in *The Long Voyage Home* he doesn't explore the region where these two tones and views of life meet and conflict). Many directors, cameramen and writers are, deliberately and cultivatedly, 'chameleons'—specialists in 'adjusting' their style to that of their directors or actors—giving the paradox that substantial contributions to a film's content and quality are made by artists who express another person's character rather than their own —a process which may be just as creative as a dramatist's expression of characters and views *not his own*, i.e., of the zeitgeist . . . *Ars est celare artem*; not all inglorious Miltons were mute.

Another kind of creative personality may come to dominate the cinema's history, not simply because of his own films, but because of his creative fertility—the German scenarist Carl Mayer, the Italian writer Cesare Zavattini, were both one-man mass movements, in that their scripts are often the salt that savours, and saves, the loaf. Creative too, to some extent, was Gregg Toland—whose deep-focus expressionism was used extensively in Ford's *The Long Voyage Home* (1940) *before* Welles took it up for *Citizen Kane* (1941). Not that Welles doesn't deserve credit; he does; but so does Toland; and Welles without Toland and Herman J. Mankiewicz (his writer) has never quite reached the same heights. Were these collaborators quite so 'passive' as we sometimes imply when we write, 'Welles. . . .'?

Although many of Hollywood's directors are *auteurs* it is quite possible to speak of an overall Hollywood 'style'—in that, whether the narrative is fast (La Cava's *Stage Door*, is surely a contender for some sort of world record) or slow (Henry King's *Snows of Kilimanjaro*), there is a certain tautness, a spareness of intention, a lack of distraction from the principal story points. There are none of the asides one finds in, say, Renoir or Becker, and which European directors generally are more inclined to entertain. Hollywood would never have invented such 'European' ideas as the *temps-mort*, or the stylistic potpourri of Truffaut. American films seem to be enclosed by their subjects, and the dramatic tensions are calculated with a Protestant rigour. European directors often deliberately relax the story so as to dwell on the sprawl and irrelevance of 'off-moments' (which after all constitute 80 per cent of life).

A notable limitation is the Hollywood tradition that it's cissy to pan where a cut would do—the latter being faster, smoother, tauter. The preference for camera-movements over cuts is primarily a European tradition (Murnau, Renoir, Ophuls) which Hitchcock's *Rope* reduced to a pedestrian *exercise de style*. In general it seems true to say that Hollywood directors show less variety of theme and approach than European ones, basically because Europe is culturally more diversified than America, dedicated as the latter is to the moulding of immigrants into one cultural pattern. None the less, a few directors, for example, Hitchcock (sometimes), King Vidor or Samuel Fuller (if only by his customary ferocity), show a 'European' extent of individuality, whereas, say, Hawks and Preminger don't.

Of course, one can group individualists, in America as in Europe, into 'schools'. After Preston Sturges 'died', his vein of sick humour was asserted by Billy Wilder, from whose failing grasp the torch was snatched up by Stanley Kubrick. In fact one can group and re-group Hollywood directors in all sorts of ways, depending on which points of style one finds interesting. There are 'soft' directors (Frank Borzage, Allan Dwan) and 'bleak' directors (Hawks, Jack Arnold, Boetticher), 'muscular' directors (King Vidor, Fuller, Richard Fleischer, Anthony Mann) and 'tight-lipped' directors (Lang, Mann, Hawks). There are 'women's directors' (Cukor, Minnelli), 'theatrical' directors (Cukor, Wyler), 'actors' ' directors (Cukor, La Cava), 'novelist' directors (Mankiewicz, Brooks). There are 'TV' directors, whose visuals are often ragged (like Delbert Mann's, and Frankenheimer's, except when he carboncopies Hitchcock) but who have a powerful acting sense. There are 'plush' directors (George Sidney, Douglas Sirk, Quine, Edwards). There are the 'tearaways' (Don Siegel, Phil Karlson). There are directors whose *forte* is what we have called *mise-en-scène*—Nicholas Ray, Boetticher, Minnelli, Jack Webb. Douglas Sirk approaches a plush weepie like *Imitation of Life* with a dry calculation-in-excess, resulting in a sense of lonely alienation which to the style-sensitive eye is not unlike Antonioni's: the apparent dedication of a whole town to a coloured mammy's funeral isn't unlike the interplay of crowds and emptiness in *L'Avventura* (1959). This doesn't, to my mind, justify calling Sirk brilliant, or even lucid, though it justifies not ignoring him; but what is interesting to notice is that the commercial cinema, by curious processes of its own, is often ahead of 'art' films. There are essentially 'middle-class' directors (Wyler, Zinnemann, but with a pessimistic undertone). There are 'fake liberals' (George Stevens), 'flabby liberals' (Wyler) and the younger, tougher more courageous men (Wise, Brooks, Daves in his Westerns). There are even more bitter, virulent men (Aldrich, Losey). There are 'right-wing' directors (Leo McCarey,

John Wayne, Ray Milland). There are deeply ambivalent figures like Ford, Fuller and King Vidor. There are the 'intellectuals'—John Huston (who, perhaps the most interesting moralist in the American cinema, joins Losey and Bunuel in the trio of screen moralists), Arthur Penn, Elia Kazan.

But none of these directors can be contained within such a classification. Cukor's *Heller in Pink Tights* reveals his affinities with Vincente Minnelli. Wyler's *Ben Hur* resembles Fleischer's *Barabbas* in its use of symbolism, its 'staging', its sense of physique. Raoul Walsh, lyricist *par excellence* of male exuberance, endows parts of *The Lawless Breed* with a soft, feminine delicacy (or is this the contribution of an art director?). One can almost describe Frank Borzage's *Moonrise* (1948), with Charles Laughton's *Night of the Hunter* (1956) and Allan Dwan's *The Enchanted Island* (1958) as Hollywood's tattered rearguard of Griffith-spirited films. Yet, with *Wild River* (1960) Kazan returns to a romantic lyricism not far in spirit from Borzage and Dwan.

Curious affinities link otherwise completely different films and directors. The use of depth and space by Budd Boetticher (a genuine *auteur*) in *Ride Lonesome* (1959) is very reminiscent of Roman Polanski's in *The Knife in the Water* (1962) (which could easily be transposed into terms of a Boetticher Western). G. Tchouhrai's *The 41st* (1956) is Russia's answer to *Duel in the Sun* (and vastly inferior), in climax (shotguns), style and love-hate theme. Kazan is the most 'European' of American directors—his *On the Waterfront* is the stylistic inspiration for Visconti's *Rocco and His Brothers* (1960), while the immigrant story of *The Anatolian Smile* (1963) is Kazan following, in turn, the immigrant story of Visconti.

The paradox is not that the various groups of *auteur* theorists accept the films that they do but that they reject so many films which would seem to be on their wavelength. Subtle, searching and courageous films like Ray's *Rebel Without a Cause*, Fuller's *Run of the Arrow*, Vidor's *Ruby Gentry*, Lang's *The Big Heat*, Aldrich's *Attack* or Kramer's *On the Beach*, arouse the ire, contempt or, at best, indifference of the older critics, who however lavish praise on the canny escapism of John Ford's potboilers. Conversely the younger theorists, priding themselves on their sense of style, all but pass by George Sidney's *Pal Joey* or his very beautiful *Jeanne Eagels*, or even of Corman's horror rhapsodies, while applauding every time such limited stylists as Hawks and Preminger manage to move the camera from

A to B.[1] Hitchcock and Preminger, two of the Hollywood directors whom they most admire as moralists, are, to my mind, sophisticated entertainers who carefully tailor their message so as not to offend their audience; while the films of Howard Hawks, charming as they are, rarely venture outside a range of agreeable cliché which almost any other American director can handle, and at some time or other has.

Yet one can understand why Hawks' films mean so much to French intellectuals. His very simplicity can have a tonic, and a real value, as a corrective to various debilitating concomitants of European culture ('confusionism', snobbery, contempt for decision, action, efficacy, simplicity). But it is as well to remember that Hawks moves on some of the easier and simpler wavelengths of his (mass) audience's responses. Even his 'deadpan', 'tough' way with emotion, though not altogether untrue to some aspects of the American attitude to emotion, is, at its best very near a favourite American cliché, and, at its worst, corn-and-ham on wry. If Hemingway's style is tainted by the same facility, it has an overtone of pain, of waste, which Hawks, more sentimentally ignores.

Hawks' films have shown a remarkable consistency (which is also a tedious monotony) throughout his long career, with the paradoxical result that though his films are full of American cliché they are also identifiable as the work of an *auteur*. He has all the insidious convenience of typicality; his individuality is in his flawless typicality. In his perfection, there is, undoubtedly, an authentic sophistication—if that implies that he has made decisions about the importance of human moods and meanings. Yet, if sophistication means humanity, variety and subtlety, then his films are generally simpler and more facile than their nearest comparisons. Thus his *Scarface* is simpler than Wellman's *Public Enemy*, his *A Girl in Every Port* is a sardonic counterpoint to Tay Garnett's *Her Man*, his 'satires' are innocuous compared to Wellman's *A Star is Born*, his *Gentlemen Prefer Blondes* is eclipsed by Wilder's *Some Like it Hot*. But if 'sophistication' means a sardonic attitude to humanity, a deadpan humour which, under the pretext of toughly controlling emotion, also all but denies it, then the very limitations of his films enable these tensions to emerge more sharply.

For much the same reason, his early films have 'aged' very well—

[1] Perhaps this is unfair, in that they are stressing the simplicity, economy and sobriety of Hawks's style.

or, more accurately, perhaps, they suit current taste. Wellman's *Public Enemy*, with its serious appeal to primitive sociology, with its complex counterpointing of sympathy and contempt towards its central figure, now 'creaks', in the context of our changed ideas and assumptions, whereas *Scarface*, with its complete lack of interest in anything except revealing that Scarface is not only a rat but a coward too, who cannot but destroy all his friends and then himself, is extremely naïve, but has a near-classical simplicity, of 'thrust', form and thought. Garnett's *Her Man* is now conspicuously vitiated by the sentimentality of Helen Twelvetrees, a latterday Dorothy Gish awkwardly 'framed' in a saloon: the point of Hawks' counterpart is the real cynicism of the equivalent character (Louise Brooks). The toughly cynical stoicism which Hawks adopted very early in his career avoids all dramatic exaggerations, and so suits, not only the modern 'deadpan' rhetoric, but our aptitude for debunking and de-sentimentalizing.

My own reaction is to find the other films *more* interesting than Hawks', just *because* they have dated, and so say, to me, something new; whereas Hawks' merely say, with a special deftness, what innumerable American films are interminably, and boringly, saying.

Even so, his films authentically express the streak of stoicism in the American character. The ruthless thrust of the categorical imperatives of the Calvinist conscience has been transposed into another set of values. It has been cut away from any belief in God, or even of reward, which is a bait, an inspiration, rather than an end. Hawks' 'buddies' are loyal, with a conscious purposelessness, in defeat and death. 'Fun' morality is accepted, but, more often than not, with a certain misogyny and masochism, as from a puritan residue, and from the feeling that pleasure is more of a threat to one's stoicism than pain. The overriding purpose is, in the end, the achievement of one's manliness, usually (and sentimentally) squared with a dour, cagey, wry moralism, in which puritan extremism ties with a sullen scepticism. These assertions enable Hawks' films to check their nihilistic trend, and to endow life with some sort of moral meaning. His tightlipped stoicism—nihilism—isn't altogether unevocative of an existentialist mood—even though the 'solidarity' is matched by a brutal competitiveness. Otherwise, Hawks' summary way with any philosophical issue is as far from existentialism as the Marine sergeant's taunting, 'Do you want to live for ever?' For much of its length, *The Big Sleep* admirably catches the Chandler mood. But the sadder implications of that mood are lost in a sort of spirited non-chalance, and one may, in the end, prefer Dmytryk's less perfect, but warmer and sadder, *Farewell, My Lovely*. Huston's *Treasure of Sierra Madre* and *The Misfits* are 'tragic critiques' of the Hawksian ideal, respecting it, fairly, but going beyond their tough conformism to a profounder humanism. Perhaps Hawks' best films are those in which, without losing the shock of his terseness, he goes some way beyond it; in *Sergeant York* (co-written with John Huston) and *The Big Sky*; while *The Big Sleep* and *Red River* have the virtues of a *petit-maître*.

Preminger is another minor figure with a, to my mind, inflated reputation in *auteur* circles. He is at his best in the 'modest' films made between 1944 and 1956 when he had emerged as a producer, but was still 'trapped' within the system—*Laura*, *Fallen Angel*, *Angel Face*, *The Man With the Golden Arm* and *Anatomy of a Murder*. All these films have a real feeling for the enigmatic quality (and the cynical undertow) in human relationships, and an authentic atmosphere of sordid anguish. But the ambiguity *in* these small-scale subjects gets into the treatment *of* the latter, bigger themes, which consequently become as boring as they are non-committal, Preminger carefully implying a cynicism which he equally carefully never crystallizes. If he makes *Saint Joan* there's Shaw's play for the respectful agnostics, Greene's screenplay for the Catholics, Jean Seberg as an identification-figure for the teenagers of the Middle West, Richard Widmark for the 'industrial halls', and Anton Walbrook and John Gielgud for the 'carriage trade'. This sort of calculation is common enough, in films, but Preminger's too often shows. His *Exodus* does for Israel what George Stevens' *Giant* does for Texas (nothing, in Cinemascope), while on the most controversial issues of all *Advise and Consent* and *The Cardinal* contrive to see all sides of the question, so disturbing everybody a little and nobody much; a mountain-size framework produces a mouse-size thought, and I don't have much hesitation in preferring to *Advise and Consent* Franklin Schaffner's *The Best Man*, to *The Cardinal* Richard Brooks' *Elmer Gantry*, to *Anatomy of a Murder* Wilder's *Double Indemnity*, and to *The Man With the Golden Arm* Wyler's underestimated *Carrie*. Preminger's best films are part of the 40's wave of 'tightlipped misogyny', notably, Vidor's *Gilda*, Hughes' *The Outlaw*, Stahl's *Leave Her to Heaven* and Welles' *The Lady from Shanghai*. Even his masterpiece, *Laura*, is one of a deluge of 40's films about portraits and missing women (such as

Hitchcock's *Rebecca,* Robert Siodmak's *Phantom Lady,* Albert Lewin's *Pandora and the Flying Dutchman,* William Seiter's *One Touch of Venus* and William Dieterle's *Portrait of Jennie,* the last a favourite of Luis Bunuel's). That most of Preminger's films show the mark of a definite artistic personality is beyond question; nor are his less satisfactory films devoid of interest. But I wouldn't see him as other than a minor Hollywood figure.

Given the Hollywood system, it's evident that few directors' names can be a guarantee of quality. For example, Lang's *The Big Heat* is a key film, in its atmosphere of bitterness and corruption; the attempt to repeat its success in *Human Desire* results in a limp, dull film, while *The Blue Gardenia* has none of the merits, and few of the mannerisms, of a Lang film. Similarly, Ray's *Party Girl* is as inept in its thought and feeble in its dramatic punch as his *Rebel Without a Cause* and *The Savage Innocents* are complex and moving. Donen's musicals are classics or near, with or without Gene Kelly as his collaborator, yet his later comedies are insipid. It may be just coincidence, but all Hitchcock's films for Paramount and Universal are at least interesting, while all his films for Selznick and (bar *Strangers on a Train*) Warner's, are below par. Indeed, Hitchcock's case is interesting. There has been a certain amount of controversy as to whether (as the '30's school' and the *Sight and Sound* team maintain) his early British films are by and large superior to his post-war Hollywood films (which are championed by *Cahiers, Movie* and Robin Wood, in his extremely interesting study). But the question seems to me awkwardly posed. There are certainly general differences between the periods (as well as underlying similarities), and, within each period, some films are richer than others. And my own inclination would be to ask which are the best films of each period (and which have merits which are typical of neither one period nor the other)? *Sabotage* (1936), *Strangers on a Train* (1951) and *Psycho* (1961) seem to me to enable the receptive spectator to live more fully through more challenging experiences than say *Secret Agent* (1936), *Notorious* (1946) or *Marnie* (1964).

And I don't see any reason to make of Hitchcock a 'consistent' *auteur* who never falls below his own best. It is possible to point to certain limitations which even his best films don't altogether transcend. It is arguable that, *Psycho* apart, Hitchcock has never unleashed the full weight of his irony, misanthropy and moral disquiet, and that he has too often too carefully tailored them, restricting himself to 'intimations' of what he thinks the public will enjoy without resentment. (Indeed he makes a point of it: so-called *Stories They Wouldn't Let Me Do on TV* appear in paperback anthology.) And yet, Hitchcock does say *some* things, not only *despite* the system, but *by means of* the system. When all the sad truths about Hollywood have been allowed, it is doubtful whether it cramps its best directors' style as much as the Victorian climate of opinion constrained our Victorian novelists. Indeed, if we allow the least literary status to, say, Robert Louis Stevenson, it becomes very perverse indeed to rule out even the 'middling' films of Hitchcock, Hawks, Ray and so on.

Quite apart from any question of exterior constraint, the greatest novelists may vary a good deal in quality, for purely personal reasons. In any case, even when an artist is exceptionally consistent, one may wish to acquaint oneself with only those works of his which have a marginal superiority over the others. Few readers would want to read every play by Samuel Beckett, for example, not because they're not good but because each is a corollary of the other.

Every spectator will of course have a greater temperamental affinity with some *auteurs* than with others; and to a great extent the broadening and mellowing quality of art comes from adapting oneself, so as to take on the sensibility of those *auteurs* who are least congenial to one's own responses. Further, the minor films of a major artist will naturally attract more intensity, more awareness of response, from their context, than the best films of minor artists, even when these, in a one-for-one comparison, are more interesting or true than a great man's failures.

Yet perhaps the best way of 'valuing' Hollywood—or any category of films—is not by selecting certain *auteurs* as 'in' and others as 'out', but by picking out the best films of (for example) Aldrich, Arnold, Boetticher, Brooks, Cassavetes, Daves, De Mille, Donen, Dwan, Ford, Fuller, Hawks, Hitchcock, Huston, Kazan, Kubrick, Mankiewicz, Mann A., Mann Daniel, Mann Delbert, Minnelli, Ray, Sidney, Sirk, Tashlin, Wilder, Wise, Wyler, Zinnemann *et al.* Thus one's canon of 'great', or 'key', or 'interesting', or 'useful' films has vastly greater variety, and one is also saved from having to see the dreary, pusillanimous, or repetitive films which all these directors have perpetrated from time to time. In just the same way, novelists can fall below their own best standards, without literary critics feeling obliged, either to rally to their defence, or to write about them with contempt.

5 · Caligari is Dead—Long Live Caligari

'Expressionism' is as undefinable a category as 'realism', which it resembles in being not only a classification for certain works of art but also an urge which underlies all art but becomes particularly obtrusive at certain times and places. Our concern here is not with tracing the history and development of screen expressionism, but, first, to replace some of its stylistic traits in their context, so as to further our understanding of style in the cinema, and second, to suggest the relevance, to the present, of a critically still unfashionable mode.

In their *Dictionary of Art and Artists* Peter and Linda Murray describe expressionism in painting as, 'The search for expressiveness in style by means of exaggerations and distortions of line and colour; a deliberate abandonment of the naturalism implicit in Impressionism in favour of a simplified style which should carry far greater emotional impact. In this general sense of emotional force Expressionism is a feature of non-Mediterranean art in general, Grunëwald being the standard example. . . . In the more limited context of modern art, the Expressionist movement may be said to spring from Van Gogh's use of drastically simplified outline and very strong colour . . . the principal exponents . . . were mostly German (or at least 'Nordic', like the Norwegian Munch). . . .'

From this angle, a characteristic of Expressionism is that the feelings portrayed invade, swallow up the 'otherness' of the outside world. English romanticism knows this impulse, and uses it, without actually abandoning itself to it, restricting itself to what is, for all the rhapsodic use of the 'pathetic fallacy', a conscious search for the soul of man, for *his* harmony with the world, rather than for any 'Music of the spheres' in itself. Wordsworth and Shelley consciously make of every realistic object and element a sounding board for their own personal feelings. But German romanticism went further into transcendentalism; the artist feels that he is expressing the 'inner soul' of Nature, of the outside world. Cooler, more sceptical souls will value such art for its picture, not of the outside world, but of introverted sensibility, so 'reducing' it to a more 'English' romanticism.

From 1830 on, English romanticism gradually ebbed, vitiated partly by the English blend of puritanism, compromise, snobbery and general anti-emotionality, and partly as the more extroverted problems of social realism became increasingly obtrusive on the literary scene. But German expressionism, whether consciously subjective or avowedly transcendental, struggled to portray complex social problems as if they were metaphysical issues or 'extroverted spiritual states' through which the artist-spectator-hero must make his 'way of the Cross'. Sometimes, as with the playwright Ernest Toller, the realistic awareness prevailed over the 'Messianic' spirituality; other playwrights, more conscious of spiritual angst than of social problems, remained mystics; a few found it easier to come to terms with Nazism than with the democratic rationalism underlying social realism.

Sometimes the expressionist artist portrays 'real' objects, which are lyrically 'convulsed' by formal style—as the sun and sky in Van Gogh are dissolved by the slap and slice of brushstrokes. Sometimes he concentrates on the emotive effects of abstract forms (though arguably all abstract art is either abstract expressionism, in that the gestalt of forms suggest tensions and therefore feelings and often ideas, or it is nothing. From this point of view, tonalities of sturm and drang are simply more easily recognizable as 'abstract expressionism' than, say, the paintings of Piet Mondrian). Sometimes the Expressionist uses passionately heavy symbols, blurring the idiomatic and spiritual frontier between expressionism and Surrealism.[1] Of course many artists use several methods, at different times or all together.

[1] The rigorous anti-anthropomorphism of Robbe-Grillet is thus at the opposite end of the literary spectrum to expressionism, which has however this advantage over the more sceptical literary genre currently fashionable: an artist who endeavours to tell us everything about everything is more likely to say something interesting than an artist who aspires to tell us almost nothing about almost nothing. That said, the *nouveau roman* has a certain lyrical charm, in carefully chosen extract, and by its very pedantry creates a mood of nihilistic solipsism which is not unexpressionistic itself.

The parallels with cinema expressionism immediately present themselves. It is notably a German movement. There is a similar heaviness, symbolism, and sense of *haunting* about such Nordics as Sjostrom and Bergman. (We might also speak of a Slav expressionism, ranging from the Czech Gustav Machaty's *Ectasy* to *Ashes and Diamonds* by the Polish Andrzej Wajda, *The Crime of Dmitri Karamazov* by the Russian Fedor Ozep, and even Eisenstein.) The starved, haggard, nightmarish quality of so many German films of the 20's is prefigured by Munch's *Abend Auf Dem Corso Karl Johan* (1892). The turning away from naturalism is paralleled in the German preference for huge studio sets and elaborate technical effects rather than location photography. There is a similar 'simplification of outline'. In such films as Paul Leni's *Waxworks*, Murnau's *The Last Laugh* and Joe May's *Ashphalte* the storyline is very simple (so simple that the films can move very slowly). The relationships of the characters are all reduced to broad, primal attitudes and urges. The acting concentrates, not on the ebb and flow of people's behaviour, but on broad, forceful postures and gestures. Thus the film is reduced to a series of *basic* moments each of which is then emphasized and 'accordeoned out'—giving the characteristic 'heaviness' of German silent films. But this 'exaggeration' is meant to express the basic, the key, attitudes and emotions, in all their vehemence and purity.

Even the décor is subordinated to the lyrical surge. Leni's *Waxworks* is a fascinating example. A fairground showman asks a poet to write three stories round his collection of wax figures, notably Haroun el Raschid, Ivan the Terrible and Jack the Ripper. The episode of Haroun and the baker's wife is an orchestration of soft, doughy, round shapes—turbans, bellies, ovens, rings, minarets, chessmen, spiral staircases which coil like intestines. The Ivan episode is stiff with sharp, dark, iconic shapes—Ivan's angular form and jutting beard, an arrow slanting from a stiffly slumping back, bars across windows, low, heavy roofbeams. The Jack the Ripper episode is a slow drift through the mysterious land of photographic superimpositions. Not only are the *forms* of the décors different, so is the *texture*. Those in the Haroun episode are soggy and flabby, like the Caliph himself; the Ivan the Terrible sequence is in the key of carved wood. Jack the Ripper is a world of dim, celluloidy transparencies.

There is more expressionism in realism than we usually realize. When Carol Reed tilts his camera in *The Third Man* he is superimposing 'expressionism' on a realistic setting. Background music, most acting, is expressionist, in the sense that it endeavours to 'express' emotions. In this sense, the difference between 'expressionism' and 'realism' is simply the degree of 'poetic licence' which the former allows itself in its handling of the visual appearance of things. If Robbe-Grillet's 'new' novels seem extreme it is because they attempt (unsuccessfully) to purge realism of any expressionist element. Where there's emotion in art, there is expressionism, of a sort. The beautiful smokescapes of Flaherty's documentary *Industrial Britain* are as subjective and visionary as the sheerest expressionism, though idealistic rather than tormented. But we can usefully contrast *realism* and *expressionism*, or speak of a battle between magic (Méliès) and daylight (Lumière), studios (Méliès) and location (Lumière)—so long as we remember that each style derives its meaning only from the implicit presence of the other.

Between them, Siegfried Kracauer, in *From Caligari to Hitler*, and less moralistically, Lotte H. Eisner in *L'Ecran Demoniaque*, have studied the social implications, the aesthetic origins, of expressionism in German silent films. Our purpose here is rather different: to see expressionism as a particular kind of 'style', as well as an often ignored, but ubiquitous, tradition, a constant, if unnoticed, diastole to the systole of realism.

We should perhaps make some sort of rough distinction between 'expressionism' proper and mere elaborateness of visual organization. Dreyer's *La Passion de Jeanne d'Arc* is visually very expressive, but Dreyer does not *distort* reality. We feel an emotional weight and angst which may remind us of expressionism, but it is created by very careful selection of reality, rather than by overriding it. In *Caligari* on the other hand an emotional shudder runs through everything—the streets, the doors, the windows, stagger and totter, just as if 'the time is out of joint'. Paths and fields are broken up into spikes and shards, roofs become mere huddle of splinters, while the asylum has an oppressive, massive solidity and order. However, *Caligari*, like *Waxworks*, asserts an extreme of expressionism—and exactly when the use of light, shadow, and objects becomes 'expressionist' rather than 'realistic' is impossible to define. In the end it's a matter of the spirit. An 'expressionistic' film has a more dreamlike feeling, a sense of blurring and vagueness, of heavy but undefined emotion, which *looms* oppressively without being analysed or explained.

By 1925 'pure' expressionism is virtually ended: from then on the films of Lang, Murnau and Pabst use the full range of expressionistic devices, and retain something of the expressionistic mood, but reconcile them with a more or less realistic framework and surface.

Thus Murnau's *The Last Laugh* relates to social circumstances of the time as concretely as *Bicycle Thieves*—with a lost uniform instead of a stolen bicycle. However, the film's visuals owe everything to expressionistic emphases. These are not a matter merely of 'heaviness', but of sensuousness. The porter's shiny tower of a uniform contrasts with the drab, deathly whiteness of lavatory linen stacked in a cupboard. The light has a grey, dusty, dispirited quality. Like Lang, Murnau loves to show characters puffing at fat cigars, and then showing the smoke drift and swirl up into the lamplight, glinting, diffusing and darkening, creating an ominous atmosphere. The sprightly, glossy twirl of the hotel's revolving doors is matched with the scurrying past of dark pedestrians and cars on the murky street beyond, and echoed later in the heavy, fateful closure of another pair of doors, down in the lavatory catacombs.

Equally *physical* is Jannings' acting. Expressionistic theory (as highly developed as 'Method'ism) required its actors to aim above all at simplification—catching the *one* important stance or gesture—and then intensifying it. It's not intended to show 'how people react in reality', but to evoke the full emotional surge, as it is 'at heart'. It's not so much to be 'looked at' with the eye, coldly, as 'felt with', by empathy, in one's body—the sense of strain, alertness, abandon in the posture transmit the subtleties in the emotion. (Plate 22) Looked at as 'realism', it's easy to find Jannings' performances ludicrous—one eye narrowed to a slit, the other glaring like a soup-plate—just as it's easy to find 'rhapsodic' poets like Keats and Shelley ridiculous if one reads them without sympathy. But it has its own authentic, pantomimic power. Jannings allowed himself to stray as far from 'realism' as comedians do—one can speak of 'slow' expressionism, like Jannings's, and 'fast' expressionism, like Chaplin's (or Jerry Lewis's). The middle term between them is exemplified by Catherine Hessling in Jean Renoir's *Nana* (1926), where she gives what is both the best and the worst performance in the history of the French cinema. With her petal-light limbs flung out into Napoleonic postures, her bee-sting mouth pouting in her heart-shaped face, her eyes narrowed till the pupils disappear under a palisade of lashes, her fluttering precocity and jagged stances, this awkward blend of Chaplinesque quicksilver and marionette fixity comes, if only the spectator will adapt his response, to make at least as much sense as modern 'Method'ism.

Similarly, the expressionistic fondness for 'symbol' owed nothing to a code of dry meanings, everything to what René Huyghe, speaking of the painter Roualt, calls 'the emotional reverberation of sensation'. Just as the acting is based on *physicality*, a sense of *the body as pure emotion*, so the symbol acquires its meaning from sensuality. In Paul Wegener's second version of *The Golem* curving ceilings with their coracle-like domes make one's spine hunch up, the huge, claw-shaped hinges on sinister doors are like cruel fingers—it is through this physicality that the symbols have meaning.

In modern American films, on the other hand, objects pick up their symbolism by their role in the story—thus both *Rebel Without a Cause* and *On the Waterfront* have 'jacket' motifs—Dean 'inherits' Sal Mineo's, after his suicide, Brando that of Eva-Marie Saint's brother, for whose murder he is partly responsible. Ingmar Bergman's films mix both techniques; as Peter Harcourt has pointed out, the opening sequence of *Sawdust and Tinsel* with its emphases on cannons, clothes and the sun, endows inanimate objects with an enigmatic significance and a tempestuous energy.

Many of the German silent directors had in fact a visual rather than a literary background. Lang trained as an architect, Murnau was an art historian, Leni a painter. The soul of the films is always *in* the surface offered to the eye. *Metropolis* with the variously dulled and frantic movements of its factory-slaves, its crowds pouring like a torrent through narrow spaces, its lights flashing round the uneven rocks of a narrow catacomb, its floodwaters first seeping, then trickling, then hurtling, with an almost 'musical' development, is a metronome-and-protractor film, like *Intolerance*. Lang's American films have a 'realistic' appearance, but are just as 'visual' as his German. He is a master of so arranging his characters in space that a kind of nameless, fatalistic suspense palpitates between them. Slow, intermittent, dragging movements are his speciality—whether of trains in *Human Desire*, or of doors and people in *The Woman in the Window*. *Tigress of Bengal* has a careful colour symbolism (spoiled in the wretched English prints); good is a matter of dull buffs and plain whites, evil is mosaics of rich, glinting patterns. The beauty of evil and the colour-poverty of good connects with his tragic-ironic view of life. Lang's story sense may be shaky, even his orchestrations of movement less inventive than they were in the 20's. Perhaps only those of his films are masterpieces which combine their visual richness with a satisfying dramatic line. But his consistently expressionistic idiom is suggested by the similarity between these two scenes, one from *Metropolis* (1926), the other from *Fury* (1936) (Plates 20–21).

Expressionism in France seemed less successful than in Germany, and one can even say that, after lying quiescent during the socially-conscious 30's and 40's, it doesn't come to fruition until Truffaut's *Les 400 Coups* (1959). In the 60's as in the 20's, the French movement would be more aptly described as an impressionism, or at least as an attempt to turn an impressionistic sensibility and idiom to romantic and expressionistic aims. The procedure is possible, as the paintings of Van Gogh demonstrate. But when, in the early 20's, Delluc, Dulac, Gance, L'Herbier, Jean Epstein and the other intellectuals who were faced with the task of artistically and economically reconstructing French film art from its wartime collapse, they constituted a sort of 'new wave', usually called 'impressionist', because they were very concerned with lyricizing psychological, subjective 'impressions', whether of the outside world, or of mental reality (a 'stream of consciousness' in opticals). Instead of the Germans' slow, heavy mime and architecture, their films disintegrated into a mercurial flurry of optical distortions, superimpositions, first-person shots ('the camera becomes a snowball' wrote Gance proudly) and hectic montages. As Jacques Brunius remarks in *Experiment in the Film*, 'In *Le Diable dans la Ville* (1926) Germaine Dulac doubled the image to indicate violent emotion in one of her characters. I do not know whether my eyeballs are peculiarly stable and unemotional, or simply whether I have never been sufficiently moved, but no such affective diplopia ever effected me, and a vision of this sort on the screen conveys nothing to me at all.'[1] Other pests described by Brunius include 'crick-necked camera', soft-focus, gauze, and 'cubist' décor. 'Fortunately at this time the trucks in French studios all had square wheels, and the impossibility of moving them spared us for another few years the annoyance of irrelevant tracking shots.'

[1] The concentration on the 'perceptual notation' prefigures the 'solipsistic-nihilistic perceptual pedantry' of Robbe-Grillet. This French screen impressionism lacked that careful exploration of visual sensation that was the procedure of an earlier impressionism—in fact it was too careless even for its own slaphappy lyrical purposes, lacking also the strong emotionality of Van Gogh. It was an aesthete's mode. Godard today has a similarly 'darting' eye for visual details, 'cool' rather than emotional; at its worst, a 'flip aestheticism', at its best authentically lyrical, in a solipsist-nihilist key.

Epstein's *La Chute de la Maison Usher* (1927) is an interesting, if finally only spasmodically successful, attempt at combining intensely lyrical location-shots (the dank, gloomy winter countryside, all mud and bare branches), impressionism *à la* Dulac (a plethora of 1st-person shots and 'arty' super-impressions—a forest of white candles 'walking through' a forest of black trees), and expressionistic décor (the House itself). It is a fascinating potpourri of the bad and the brilliant—in one slow-motion shot, a stack of books falling forward from a cupboard seem to be sagging, crumbling like a very old corpse. . . . The comparison with Corman's version is fascinating, especially since both films combine two Poe stories into one.

By about 1931 the French had given up such impressionistic-expressionistic cocktails. The great French films of the 30's are all in the tradition of a slightly literary realism. One director alone, in two films, achieves the perfect integration of the three idioms: Jean Vigo, with *Zero de Conduite* (1933) and *L'Atalante* (1934).

By the late 20's German expressionism and realism had reached the compromise exemplified by E. A. Dupont's *Variété* by Pabst's *Pandora's Box*, Joe May's *Ashphalte*, Fritz Lang's *M*, all of which, more or less acceptable as 'realistic', use a visual language derived almost entirely from expressionism. Streetscapes straight out of silent German films (huddled roofs, twisted windows) turn up even in British films—Dupont's *Piccadilly* (1928), Hitchcock's *Murder!* (1930). But though expressionism sensitizes and strengthens the camera's language, it can't be said that expressionism as such infiltrates world cinema. In the early talkies words seemed to discourage the lyrical simplicities of the silent film. They enabled plots to move much faster, and moved the acting and the whole 'tone' steadily towards the underplaying which passed for realism in the 40's.

The main exception is the out-and-out horror film, which flourished during the Depression, and which, by definition, rules out 'common sense', so as to unleash nightmarish emotion. In painting too, there is a general connection between expressionism and nightmare, that is, the primitive, morbid, uprush of subrational emotion, and this link characterizes the German silent cinema. In its storyline, *Caligari* is pure penny dreadful. Murnau's *Nosferatu* (1922) was the first screen adaptation of Bram Stoker's *Dracula*. American Depression-era horrors retained the germanic bestiary (*Dracula*), its trickwork (*King Kong*) and studio-sets (Frankenstein's tower and crypt); even the flashing of machinery during the Monster's resurrection is prefigured in the creation of the robot in Lang's *Metropolis*.

The acting is often a dreamlike pantomime (Karloff, Lugosi). There is a procession of 'tyrant figures' like that which Kracauer notices in German silent films (for Haroun el Raschid, Ivan the Terrible and Jack the Ripper read Count Dracula, Count Zaroff and the Frankenstein Monster). There is a similar interest in tortures (Zaroff and Fu Manchu) and waxworks (*The Mystery of the Wax Museum*). But all these films are only just beginning to return into critical fashion. . . .

Nor have critics been very appreciative of those directors in whose works expressionism led a subtler existence, as a visual style. Of Joseph von Sternberg it can safely be said that if expressionism hadn't already existed he would have invented it. If his storylines incline to be a little top glib, his visuals are so impeccable, so rich, as to poeticize both the most arrant artifice (Marlene in 'Morocco' trotting out into the desert on four-inch heels . . .) and the most casual detail (a candle on an unlit stove, a boy poking his head round the side of a wooden mannequin). Straight from German expressionism is his sense of fate (suggested by the menacing dredger in *The Salvation Hunters,* the maze of nets in *Macao*) and of moral ascendancy and humiliation (Jannings, pompously: 'I am the professor of English at the local school!' Marlene, coolly: 'Then you should know enough to take off your hat.') His décor is completely controlled: its grotesque, suffering masks, its cages, its animals, are as expressive of the characters' souls as the expressionistic distortions of *Caligari*.

Near the end of *The Devil is a Woman* a train emerges from a tunnel; only Von Sternberg could make of its appearance a little poem. The sun is behind and above the tunnel, which forms a squat black mass far away down the line. First we hear the train approaching. Then we see the white smoke jet out amidst the framing blackness. Abruptly its grey-white pillar billows up into the sunlight. At last the black square mass of the locomotive itself slides out into the glare of sun, towards us, and blacks it out. These tonal reversals in and round a steadily thrusting-out object are quite hypnotic. Some of the visual jokes are admirable. Marlene dons insolent white to visit her lover in prison, and, to visit him in hospital, funereal black. As Lionel Atwill enfolds Marlene in his arms, she holds in her arms a goose in a cage.

The heavier, foggier aspects of expressionism inspire the lighting of Lang's *Fury* and *You Only Live Once*, Ford's *The Informer* and *The Long Voyage Home*, and Welles' *Citizen Kane*. Perhaps the last burst of Hollywood expressionism is the heavy shafts of light in the condemned cell scenes of Siodmak's *Phantom Lady* (1945). By the early 50's, expressionism seemed altogether exhausted. *Citizen Kane* and *Ivan the Terrible*—two studies in megalomanic solitude—seemed like whales stranded on the shores of fashion.

When the cinema wanted to be 'expressionistic', it had to find a location which gave the psychological effect a realistic 'pretext'. And it did (for the expressionistic urge can never die). The maze of mirrors, the clammy aquarium in Welles' *The Lady from Shanghai*, the empty fairground in Kubrick's *The Killing* (with the loudspeaker booming, 'We—the dead—welcome you . . .'), the planet Metaluna in *This Island Earth*, the blitzed church, the huge crucifix hanging upside down, and the rubbish dump on which the hero dies kicking and writhing in Wajda's *Ashes and Diamonds*, the complex symbolism of Ingmar Bergman (in *Summer Interlude* a woman walking on a windy, rainy path suddenly resembles Death . . .), the glossy clinic of *La Notte*, the children's downriver drift, watched by forest animals, in Charles Laughton's *Night of the Hunter*, all, in different ways, draw attention to themselves as overpowering mood, as whirls of intense emotion.

Two technical developments of the 50's pushed the pendulum of style slowly back from the 'realistic' to the 'expressionistic'. Magazine photography was controlling and exploiting such effects as blurring, grainy texture, out-of-focus, 'bad' light, 'wrong' exposures, and all the 'mistakes' which have vastly increased the camera's repertoire. For the movie camera too faster emulsions, simplified lighting, in or out of the studio, and smaller cameras permitted far greater variety, nuance and subtlety in location photography and movement.

The change can be seen as far back as Dassin's *Du Rififi Chez les Hommes* (1955), where the crazy streaming of trees reflected in a car windscreen mirrors the delirious, the *internal*, world of its dying driver. The director no longer has to *create* an effect, as did Wiene, Lang and Murnau. Now he has only to *spot* it. The 'camera stylo' is nothing new; a walking camera *à la* Coutard is used in Epstein's *La Chute de la Maison Usher* (1927), in Vigo' *A Propos de Nice* (1930) in Dreyer's *Vampyr* (1932), and many other places besides. What is new is the ease with which the director's visual *impressions* can be caught. At last his personal world can easily become a subjective, an expressionistic, world. American *avant-garde* had been developing such effects consistently for many years, but in the popular cinema the most useful milestone is perhaps the opening sequence of Truffaut's *Les 400 Coups*. The camera glides past blind brick walls, desolate warehouses, glimpsing intermittently, the Eiffel Tower stalking far away, like a pale ghost against an iron sky. Paris is suddenly chilled to one boy's feeling of utter desolation and solitude. The boarded-up windows become gouged-out eyes. This is a dead planet, one man's Metaluna. The visuals are one long, desolate wail. But the music is mildly sprightly, the music doesn't care too much, there is a discontinuity in the feelings—a discontinuity which comes closer to the surface in the 'cool' mode, the 'flip tragic' mood, of Charles Aznavour in *Tirez Sur le Pianiste*. The scene where a lover's-eye-view panning-shot round their bedroom is superimposed over a shot of the two lovers lying in bed is the consummation of the white candles-black forest effect in *La Chute de la Maison Usher*. At last such effects have emotional relevance.

Simultaneously, in America, Roger Corman and Floyd Crosby develop a colour expressionism, at its most dazzling in the delirium sequence of *Tales of Terror* (1962). Certain Saul Bass credits (like the prowling cat in *Walk On the Wild Side*) point the way to an expressionism based less on traditional 'painterliness' than on the newer idioms of graphic design.

The contemporary audience which accepts the 'false-time' jump cuts of Godard's *A Bout de Souffle* and Desmond Davis' *Girl with Green Eyes* is an audience which will take the cinema screen as, not a *literal* reality, but a 'mental world'. So with the 'puzzle worlds' of Resnais' *L'Année Dernière à Marienbad*, Fellini's *8½*, of Welles' *The Trial*, all of which are, in some sense, expressionistic films. Again 'realism' becomes merely a means to an end, a convention which can be accepted or ignored, whichever the artist prefers.

Still untapped possibilities loom. The difficulties are less of *inventing* and *controlling* effects, than of making sure that they have some emotional relevance. One can distort colour by using tungsten stock by daylight and daylight stock by artificial light. One can alter hues and shades by over- and under-exposure. One can throw backgrounds slightly out of focus to produce a 'dreamlike haze' (an effect already abused in magazine advertisements), or throwing images completely out-of-focus so as to create evocative patterns (corresponding to semi-abstract expressionism). Thus in *Lueurs* (1950), Dr. Thévénard let the camera dwell on a convict's cigarette smoke as he languished in his cell, and evocative music gave the smoke fleeting resemblances to blurred memory-images—a fairground, a girl. . . .

Colour commercials have developed a new sensuousness which the artist might well take up, deepen, and use in a disturbing or sinister way. There's no reason why one shouldn't re-explore certain silent 'effects'—masking, shooting through thin cloths. One might alter photographic textures by reshooting scenes projected on to suitably textured or uneven surfaces—thus in Michael Powell's *Peeping Tom* a film-within-a-film is seen on the hero's Harris Tweed jacket, and a face blurs into a skull. Losey does something like this in his use of a convex mirror in *The Servant*. Its bulge distorts the space it reflects, and therefore not only the relationships but the bodies and postures of the people in the room. Different colour stocks might be used in adjacent sequences or even shots. And as Von Sternberg has remarked: '. . . still photography as distinguished from motion picture photography has one enormous advantage which one day will cease to be: that is the treatment of the surface of the photograph. Choice of grain in the paper, paper, manipulation of the negative, the enlargement of an interesting detail, can salvage otherwise uninteresting work and make it effective. It is only a matter of time when such manipulation will be incorporated into our work.'

The greater the range of possibilities at the artist's finger-tips, the greater the importance of disciplined selection, of exact control. Effects must never be used in a random or pretentious way, that is, so that by drawing attention to themselves they disrupt instead of reinforcing the overall emotional substance. But that problem is a perennial one, it exists in one form or another with the simplest techniques—pencil on paper. Meanwhile the cinema stands on the brink of another leap forward in its artistic development.

6 · Architecture in, and of, the Movies

A. The Rape of Architecture by Drama

Carl Dreyer has argued that the cinema's closest relative is architecture.

It may seem paradoxical to compare the most mimetic (photographic) of the arts with the construction of a new reality, and a dramatic art with a 'Utopian' one. Equally unexpected is the *rapprochement* of the most fluid of all visual media with the most solid and static.

Yet the paradoxes hold. For, by its nature, the cinema is a *beau monstre*. Like the theatre, it centres on actors. *But* its tempo-spatial flexibility approaches the novel's. *But* it is predominantly visual—flat, like painting. *But* its visuals exist in *movement* and *time*, so that its plasticity has musical components. *But* its photographic quality precludes music abstraction, suggesting a very literal realism. *But* seeing a film is notoriously a dreamlike experience. . . .

This blend of realism and onirism provides the clue to Dreyer's meaning. The cinema's mimetic fullness (photography, movement, sound) permits the creation of a *self-sufficient* world. Like the architect, the film director weaves diverse media into a 'new' reality.

The traditional division between the 'dramatic' and the other arts is only part of the story. Dramatic ugliness and tensions, even the tragic end, occur within aesthetic 'distance' and form part of an ultimately agreeable existence. The character dies, but author and actors enjoy our enthusiastic applause. Through vicarious experience, katharsis and enhanced understanding, drama, like architecture, improves the world.

And architecture, in its way, implies drama. There is the possibility of displeasure. An effective building, like a circus acrobat, might be graceless, but flies through the air with the greatest of ease. Its 'suspense' is non-representational, but exists as intensely as that of music. As Keats and Freud agreed, there is no beauty without melancholy, no thrill without anxiety, no elegance without the remembrance of pain. Creativity treads a tightrope between complacent 'good taste' (too little 'danger') and bad taste (an emotional 'unhappy end').

Architecture's immobility makes it the natural complement of the movie-camera. The basic architectural experiences—standing in a space, looking around, and walking along a corridor—find their equivalents in the screen frame, in the panning shot (the camera turns its head), and the tracking shot (the camera walks forward or backwards). Though the screen is flat, the camera's reticulation of movements in space confer on the succession of images (the sequence) a quality of space-in-depth, controlled and orchestrated.

Architecture has been described as 'frozen music'. When the camera moves, the roofline flows past us like a river. The camera tilts rapidly up, and banister and staircase cascade down. The cinema is 'unfrozen architecture'.

In the opening shots of Thorold Dickinson's *Overture* the swooping camera counterpoints the inner lines of the U.N. building at Lake Success with the opening theme of Beethoven's *Egmont* Overture. Space becomes time, balconies and musical phrases leap out together. The cinema *is* an architecture (and is the best medium for recording architecture).

B. How to Make a Building Omelette

But the film hurls form into a melting-pot of its own. It abducts, reforms, deforms, all it shows. Above all, as we shall see, it perverts its emotional sense.

When in David Lean's *Great Expectations* Pip as a boy calls on Miss Havisham her room is huge, cavernous. When Pip as a man (John Mills) calls on her it is stuffy, cramped. The room is the same. The camera lens is different. The camera is a born liar.

It commits every conceivable offense against the human scale. It is the anti-Modulor. The cloak of a foreground figure rears up over the palace beyond. Cut—and that monumental figure now becomes a tiny dot stranded in the forecourt, dwarfed in its turn by a foreground vase. The cinema's mobility *explodes* architecture.

The camera glides up the outside of a wall, and swoops from window to window. It glides 'through' walls from one room to another, creating a sense of magic ease, of liberation from gravity and mural impenetrability. In Jerry Lewis's *The Ladies' Man* the camera tracks back from an ordinary two-shot to reveal an entire mansion in cross-section. It doesn't reduce the house to a dolls' house; it makes the spectator feel he has become God's right-hand-man. Or empty rooms may be barricaded with shadows which appear as beams of black light. . . .

Films may convert space into time. Roger Corman's *The Man With the* X-*Ray Eyes*, is one of the 'pulp' films that fascinate pop-art addicts. The guilty scientist (Ray Milland) runs down a fire-escape, and superimposed over a 1st-person-shot of his feet hurrying down the steps, endlessly, endlessly, appear newspaper headlines announcing his escape. A mere 'metaphor'? But it shows that, in the spectator's mind, space was 'merging' into time. In *Hoven Zo* (*Steady*), Herman Van Der Horst's documentary on the reconstruction of Rotterdam, the camera, identified with a steam-drill, plummets down past tower blocks, which conversely seem to be thrusting up into the sky with a phallic indomitability; or like intention directly translated into fact. Thus camera style becomes metaphysics.

Jean Cocteau's *Le Sang d'Un Poete* opens with a factory chimney beginning to fall. Seventy minutes later it concludes with the chimney hitting the ground. This 'time-split' establishes the onirism of the intervening story (for back in the 30's dreams were thought to be all-but-instantaneous). But it harnesses also the thrill and awed chill we feel watching demolitions. We hold our breath, because as the chimney falls, we fall. That crumbling chimney is the spectator's own body 'dissolving', and through kinaesthetic empathy it triggers emotions of failure and death.

Louis Feuillade's *Les Vampires* (1915) is a pulp serial celebrated by the Surrealists and latterly revived with great success at the National Film Theatre. Perhaps its most beautiful sequences show criminals clambering about Paris rooftops, clad in black catsuits and Ku Klux Klan hoods (as to be completely inconspicuous). Their presence, akin to Chirico's geometrical figures, transforms the real, shot-on-location roofscapes into a world as hallucinatory as Chaval's Dream Palace at Hauterives. The roofs become moon dunes, the chimneystacks a cubist vegetation or lunar cacti.

C. Architecture as Metaphor

At the other extreme, architecture is a favourite image for social pressures, for society itself. The camera needs visual metaphors; and architecture is a man-made landscape, a man-made environment. Elia Kazan's *On the Waterfront* concludes with the dockers returning to work, strengthened by their new-found spirit of 'one for all, all for one', which will make an authentic unionism possible. But a grim steel shutter closes down on them. The docks in which they work are a prison. Their next fight is just beginning.

More subtle and evasive is the meaning of an extreme long shot in a John Ford Western, *My Darling Clementine*, showing three masses echeloned against the desert. Nearest us, the half-built church; beyond, the saloon; beyond again, a craggy massif. The formal echo summarizes the nascent West: the Protestant ideal; its brawling antithesis; and, over and above these, *their* antithesis, silent, sullen nature. The finest is the most 'fragile' of the three. Civilization seems a raft bobbing on vast sea, the third 'block' being—a tidal wave. . . .

A fundamental equation of the cinema's is: landscape=state of soul. Architecture may constitute an X-ray photograph of the heroes' minds. If in *Rocco and His Brothers* Visconti stages a quarrel, between a newly urbanized peasant and a *dolce vita* call girl, on top of Milan cathedral, and then cuts and cuts jaggedly, hectically, it is because that cathedral, like the moral framework of their lives, is a giant ship keeling over beneath them. Christendom 1960 is a *Titanic*, sinking fast.

In Claude Chabrol's *A Double Tour*, Antonella Lualdi lives in a house one of whose glass walls lets a green field with poppies into the room. Between us and the picture window is an aquarium, and tropical fish slowly drift across the scenery, like living gems. The strangeness of all this transforms physical beauty into a spiritual power: the flesh (Lualdi), a *fin-de-siecle* preciosity (fish-gems), and nature-merged-with-structure (or, a new classicism) which has room for the romantic urge.

In many ways, the cinema deprives architecture of its autonomy, makes of it a symbol whose meaning alters with content. The concept of *objet trouvé* isn't inappropriate, for directors currently depend on finding buildings with emotional possibilities. The vast complex of rooms in Orson Welles' *The Trial* is not the studio construction it may seem, but the derelict Gare d'Orsay in Paris 'merged' with a Yugoslavian exhibition hall. The supernatural 'zone' of Cocteau's *Orphée* is the ruins of L'Ecole Militaire. It is not photography *per se* which makes these fantasies so convincing, it is the concrete specificity of their sustained architectural metaphor. Here architecture takes a thoroughly creative role. Eisenstein didn't think of a massacre on some steps and then select the Odessa Steps; the Steps inspired the staging. Carl Dreyer, while searching for a visual style for his *Vampyr*, came across a flour mill and derived from it the idea of a vampire film in the key of white.

D. The Rise and Fall of Expressionism

When photography was less sensitive than it is now, the director could control his environment only by building it in a studio. The facility of exaggeration led easily to expressionism.

Weine's *The Cabinet of Dr. Caligari* (1919) was not the first expressionist film (contrary to academic myth: its principal predecessor was C. A. Bragaglia's *Perfido Incanto* (Italy, 1916). But Weine's film initiated the screen's first concerted attempt to emotionalize architecture, along principles derived from Max Reinhardt's stage décor and the theories of Edschmidt. Seen through the mind of its madman, the streets and façades of *Caligari*, painted on intersecting back-cloths, were shattered into spikes and shards; ceilings warped and drooped, buildings were paper scraps. In Weine's *Raskolnikoff* (1923) the guilty student slept under a clutter of black beams which seemed to be pressing down upon his head like a vice. As he climbed the rickety staircase to the murder room, its tottering banisters were so many needle-like shapes, hysterically pointing the way. But as he backed hysterically out of the room, they seemed to be falling away behind him, letting him fall into the horror. . . .

Expressionism soon revealed two tendencies, the *paroxystic* and the *decorative*. In contrast to the flimsy, staggering structures of the madman's vision, the asylum in *Caligari* is a cool, heavy, immovable, three-dimensional structure. The enigmatic Dr. Caligari himself is awaited. From which of a row of three dark arches will he enter? The suspense turns the arcade into a labyrinth concealing the minotaur of authority. The asylum architecture has a strong, but slightly barbaric, feel, and one's feeling that its symmetry is hierarchic to the point of feudalism is confirmed by Fritz Lang's two-part *Nibelungen* film. There medieval orders of chivalry are associated with halls of chessboard patterns and a brutal solidity. Thus these apparently 'decorative' designs reveal their emotional tensions, and, as Siegfreid Kracauer suggests in *From Caligari to Hitler*, points to the house style of the Third Reich.

The madman's flat confusions oppose a brutal order; their linking term is the *maze* from which issues *tyranny*. Mazes, mirrors, the interplay of spotlights and drifting smoke on architectural forms, the tension and mystery of winding staircases, the squalor of crooked streets, are among the visual motifs which dominate German expressionism, whose inspiration is the reaction to the economic instability of post-Versailles Germany by a profoundly Junkerized *bourgeoisie*.

Abandoning expressionism in the late 20's, German directors transposed these visual motifs into realistic settings and subjects. The ominous atmosphere characteristic of all the films of Lang (who trained as an architect) is created by his feeling for small, slow movements isolated in empty, rectangular spaces. The films of Pabst are built on the motif of a sharply angled passage flanked by dark masses. The passage may be a mineshaft along which flames are leaping (*Kameradschaft*, 1931), it may be lorries driving out of a barrack square (*Jackboot Mutiny*, 1955), it may be tunnelled out of an enigmatic chiaroscuro by spotlights, but the implied or stated Z, with all its tensions, gives all the films of this celebrated 'realist' an emotional undertow as powerful as expressionism's. Lang's colour *Tigress of Bengal* is another of the 'pulp' subjects whose formalism has enraptured the writers of *Cahiers du Cinema*, critical seedbed of the New Wave. In her white, almost *bleached*, clothes, the European girl, wanders through the Maharajah's Palace in search of her lost brother. First, by daylight, she strolls past vivid, coloured mosaics, orderly and rectangular. Then she strolls past dark, purplish murals —the colours are rich, but sullen, brooding, the forms more confused and hectic. At last, leaving daylight behind, she ventures into the catacombs, the palace corridors now yielding to a rocky irregularity of form.

Architectural forms strike off bodily motifs. In the temple, dwarfed by the gigantic statue of a goddess, Debra Paget dances, with lubricious legs-astride movements of her torpedo-shaped thighs.

Meanwhile the exploring architect clambers up a catacomb-chimney, his straddled legs 'rhyming' with hers.

In Dreyer's films architecture plays a major role. The hero of *Vampyr* arrives at an apparently deserted inn. He hears a voice and seeks its source. The camera tilts up one corner of the house, pans across the diagonal slope of the roof, and discovers a woman in an attic window. The camera moves along the edges of the building, which we always thought of as a volume. The house becomes a collection of edges, a set of blades, a slice of the sky stolen by man to live in.

Later, the hero dreams that his corpse is being carried past the church in a glass-windowed coffin. As if through his eyes, we see the sky and trees above us—and then the front of the church rears over us, turned on its side, quivering slightly as if with the movements of the coffin. It moves slowly over us, and away off the screen, and we, the not-quite-dead, destined for burial in unconsecrated ground, feel as forlorn as men in a lifeboat when the great ship they have attempted to hail moves steadily away.

By contrast with the human eye, the camera has 'tunnel vision', and Dreyer uses this visual concentration to render structures *unsteady*. The camera looks down across a room so that the far skirting is an uneasy tilt across the top edge of the screen. The furniture, or such floor-coverings as a heavily-patterned carpet, emphasize the floor's climb 'up' perspective hill, and it is as if the room were heaving under strange pressures. Wide-angle lens permit a whole web of such effects, involving also the angles of furniture and the human body. Degas' *Le Tub* (1888) anticipates them, but in Dreyer the effect is specifically of a building under the torque of disturbing spiritual forces.

The house in *Vampyr* is *also* a matter of flat planes. A door in a near wall opens to reveal a further wall beyond; the house has a Whistlerian flimsiness, even preciosity. 'Safe as houses?' No, a house is only a maze of planes, partitions between which the uncanny emanations freely flow—the fluidity suggested for us by a gliding camera.

Dreyer's *Day of Wrath* (1943) emphasizes *bourgeois* love of property as a spiritual evil. Heavy shadows, emphasizing solidity of form, an immobile camera, and 'rectangular' placings in space, render buildings and furniture dark and massive. In their stiff puritan clothes, the people themselves seem rigid as oak or teak. But when the flames are lit round the foolish old woman who has become the scapegoat for repressed hatreds, the hot air rising from the pyre makes the stone church beyond *tremble* and *shudder*. . . .

Despite the achievements of such lonely souls as Dreyer, the 30's saw expressionism in eclipse. In the popular cinema, almost its last stronghold was the American horror film. James Whale's *Frankenstein* (1931) and *Bride of Frankenstein* (1935), for whose lyrical power even the documentarist John Grierson had a grudged respect, are glorious specimens of what one can only describe as 'slaphappy Gothic.' There are among those artistic hybrids found only in the popular arts, the result of sophisticated people working for a hick audience, now subverting the formula with private parody, now hitting on a unique blend of subtlety and popular myth.

There are architectural jokes. In the middle of a deliriously cobwebby sepulchre, Dr. Praetorius warns Baron Frankenstein to, 'Mind the step.' As a laboratory, the too-audacious Baron uses a dilapidated stone tower on top of a hill. The Freudian symbolism of this topography (a phallic erection on testicle hill) is duly enhanced by the details of the process of carcass-revivification. The corpse, laid out on a stretcher, is hoisted to the top of the tower, preceded by an electrical 'pylon', which screws itself up into the nocturnal storm, whose energies are further tapped by a flotilla of kites. The thunderstorm, the lifting of the 'unborn' body, the erection of the spire, the floating of the kites, the crackling and sparking, introduce a plethora of classic orgasmic symbols. The reference is not only Promethean (stealing fire from the heavens), it is also to a gigantic, monstrous, erection—the megalomaniac 'hubris' of the scientist, creating life without the aid of God, or of woman. Grand finale: the Monster (Boris Karloff) is scorned by his Bride (Elsa Lanchester), who is an improved model, and only loves her maker (Colin Clive). Vengefully the lumbering old Mark I pulls the wrong lever, whereupon Tumescence Tower literally blows its top.

E. A Lyrical Realism

The 40's and 50's are under the sign of realism, and, predominantly, architecture 'is' society. Many young critics, preoccupied with screen aesthetics for their own sake, find it hard to respond to such films of de Sica's as *Bicycle Thieves* (1948) and *Umberto D*, whose style seems so cold and plain.

But 'cold and plain' is the key. The streets down which the workman searches for his stolen bicycle have a bland, callous indifference to the desperate individual. In endless successions, skeins of terrace houses, lofty apartment blocks, become symbols of a society built out of privacy, indifference and a human 'absence'. De Sica's sense of Rome reflects his curious blend of Franciscan sentimentality and Marxist hard-headedness. And the 'coldness' of his films prefigures Antonioni's, whose evocation of 'alienation' transposes this critique of capitalism from the proletarian-economic sphere to the *bourgeois*-spiritual.

In the films of de Sica, Visconti (and of their Indian disciple, Satyajit Ray) architecture plays an interesting syntactical role in articulating the image. All three have to deal with poor people living in very crowded conditions. Continual close-up would abolish the sense of *man in his environment* so essential to the films' theme; so individuals are isolated by creating within the frame smaller frames by walls, windows, railings, or other spatial 'vignettes'. Often the character isolated is an unimportant one—a lonely grandfather shaving—while the story proceeds 'round' him, in terms of movement and dialogue. And we become aware of the loneliness in crowds, of lives proceeding beside lives, of individuality everywhere.

Neo-realism died, briefly, around 1953, killed partly by audiences' dislike of its drabness, partly by government dislike for its picture of an Italy where people were poor and it rained all the time. Around 1960 the 'economic miracle' and a governmental 'opening to the left' presented it with a new battery of themes, and it could call on the talents of the 'school of Visconti', a bunch of very highly cultured young Marxists. One film must stand for many (by Bolognini, Pasolini, Patroni Griffi, Rosi, Olmi, *et al.*). In Lina Wertmuller's *The Lizards*, long white lines of sun-baked stone houses evoke all the harsh torpor of Southern feudalism. A boy dares outrage tabu and address a girl, unchaperoned, in the street. A God's-eye-view camera looks down on the boy as he overtakes the girl and walks alongside her. The pan continues through its 90° so that street and houses keep slowly over, and 'up' is slewed to some indistinct area to the left of the screen. The lovers walk on in a disordered, strange, *weightless* world—the effect is so uncanny that we know they will just let the matter drop.

F. The Architecture of Alienation

Richard Smith remarked in *Ark 19*: 'In *Little Caesar* (1930) Edward G. Robinson's set-up as a minor monster was straight from the Bauhaus stable. . . . Later, modern styling became associated with a new bogey man in the communist agent who, while obviously living in the same world as we, could not have settings impinging on the audience's dream world. So the as yet unacceptable modern was called into service, along with the use of modern art galleries and modern music as front organizations.'

An overt anti-egghead bias operated too. But it's less the heroine than the vamp who wears next year's clothes and keys next year's behaviour. So modern stylings gradually percolate from the villain to the hero-villain, and, via the psychiatrist, to the hero, and from the snooty hotel to the cosy home.

But a curious thing has happened to what the man-in-the-street thinks of as 'modern' architecture. Just as curtain-walls and tower-blocks are becoming familiar, so the screen portrays them as cold, remote, bland. Tati preferred the unfunctional ramshackle home of *Mon Oncle* (1958) to sterile *bourgeois* gadgetry. In Marcel Camus' *Orfeu Negro* (1959) a steel-and-glass office-building becomes a silent, shining sepulchre, past which winds the joyous snake of a Brazilian native carnival. In Louis Malle's *Ascenseur à l'Échafaud* (1958) a modern office-block evokes the larger trap, which is society. Seen through its glass walls, the windows in the block opposite are rows and columns of eyes staring at the hero as he murders his unscrupulous boss. As he escapes in the lift, a power cut traps him between floors—another image for *the system*, and an aesthetically pleasing converse to the sinister of open space. In Resnais' *Hiroshima Mon Amour* (1959), the new buildings, the glittering neon streets, past which the heroine wanders, are not just the cynical will-to-live of the Japanese people, shaming her 'idealist' clinging to her martyrdom in a cellar. They also represent a schizoid obliteration of the pain of Hiroshima, of the past.

In all these films the equation architecture=society is dominant. A world of rapid moral and spiritual change is a world of 'alienation'. Joan Littlewood's *Sparrows Can't Sing* (1962) half-domesticates current styles. A block of shiny flats rear over us imposingly; a feckless young Cockney gadabout (Barbara Windsor) leans over her balcony and yells down to her sort-of-husband, 'Don't forget to get us some lemons, love.' Not even modern architecture can awe the Cockney soul.

Occasionally architects' Utopianism can shade over into what feels like totalitarianism. One can still talk to people in the L.C.C. Architects' Department who want open-plan apartments imposed on people for whom one of the nicest things about quitting their overcrowded old slums would have been an orgy of privacy. There's no easy answer to such clashes of taste, involving so many factors. In Antonioni's *La Notte*, a man is dying in a cancer clinic, whose, sleek, lavish lines are, somehow, an outrage—that is, an architectural metaphor for the way in which our optimistic, utilitarian rationalism smooths over human pain, therefore emotion, therefore communication. In this context, its elegance, like the charm with which Plato invests his totalitarian visions, is as sinister as a title like 'The Ministry of Peace'.

It's almost as if human nature prefers a slightly messy, random environment, not too ugly, but full of holes and corners and accidents and possibilities of ugliness, to suit its essential ambivalence. In films like *La Notte* we see the human mind making 'Utopian' architecture 'sinister', i.e. congenially ugly.

The animus is not against modernity specifically, but against the manner in which society dwarfs the individual, while uprooting (by rapid change) and manipulating him. It is with a seething hatred that King Vidor's *The Crowd* (1927), Billy Wilder's *The Apartment* (1960) and Orson Welles's *The Trial* (1962) show us a vast open-plan office—for its 'sociability' is an imposition of routine and of what David Reisman in *The Lonely Crowd* calls 'false personalization'.

In the films of Antonioni, architecture and landscape are inseparable. Throughout *L'Avventura* (1959) one broad, flat landscape after another drags itself wearily up the long, slow haul to the horizon. Limp roads lead the eye to clutters of irrelevant shacks. Buildings, cars, squares, are arranged with elaborate casualness, in unsettled snips, fragments of a jolted jigsaw, some of whose pieces are tracks and pans. They are linked raggedly. A slow motion earthquake is on. The perspectives are a web of emptiness.

We first see Claudia (Monica Vitti) waiting for Anna (Lea Massari) outside Sandro's house. She peers in through the doorway at a cold white corridor, hesitating before entering the labyrinth of his cold doubts. There are many such corridors in the film. The search for Anna after her disappearance is a *narrative* labyrinth, whose horror is that it dissolves into a grey mist of guilt. There is the corridor of the train in which Claudia and Sandro first toy with the idea of flirting. There is the long corridor down which Claudia runs in panic as the once-spontaneous Guilia and the sex-obsessed young painter make love. Her final search for Sandro, takes her down corridor after corridor, towards one vanishing point after another, until the pursuit becomes a dreamlike motionlessness. She is on the nightmare treadmill of their life together.

The strangely-deserted town of Noto, we remember, was completely destroyed by an earthquake in the eighteenth-century, and reconstructed—as Sandro, an architect, would have liked to reconstruct Italian society today.

Resnais' *Muriel* (1963) translates modern deracination into architectural terms. Boulogne, like Hiroshima, is a 'rebuilt', that is, an amnesiac, town. A stranger asks for the town centre and is told, 'You're already there.' So much for civic spirit, for society as an organism. The heroine (Delphine Seyrig) lives among the antiques she sells—her home is a *musée imaginaire* in a shop, exemplifying all our cultural confusions. Her son lives in a rickety adolescent 'den' on a farm—as if all that wasn't complacent suburbia was banished to the periphery of consciousness. Nature—Pan—is only a desperate old tramp among the bunkers, vainly seeking a mate for his goat, while the human characters, with Proustian sterility, chase their memories, revealed mainly as illusions and lies except for the shameful secret of torture in Algeria. Neons and plate glass create a maze of reflections amongst which the peripatetic characters intermittently fragment. Only in the rusty iron lacework of an old railway station does there linger any romance, any magic. We are told about a block of new flats which capsized before they were occupied—an absurd accelerando of 'planned obsolescence'. Images of new white concrete blocks suddenly outcrop on to the dialogue, irrelevantly. In a haphazardly decorated flat, the windows become glassy spaces, unfinishednesses in the walls. If *Hiroshima Mon Amour* was, in essence, one long tracking shot through a maze of distractions, to the minotaur of a past trauma, *Muriel* is *pointilliste*, a mosaic of short, static shots catching a clutter of trivial, nervy, notations, movements, moments.

By the same token, *L'Année Dernière à Marienbad* is a lattice of dislocations and contradictions. One thinks of the x-dimensional architecture of M. C. Escher. For Dilys Powell its theme was 'time, memory and love', for Eric Newton it was 'place', and the terms are tautologies. This—clinic? hotel? limbo?—is the apotheosis of the 'amnesia' themes of *Hiroshima* and *Muriel.* Perhaps the palace dreams the people? . . . or perhaps they, elegant and lovely, and it, are the potential fullness of our lives: remote, frozen and two-dimensional because they are only wish-fulfilment images of ourselves, with no more substance than the nostalgia of 'if only. . . .' Thus they can exist only on the *brink* of freedom.

With its chessboard parquets and chandeliers like dream blossoms this intellectual structure is an Enchanted Palace whose Sleeping Beauty, instead of lying in a glass coffin, dances the icy minuet of schizoid grace. Similarly, under the ideal turbulence of the Trevi fountain, Marcello in Fellini's *La Dolce Vita* is about to embrace his dream princess (Anita Ekberg) when—the fountain dries, dawn descends, like a shutter.

G. The Pathos of the Baroque

'Baroque' is a conveniently vague and distended word to describe the sumptuousness of these films. Laurence Kitchin points out that in Carol Reed's *The Third Man* (1949), Viennese baroque seems 'a pompous gesture from the past' by contrast with the frenzied squalor of contemporary intrigue (which, we might add, climaxes in the architectural negative—a sewer). I don't see, with Mr. Kitchin, that its use of formal architecture makes *The Third Man* a dominant influence on the 60's: it derives from the formula of 'incongruous settings' beloved of the 40's melodrama; its director's stock has been plummeting for years; and the exquisite attention paid to the niceties of architecture by Visconti and Antonioni evolves from Italian film traditions. In fact the Italian films reverse the irony of Carol Reed's film. Baroque turbulence seems suddenly energetic, confident, everything the contemporary characters aren't, with their indecisions, their routines.

Fellini's delicate sense of open spaces and masses goes with narratives drifting from encounter to encounter and apply a *mise-en-scène* opposing continuous, indecisive movement to homes and palaces. The travelling entertainers of *La Strada* (1954) carry their motorized shack like a snail's shell. Restlessness is imparted to the 'closed circles' of *La Dolce Vita* and *8½* by the camera's surging, stabbing movements round characters who walk as they think. The peripatetic becomes nomadic. The most imposing architectural mass in *8½* is a scaffolding surrounding a gigantic rocket which is only a film set, for a film which isn't made. Illusion of an illusion . . . Orson Welles' *The Trial* offers a prime specimen of paranoiad baroque. Using in some sequences an incessantly roaming camera, in others a flurry of quick cuts, Welles makes all space fidget. Taken on the diagonal, the rectangular jut of concrete balconies outside K's flat becomes a double lightning flash. Apparently separate locales—the bank, the tribunal, the lawyer's suite, the Ministry of Justice archives, the cathedral, the painter's 'cage'—are revealed as one agglomeration—the system in metaphor. K has long been in the whale's belly. Welles simultaneously 'explodes' space (cutting), shuffles (fidgeting) and 'agglomerates' it.

Any incongruities are happily exploited. The columns of the Gare d'Orsay appear incongruously in the cathedral, and in the lawyer's suite, among the forest of candelabra.

There exists a curious tension between the efficiency of the system (one thinks of *1984*) and its dilapidated architecture (evoking prewar European bureaucracies), a contrast underlined by K's modern equivalent. The dilapidated, peeling architecture gives the system an 'Oedipal' quality of which Welles is presumably aware, for the dialogue abounds in Freudian puns ('oval/ovular', 'phonograph/pornograph'). Thus the film links the '1984 syndrome' with the *bourgeois* conscience and love of law and order—an accusation characteristic of Welles's Nietzschean streak. The hollow grandeur thus implied is also a favourite architectural and thematic motif of his, reaching its apogee in *Confidential Report* (1955). His wide-angle lens and low angles enable tycoon Arkadian to dominate us; but also turn the walls and ceilings of his castle into converging, unstable, tottering affairs, a house-of-tottering-cards. Such shots are Welles's 'signature'.

H. Expressionism Rides Again

During the 40's Xanadu in Welles's *Citizen Kane*, the palace in Eisenstein's *Ivan the Terrible* and the Beast's castle in Cocteau's *La Belle et la Bete*—where living arms held candelabra from the walls—seemed the last bastions of screen expressionism. Less individualist directors compromised with realism by setting their stories in poetic locales. *The Third Man* might be subtitled 'Tales from the Vienna Sewers'. Welles's *The Lady from Shanghai* is famous for its love-scene set in a sombre aquarium (so that the silhouettes of shark and octopus would comment on the courtship), and for a final gunfight in mirror-maze (a superb perversion of architectural space which Welles remembered in *The Trial*, with the camera racing past alternate mirrors and spaces so that K sees Romy Schneider beyond her face; and his own image, alternate at machine-gun tempo).

Fast emulsions and pistol-size camera have vastly facilitated what we may call a 'flip expressionism'—subjective effects 'imposed on' reality simply by juggling with exposures, movements, and so on—as we saw in the case of Truffaut's *Les 400 Coups*.

Directed by Jacques Doniol-Valcroze (editor of *Cahiers du Cinema*), *L'Eau à la Bouche* (*The Game of Love*, 1960), commits one of the most creative outrages ever perpetrated on architecture by a film director. Its very uniqueness is my excuse for recurring to an example I have cited elsewhere. Its story is a little piece of bittersweet, about three pairs of young lovers switching round during a week-end in a Perpignan castle. The castle is a real treasure of nineteenth-century *bourgeois* pretention, blossoming neo-classical statues, tapestries and paintings galore of Greek Gods up to their various amorous adventures. Their fullblown flesh and gestures contrast deliciously with the cool ways, the tight trousers and relaxed sambas, of the modern girls. Throughout the film an ever-moving camera rises to a crescendo of vivacity in two visual climaxes where the camera weaves itself round staircases. Up the grand staircase the pompous butler, teased beyond endurance, pursues the provocative maid, frantically tearing her clothes off one by one as she flees. And later, when the most sensitive girl, a loser in love, is missing, and her friends fear suicide, a *concierge's* knowing little daughter (actually the director's), gravely bouncing her yo-yo, leads the anxious adults along the ups and downs and ins and outs of an iron fire-escape that twists and bends across the roof to the little corner where the girl has hidden herself to weep. And there is a quite stupendous sequence where the camera thrice races round the castle, in whose huge bulk, set suddenly spinning, three lighted windows signify that three couples are revelling in the delights of the flesh. That intoxicated castle is the castle of worldly delights. . . .

The renewed popularity of fantasy, at all intellectual levels, has offered screen architects several unusual problems. In Roy Rowland's *The 5,000 Fingers of Dr. T*, the prisons of the malicious Dr. T include a staircase every one of whose steps is of a different, and inconvenient, height. (Dungeon architecture would be an interesting new field; after all, a 'good' dungeon reverses most of the usual functional architecture, e.g. it should drive its occupants mad.)

In film studios, the current horror-cycle ensures that more ruins are being built than at any time since the Gothic revival, and some essays in science-fiction architecture are looked at in more detail in our last chapter.

But in this necessarily incomplete survey we have limited ourselves to the *dramatic perversion* of 'normal' architecture rather than to sheer fantasy, or, on the other hand, the screen *presentation* of existing architecture. As it is, we can only lament our failure to dwell in appropriate detail on such films as Eisenstein's *Ivan the Terrible* and Jacques Rivette's *Paris Nous Appartient*, two vastly different essays in paranoiad architecture; or the tormented baroque of Wajda's *Ashes and Diamonds*.

7 · The Cinema's Art Gallery

During the last twenty years, films about the older visual arts have ceased to content themselves with being passive, and therefore generally flat and dull, records of their subjects. They have ventured on to a variety of tasks, not only of popularization, but also of criticism and translation. Over the next twenty years, this use of film seems certain to increase substantially; and a summary of some of the aesthetic and spiritual problems involved can illuminate some resources and effects of the cinema medium.

In contrast to reproductions on the page, the cinema puts the painting back on the wall. Indeed, there are fewer distractions than in an art gallery. The camera can move towards and around a piece of sculpture, so creating more 3-dimensional awareness than is possible on printed page or projected slide. In contrast to a batch of slides, it can offer an unlimited number of subtly different viewpoints. Certainly, the cinema's controlled temporal continuum makes it difficult for the spectator's eye to 'browse', at leisure, over the work of art, and in this respect it is inferior indeed to both the printed and the projected still. But it has some compensation in its power to direct attention, to move smoothly from the whole to the detail and back, to relate details, to analyse, order, reorder.

The traditional association between colour cinematography and hot garish hues springs from a conjunction of diverse factors, notably, the inaccuracy of dyes, the hazards of printing, Hollywood's working for popular taste, and the visual contrast between the brightly-lit film and the surrounding darkness. Within the last two decades, the range and sensitivity of colour-system have improved beyond recognition, and colour film has repeatedly proved itself capable of soft, cool, sensitive, even 'white-on-white' effects. Variable printing remains a (minor) problem, and the light-darkness contrast often facilitates concentration on painting's actual colours (nor, after all, is the art-gallery the 'natural habitat' of many artworks). Although film reproduction is less accurate than the best ink-and-paper printing, its shortcomings are less grave than is often assumed.

For most purposes, the most accurate system is Technicolor, but it is not cheap (and the laboratories require a minimum run of forty prints). The majority of art films are filmed in a process which for most purposes is as satisfactory, Eastmancolor (the professional 'big brother' of Kodachrome), and Warner-, Pathe-, Metro-, Columbia-, and De Luxe Color are merely other names for the same process. The German Agfacolor process gave rise to various adaptations, notably Anscocolor (U.S.A.), Sovcolor (U.S.S.R.), Ferraniacolour (Italy) and Gevacolor (Belgium). The Agfa family tends to a softer colour quality which can be restful, although in fact less accurate than the two American groups. Sometimes it tends to juxtapose 'bleached' areas with one, predominant colour (often, in Ansco, green; in Ferrania, red; in Sovcolor, salmon). By far the truest is Gevacolor, though in dark hues it tends to a certain 'plumminess' (which can be appropriate, e.g. in certain 'firelight' interiors). But over most of the range, it offers a sensitively creamy, pastelly quality (which can most happily render the *clarté* of medieval landscapes).

Over- or under-exposure changes not just brightness and darkness, but the actual colour-hue. John Huston, in filming *Moulin Rouge*, over printed a black-and-white image over its colour 'twin', so as to attain a suitably 'rough' visual texture. Thus the film-maker is far from being the passive slave of his system's characteristics; photography and printing allow him considerable scope for manipulations to suit subject, thesis and style.

Apart from these 'aesthetic' points, there is a practical convenience; the film with commentary and comparisons is, virtually, a lecture packaged for distribution. Further, cinema and TV possess a blend of familiarity and glamour which, for the wider public, is far more 'living' than the characteristic accent of art gallery and lecture room, and thus can serve as a useful intermediary.

Yet the most resourceful interpretations of works of art in cinematographic terms run into all the snags that beset any translation. The cinema image is two-dimensional (and 3-D depth too 'laminated' to feel real). Again, the cinema sequence breaks a canvas down into a series of details, that is, a *series* of compositions in time. Where the elder visual arts suggest movement by static forms, the cinema medium inclines to endow static forms with movement (e.g. as the camera moves across the canvas). The quality of reproduction is insufficiently good for a single 'still' of a painting to constitute a whole film; cinematically, such a procedure would be so uncongenial to the medium as to be unbearable; a lantern-slide is not a film.

The 'otherness' of the film medium forces the director who wishes to subsume a work of art into his film to decide, first on his exact purpose. He may, for example, use the work of art as 'raw material' for his own distinct artistic purposes. But let us suppose he is concerned with presenting the work of art for its own sake. Does he wish to provide a faithful 'crib', which disrupts the gestalt of the original artwork as little as possible, but runs the risk of obstructing understanding by failing to fit the cinema language? Or should he venture a paraphrase, which reads smoothly in the new medium, at the cost of a substantial infidelity to the structure of the original? Or should he take up the principle that a new medium requires a new creative dimension, and like Ezra Pound attempt to find altogether new, but 'equivalent', ideas? Or should he sidestep the problems of translation and merely 'illustrate' the artwork, using music, commentary, comparative material and other 'extraneous' elements so that his film constitutes not so much a translation *of* it as a critical essay *on* it? Or should he attempt a compromise between some or all of these functions, as many so-called art' films' quite successfully contrive?

Whatever his decision, the director (usually the dominating artistic personality of a film) will find himself caught between the Scylla of a passivity which fails to communicate anything vital of the artwork through the new medium, and the Charybdis of disintegrating the painting into a purely cinematographic gestalt. The selection of background music makes an obvious example. As a result of cinematic conventions, its absence tends to sound rather uncanny, even portentous. Moreover, the intelligent use of music offers possibilities which the director naturally wishes to exploit. Yet: music which is worthy of the artwork might well distract from it (by complexity) or (by context) transform it. But, on the other hand, music which merely underlines one aspect of the artwork is likely to overemphasize that aspect and so to bias or over-simplify its tensions. These considerations apply whether the music simply responds in a general way to the artwork's 'spirit', or whether it punctuates or underscores its formal 'events'. Well-chosen period music might establish moods of the period, and so establish the formal or spiritual links between the artwork and its period, while also setting off its cultural 'novelty' or uniqueness. Well-chosen 'contemporary' music might relate the artwork to our time, and, by implication, to all time. Or music might be composed which doesn't simply 'repeat', but subtly sets off, the nuances of what the director feels to be the artwork's form and soul. Often, the best solution is a compromise between these functions, which gives the music-track most play, avoids the obvious, and keeps the spectator on the *qui vive*, so honing his receptivity.

Yet, whichever musical policy the director adopts, he is creating a work of art which exists around and within the artwork itself. You can't make a film omelette without breaking the painting egg. . . .

Many art films are, in effect, 'packaged lantern lectures', like, for example, André Gillet's interesting *Equilibre* on Gothic cathedrals. Others belong to the 'higher journalism', and approximate to Sunday-paper articles, like Pierre Kast's *Ledoux—Architecte Maudit* or *Le Corbusier—L'Architecte du Bonheur* (France, 1956). Carl Dreyer's *Danish Parish Churches* shows that there is no hard-and-fast boundary between this kind of film and something deeper. Technical explanations, a probing camera, and modest reconstructions of basic ceremonies of past epochs quietly but firmly evoke the strange grafts of spirit and stone, of life and time, of the devotional and the functional, through which the hereafter meets the here and new.

But our emphasis here will be on those films which, with greater or lesser success, set out to preserve, or paraphrase, in film form, the thrill of an artist's vision. We can of course not hope to pass all interesting art films in review, but rather comment on a few examples through which we may explore the problems and successes of translation into film terms.

The vagaries of the art school market (film societies, schools, etc.) result in a preponderance of films which aim to introduce the intelligent and respectful layman to the main themes and finer points of an artist's vision. Typical of such films are two Leonardo films. Enrico Fulchignoni's *The Tragic Pursuit of Perfection* and Adrian de Potier's *The Drawings of Leonardo da Vinci*. The first is, as a lecture, more satisfying, even if one may object to the glibness whereby Leonardo's work, though adequately, sometimes finely, portrayed and analysed by the camera, is subsumed by the 'psychological' storyline which the title suggests. But, even if one prefers, for example, Freud's more sombre Leonardo to Fulchignoni's rather Browningesque figure, this 'reductionism' of theme is no falser than much spiritual exegesis of a traditional kind, and does throw some sort of light of its own on to the paintings. The second film is not lacking in interesting effects, as when the camera, moving across drawings of hair and water, imparts to them an 'apparent animation', and admirably brings out the angst implicit in Leonardo's convulsive line. But as a whole its success is mitigated by some reach-me-down strivings for effect, as in the commentary's phrase, 'a horse pokes its head through notes on astronomy' (a poetic device muffed), or when the music descends to the bathos of miaow effects over sketches of cats.

The commonest betrayal of an artwork by film-maker arises, paradoxically, from an anxiety to emphasize its beauty and profundity, and a consequent recourse to 'inspirational' effects or generalizations. Thus Pierre Biro's *Walls of Colour* (Turkey, 1963), a neat little exposition of Mohammedan mural designs, staggers under huge banalities like, 'Out of eternity emerges the spirit of man with its unfathomable mysteries,' while one is only distracted from the informative visuals of Arun Chaudhuri's *Jain Temples of India* by such meaninglessnesses as: 'A thousand years have tiptoed through this shrine, prayerful as a devotee.'

Indeed, a veritable curse of art films is that moralistic solemnity which so often obscures the contradictions, the anguish, the life-force, of an artist's work. Thus Guy Brenton's *The Vision of William Blake* is filmically neat enough, and the 'inflation' of Blake's drawings to screen-image size is a distortion of the more illuminating kind. But the music, with its pastoral-flute flavour, and the commentary, assimilating Blake to Bunyan, Wesley and the nonconformist tradition, relentlessly cut a poet who proudly claimed Milton for the devil's party down to the size of school-speech day interpretations of *Jerusalem*, as if Blake had never uttered the least criticism of orthodox Christianity.

For all their qualities, which are sufficiently marked to render their defects infuriating, the BBC's series of TV documentaries on prominent British artists suffer from a similar hypertrophy of reverence, a feeling that art portrays, not so much, or only incidentally, doubts, struggles, contradictions, but rather some sort of 'Third Programme' of the soul where all is lofty and deep. The simple-mindedly reverential approach adopted by John Read in his two-part *Stanley Spencer* (1956) results in a fictitious sweetness quite as unpleasant as the Box-of-Pin-Ups aspect of *Private View*. Often this is crossed with crude leftovers from romantic iconography. John Read's *A Sculptor's Landscape* is moving when it places Henry Moore's sculptures where he likes them, out on the moors, but gallingly rhetorical when it goes on to add a thunderstorm so as to get them real cosmic. Had Moore wanted a storm he would surely have wired his works for sound. The film further informs us that 'the artist sets out to enrich our perceptions', but the generalization needed less to be stated than implied through specific examples of such enrichments; and to this end the film devotes less effort than to a ripe selection of 'popularizer's ploys' which, like the thunder, are as distracting as they are ineffective. Thus, shots of the artist wielding hammer, chisel or blowlamp, or helping a common-or-garden workman pile bricks under a statue, are intended to convince the non-intellectual public that even a modern sculptor who puts holes where the torso ought to be is a practical man with a common touch, that art is an activity as matey as bricklaying or coalheaving, and, presumably, that modern art isn't difficult to understand, a Quixotic contention. For all that, the film is effective in so far as it's transparent, and the shots of the bird-headed King and Queen watching over a Scottish moor, or a flat-backed couple presiding over Harlow New Town, admirably place Moore's work in its optimum context. The companion film on *Graham Sutherland* (1954) had an audience of Slade School students in stitches—understandably, I'm afraid, as when the commentator reverentially declares that, 'He makes us see things in a new way,' and the artist, obligingly, stares at nothing in particular and shuts one eye. Equally inane, really, is the manner in which remarks like, 'He takes a walk with his senses alert,' justify aimless camera-trudges along country roads and up tree-trunks, seeing nothing that an uninspired cameraman doing his honest duty on an assignment wouldn't see. Otherwise, the direct contrasts from a Sutherland crucifixion to Belsen photographs are quite revolting and, in this context, suggest, if anything, that the artist has completely failed to render anything of what is truly atrocious in raw reality. More successful, ironically, is the same director's *Walter Sickert*, where settings (Camden Town) and artist alike resist rhetorical 'inflation'. The 'motionless' stills of Sickert as an old man have a certain eloquence in their immobility; and his happens to be a 'photogenic' personality. But it should perhaps be added that any artist's face, posture, gestures, and rooms are 'photogenic' if watched with enough sympathy—that is to say they can be used, by a sensitive and resourceful director, to express artistically significant aspects of the mind and life-history, that is, the spiritual reality. Although all these films contain sufficient 'raw material' to fascinate the art-lover, and more than justify their existence, they are guaranteed to embarass the apologist of the cinema as a *musée imaginaire*.

Those European art films which are comparable in aiming at 'middlebrow popularization' tend to be less reverential, more analytic, taking the ultimate uplift for granted and concentrating on clarifying the intrinsic struggle. The twin pioneers of the more analytical art film (during the post-war decade) were the Belgian Henri Storck and the Italian Luciano Emmer. In Emmer and Enrico Gras' *Paradise Lost*, on Bosch's *Garden of Worldly Delights*, and H. Arthur Klein and Thomas T. Taylor's study of *Brueghel's The Seven Deadly Sins*, the camera, with a self-effacing cinematographic skill, explores the canvas, dwelling in turn on each of the details which the commentator clarifies as images of medieval ideas. There is little formal analysis (except in so far as a close look predisposes to analysis) but the canvas becomes a whole world, a spiritual geography, so that the modern spectator recaptures something of the intensity of concentration, that is, the naïvety, with which the paintings' contemporaries would have received them. Here the camera, paradoxically, takes the art works out of the context of art appreciation and restores them to an interest which is not so much 'literary' as a religious holism of eye, mind and heart.

In a parallel way, Jerome Hill's *Grandma Moses* is most lucid incidentally, most lyrical, when the camera simply, steadily moves across the landscapes as if we were seeing some childlike continent from a train. The apparent simplicity of Charles and Ray Eames' *Two Baroque Churches in Germany* (U.S.A., 1959), is deceptive, however. The film is a fast, fluid, flicked-through ensemble of still photographs, ensemble views, of, first, the church at Vierzehnheiligen, then, that at Ottobeuren. Details and configurations are all so crisply juxtaposed as to bring out both the 'violence' and the 'assonances' of style. The film is only apparently simple, depending as it does on the paradox that heavy architectural patterns are 'shuffled' into a spatter of fluid, discontinuous, and therefore 'light' images, and overbearing ensembles fragmented into quick snippets. This counterpointing is none too successful as a paraphrase of the architectural effects, but a fascinating comment on them it certainly is.

As a general rule it seems that the best films are rarely those which set out to inspire the audience with love of the art, or of the artist, than those which devote great care and skill to being, simply, helpful, and achieve lyricism as a 'bonus' effect. A modest success of this kind is Sergio Amidei's *Picasso* which, despite the too-refined Spanish guitar provided as musical backcloth, examines the painter's various periods, stresses his satirical underlay, and comments on the disintegration of the human image in twentieth-century art. Its success lies in its awareness of the problems behind, and complexities in, the individual art work, as distinct from the edifying effect of art in general; and a similar sensitivity underlies the most successful attempts at transposing into film form the full impact of a painting's, or a painter's, mood. Henri Storck's *Le Monde de Paul Delvaux* is less an analysis of individual paintings than a collage of details from Delvaux's canvases, with their nude, fragile, doe-eyed women forlornly awaiting the love of sad, garbed and grudging men, while the moon shines hard and clear on the motionless locomotives, cities crumble, mountains gleam, and skeletons loiter quietly amidst empty porticoes. The monochromatic greyness of the film undoubtedly over-simplifies Delvaux's melancholy (his colours are eerier), and it's often impossible to tell which details belong to which picture. On the other hand, the camera reveals more clearly than any reproductions have done the paintings' texture and their demented minuteness of detail. Responsive music, and a poem written and read by Paul Eluard, worthily re-explore the palpitating desolation which is the painter's characteristic mood. The film itself is a work relating both to usual painterly textures (by which standards its texture is unusually realistic) and to the cinema's photographic norm (by which standards its texture is unrealistic), so that the 'melting' of Delvaux's paintings into one another becomes a film-dream in its own right, an extension of Delvaux's, an 'unidentical twin' to his. The surprises made possible by a camera which prowls around a canvas also enhance Luc de Heusch's explorations of disturbing Surrealist puns in *Magritte 'ou la Lecon des Choses* (Belgium, 1960) and Peter Schamoni's of *Max Ernst* (Germany, 1964).

The subtle cinematic style of Alain Resnais, director of *Hiroshima Mon Amour* and *L'Année Dernière à Marienbad* owes a great deal to a variety of unusual pictorial idioms, notably comic strips (which he claims taught him all he knows about editing) and Surrealism (to whose spirit he claims to be unswervingly faithful). In his early documentaries on *Van Gogh* (co-directed with Gaston Diehl and Robert Hessens), *Gauguin* and *Guernica* (co-directed with Robert Hessens), his deftly self-effacing creativity concentrates the full weight of the spectator's attention on plastic details, even when the director 'outrages' the original work of art. Thus the camera moves up to the door of Van Gogh's cottage (on one painting) and 'penetrates' it to show the interior of the cottage (on another painting); a quietly magical effect which passes unnoticed by most spectators. The English (or rather American) version of *Van Gogh* is afflicted with a painful commentary, which informs us that the painter's motive was 'to express the love he felt' and that 'he paints the misery of the poor'. But Resnais' own film has a truer sense of pain; quick tracking and cutting, producing swift scurries of images, generate a somatotonic turbulence which is analogous to that of the painter's brushstrokes—yet never becomes so turbulent as to impede our apprehension of the turbulence in the paintings. *Gauguin* makes great use of the painter's self-portraits, letting us see, in sad dissolve, the slow changes in his face, from a remote self-assurance to hurt pride and at last ingrained suspicion, and is all the more tragic in reclothing the painter's turmoil with an individual's agony. The films solve, movingly, many of the problems of 'the cult of personality' later raised by John Berger. *Guernica* intersperses paintings and sculptures by Picasso with contemporary documents and newspaper cuttings, as well as music and a poem by Eluard, to reclaim Picasso's cry of anguish from the aesthetic celebrity which envelops it, *like* complacency. In contrast to the imperceptive crucifixion-Auschwitz contrast of the Sutherland film, Resnais accepts the fact of aesthetic refinement imposed by Picasso's *Guernica* on Guernica's Guernica, and drives no spectator back to the atrocities themselves. In the opening sequences, they are evoked, through documents and sounds only. The film moves from 'flat' paintings in the first half to light-moulded sculpture in the second. And this corresponds to a philosophical modulation, from indignation at *this* inhumanity by *some* humans to a pessimistic recognition of some bedrock of inhumanity in all humanity. The film moves from newspaper 'actuality', through the caricatural expressionism of *Guernica,* to something unrecognizable and irreducible in us all. . . .

The virtuosity behind so stealthy a creative style is set off by Henri Alékan's 'intelligent failure', *L'Enfer de Rodin*. In presenting the sculptor's work the camera indulges in sideways slants, in curling and spinning movements, seeking to prolong the *élan* of art *nouveau* lines into the film's own dimension. Unfortunately these effects are, by relation to the cinema's normative syntax, so 'broad' as to distract attention from the effect of the convolutions of Rodin's own forms. Thus an honest attempt to transpose an artist's effects into film form may conceal or disrupt the artist's own eloquence. Hence a discreet counterpointing is often more helpful than a reduplication of effect. A fine example is Harold Becker's *Eugene Atget* consisting of a 'portfolio' of Atget's piercingly elegiac photographs of Paris. The camera is confronted by each photograph in turn, then moves towards it, centring on a 'detail' chosen not simply for its obvious interest, but as emblematic of Atget's grey, melancholy figures and spaces. Thus we move, as it were, into Atget's world, but before we 'reach' it, the image fades into another, which we approach, in its turn, but which, again, we never reach. Thus the camera's endless journey into the past becomes an endless yearning, a *recherche du temps perdu*, an effect analogous to Atget's attitude to his present, and enhanced for us by the poignant matching of this futile, incessant odyssey with the serenely sad, 'motionless movement 'of Erik Satie's *Trois Gymnopédies*.

Jean Grémillon and Pierre Kast's *Les Charmes de l'Existence* widens its scope from an individual artist to a whole period, evoking, solely through their canvases, the ethos of Bouguereau and his fellow salon-painters who from 1858 to 1914 gratified the French *bourgeois* taste for highflown sentiment, stern moral optimism, and an opulent eroticism piously disguised as allegorical uplift. But these canvases are not displayed for the crudely direct debunking that is the philistinism of the modern educated man. They are allowed to acquire the charm of Victorian Valentine cards, of a lost emotional opulence, and, through their direct, clumsy, but now unfamiliar, half-alienated, imagery, acquire an air of excess that becomes, at last, Surrealist. The commentary is unwaveringly deadpan in its quiet firm exposition of the solemn complacencies which the paintings illustrate. The sentiments are devalued by the pictorial excesses, yet, as carefully chosen pictorial details are cut adrift from the weak grandiosity of their compositions, and are instead swept up by the suave, smooth editing, they take on a more philosophical quality, of the 'Absurd' in the modern, positive sense. As their inept colours are sobered to grey, their blend of pedantic 'realism' and of rhapsodic subject is revealed as a true predecessor of the sentimental excesses of the silent cinema. And they provoke us to reflections far more complex than mere derision. The fades to blackness, functional enough cinematic devices, acquire, in this context, an elegiac quality. The 'dramatic' ideas become at once comic and nostalgic, that is, doubly inadequate, and, therefore, gently tragic. Yet by this change of context, by our new tenderness, they are also reimbued with their original meaning. Thus Grémillon and Kast, two highly cultured individuals, go far beyond *Saturday Book* picturesquerie, and, while smiling, or laughing, we see these paintings as those who loved them saw them, marvelling at an emotional shock that seemed poetic. Is not this an ideal of historical criticism, all the more surprising in being attained in relation to *bad* works of art?

Another category of art film seeks not so much to translate the art work itself into filmic terms, as to explain it by a close study of its physical genesis, which in some cases reveals more of a painter's intentions than one might expect. The advantages of a movie record are particularly obvious in the case of action-painting, as in Piet Von Moock's *The Reality of Karel Appel.* But there is some profit to be had also from, for example, Wango Weng and Chih Meng's *Out of a Chinese Painting-Brush.* We watch the brush of a Chungking artist streak over the paper, laying down three colours (each with a different part of the brush), during each long stroke. Our empathy with the completed, final, static line is sharpened and intensified by our empathy with the actual movements. Thus a calligraphic sensitivity becomes choreographic as well as visual, and we are introduced to the strange, but narrow, no-man's-land between the 'studied spontaneity' of Chinese classicism and certain aspects of action-painting and kinetic art.

Another, elaborate, not altogether successful, exploration of the creative act is Henri-Georges Clouzot's feature-length *Le Mystère Picasso*. John Berger, while also, of course, criticizing Picasso himself, roundly denounced Clouzot as Picasso's Delilah, degrading the artist to the level of an entertainer, and the act of painting into a virtuoso's conjuring trick. Clouzot's film is indeed devoted to watching Picasso paint: sometimes on an ordinary canvas, sometimes on a transparent canvas, so that the screen 'is' the painting (left to right reversed), climaxing in a scene where the cameraman, Claude Renoir (Auguste's Coco) asks Picasso to hurry because his reel of film is running out. Yet even this last 'gimmick' has a certain poetry, serving to exemplify the artist's astonishing adaptability to diverse media, and his imperturbable spontaneity, indistinguishable from opportunism. Throughout, it is fascinating to watch his paintings accumulate, touch by touch, or to 'select' one's own next stroke and then see the artist's. Certainly the film is scarcely a study of an artist's mind. Yet it works on two levels. For the lay, lower-middlebrow public, it fascinatingly rivets attention on a creative sphinx, while, for the scholar, its stroke-by-stroke record of Picasso's paintings is of obvious interest. On a more spiritual level, the film's presentation of artistic creation as something that appears, *ex nihilo*, arbitrarily, from somewhere behind Picasso's shining, smiling, teasing eyes, has an intriguingly duple lyrical effect. On the one hand, the black background, the sombre hues, of the film, together with Picasso's 'Mona Lisa' self-assurance, and the unpredictable succession of brushstrokes, endow the act of painting with a certain arbitrary quality, and, where one would expect to find the molten core of creative emotion, a silence, a cold, dark hollowness. Clouzot seems, by this silence, to be criticizing Picasso (along the same lines as Michael Ayrton, who denounced him as a sort of demoralizing deft monkey, assuming, and so discrediting, all styles), and, through him, all creativity. On the one hand, Clouzot's superficiality is deliberate, a solipsism prefiguring that of Robbe-Grillet ('We cannot know what goes on in another mind . . .') and it also suggests a nihilism reminiscent of Samuel Beckett's. On the other hand, his silence as to influences, motivations, exegeses, allows a kind of freedom to the painter, making him the God of his creation, sincere, moving yet unmoved; and so the film restores the now rather old-fashioned view of art as the autonomous assertions of a soul who amazes and inspires, but whom it would be sacrilege to attempt to explain in terms that did away with the element of mystery and majesty in the creative act. The ambiguity as between the nihilistic and the 'reverent' attitude results in a mood of saturnine duplicity, of exhilarating pessimism, characteristic of the director of *La Vérité*. 'Picasso's, any artist's, *vérité* is no truth at all, merely a thing which he produces. . . .' This view of art isn't, after all, so far from that expressed, more than half-seriously, by the late Aldous Huxley, among others, and though one may wish that Clouzot had asserted it *after*, rather than instead of, an exegesis of Picasso's vision, his silence, allowing the paintings to speak for themselves, has a stealthy, steely quality about it which one can respect.

Almost as 'absurd', in the modern sense, is Harold Liversidge's

Auto-Destructive Art (G.B., 1964), showing Gustave Metzger, covered in protective goggles, and wielding an acid spray, attacking a large white screen set up outside the Festival Hall: tearing at the fabric, the acid produces, on the larger scale, a random 'action painting' on the canvas, and, in the microscopic close-ups, patterns of strain, tearings and dissolutions. This concentration on decay isn't without its effect, especially as counterpointed by a, presumably involuntary, irony. For the auto-destructive process is being preserved by the camera, which has—accidentally-on-purpose?—set itself up just where St. Paul's Cathedral will appear in the distance through the largest tear. Though one can't fault Metzger's logic, the whole film, as a document, has a touching quality, for the artist's inability to assert his indifference to preservation without, briefly, preserving, seems a negation of his negations, and puts him in the same tragi-comic situation as the rest of us.

Clouzot's irrelevancies and Metzger's masochism are certainly more bracing, less sentimental, than the academicism of Guido Manero's *Sicilia Ellenica* which explores Greek ruins in Sicily and treats us to images of young shepherds playing flutes while their sheep graze among ruined temples, and other ultra-conventional images for *tempus fugit* and *plus ça change* notions. A similar quality of picturesque irrelevance is indulged in Jacques Godbout and François Bufold's *Le Monde Va Nous Prendre Pour Des Sauvages* showing, against the background of their village life, the traditional paper dolls made by a group of Indians, who will never reveal their secret significance, because 'the world would take us for savages'. The effect of mystery is, despite some exquisite colour photography, lost by the too-easy separation of inner significance and outer enigma, although this mysteriousness is itself a useful corrective to the modern cosmopolitan habit of treating primitive art-objects as if they were meant to be seen in an art gallery. More cutting is *Les Statues Meurent Aussi*, directed by Resnais, Chris Marker and Ghislain Cloquet. This study of African primitive art is so incisive in its anti-colonialism that the film was banned by the French government for many years, and has only recently been released, in a severely truncated form.

Typical examples of the more straightforwardly discursive art film are offered by two of the more successful BBC documentaries, John Read's *L. S. Lowry* and *Reg Butler*. The Lowry film (whose script was printed in *Ark* 23) is interested, fairly equally, in the painter's art and his loneliness, and the nostalgic delicacy of the paintings tragically contrasts with the treadmill obstinacy with which Lowry anticipates hostility and affects indifference: 'People say to me my people look like matchsticks. Well I don't mind what you say, I paint them that way because I see them that way.' And the form, 'People say to me . . . well, I don't care . . .' has the intonations of a paranoiad litany, heartbreaking in its juxtaposition with Lowry's painted world. Reg Butler's robust and sensitive common sense infects his whole film, for almost along among the BBC documentaries it has a touch of humour which one can assume to be voluntary. For example, Butler explains that he never had a sister and treats many of his sculptures as explorations of girls, whereupon we see him splashing black paint across a pair of stone buttocks.

Other films intersperse their exploration of the artist's work with images in which the camera seeks to show us the objective world 'on the point of' being transformed by the artist's personal eye and mind. Such 'perceptual subjectivism' can, of course, be only indicative, which is why I say 'on the point of', but it furnishes a useful intermediary between 'raw', objective reality and the artist's own work. *Rothenstein '64*, made by Lawrence Moore, a student at the Royal College of Art, is an object lesson for the BBC school. It intersperses Rothenstein's work with extreme close shots exploring the textures of trees, of stones, of weathered wood, deepening the layer of associations with all the ambiguities of pictorial richness and actual ruin, indeed, many of the preoccupations of auto-destructive art. Evald Schorm's *Living One's Life* watches the elderly Czech photographer Josef Sudak trudge, with heavy plate camera and old-fashioned tripod on his shoulder, through streets, parks and forests, only rarely setting it up before some configuration of details—autumn leaves lying heavily on shining water, a wrought-iron garden seat glinting with dew—which crystallizes his vision, one of Proustian tenderness for a lost, sensuous, richly emotional world suggested by textures and forms that are at once rich and ornate, yet abandoned and desolate.

Ken Russell's *Pop Goes the Easel* deals in a basically similar way with a group of 'pop' painters (Pauline Boty, Derek Boshier, Peter Blake, Peter Philips) whose work it relates to their happily contemporary, 'working-class-beatnik' life-style (living in 'pads', watching professional wrestling, playing pintables). The film resembles the work of the painters whose work it celebrates in that, once the first, extremely exhilarating, shock of this happy acceptance of contemporary lowbrow amusements has worn off, it has little further to offer. Its most complex and valid moment has the personally delectable Pauline Boty, dressed in top hat and tails, miming to the record of Shirley Temple singing 'On the Good Ship Lollipop'. This semi-transvestite and semi-infantilism rather beautifully crystallizes some current emotional syndromes (e.g. the nostalgias summarized by the 'tomboy' and 'dolly-girl' *personae*). The film remains a welcome breach in the BBC's obsessional reverence, and does indicate the enormous area of, not only iconography, but, more important, experience, on which 'pop' painters can draw, even if, in fact, the sheer weight of material occasionally overwhelms their powers of criticism and their creative resources.

A handful of films have essayed more general themes, rarely with striking success. Virgilio Sabel's *A Geometry Lesson* dwells on the aesthetic beauty of 3-D mathematical figures, as on the functionalist atmosphere of various sculptures, and asks what distinguishes the art from the mathematical object, but does not stay for the answer, which is presumably that a mathematical object becomes a work of art when the spectator can be persuaded to attune to it as many layers of his mind as he can reach (including the kinaesthetic sense and irrational associations), while a work of art is merely an elegant-looking object until the spectator has opened himself to it in this way. Similarly George Hoellering's *Shapes and Forms—Primitive and Modern Art* establishes certain formal 'assonances' between primitive art from here, there and everywhere, and modern art, without pausing to look at the different functions to which they are put, or their different rationales, which may give quite different meanings to similar shapes. Both films exemplify the current peril whereby a *musée imaginaire* comes to be a mere agglutination of *objets d'art*, all understood only as 'pure form', and divorced from their cultural roots, a procedure which reverses the mind-broadening potentialities of art, or its role as communication. Still, both films make interesting introductions to their particular formal 'key-signatures'.

In general, 'generalizing' films are more successful where they consider a relatively limited field, like Paul Haesearts' *Un Siècle d'Or*, which presents eight fifteenth-sixteenth-century painters in beautifully glowing Gevacolor, or his *De Renoir à Picasso* which, schematically perhaps, but usefully, divides its screen into two or three to trace the interweaving of the threads of modern art, the sensual (Renoir), the intellectual (Seurat-Leger) and the emotional (Picasso). Lou Stoumen's feature-length *Image of Love* reverses the process, using works of art to illustrate changes in European attitudes to eroticism. Though riddled by over-simplification and glibnesses, it is honest enough in intention. Plastic subtleties are beyond its scope, but it has a certain tonic effect simply by its offbeat acceptance of the fact that, though subtleties may serve to distinguish the masterwork from the merely competent or striking piece of ephemera, the masterwork doesn't consist solely of its subtleties. It also has a significant layer of meaning in common with the minor work, and indifference to this layer is, surely, a truncation of the artist's whole vision. Thus, the Venetian painters are *also* celebrating the affluence of a *nouveau-riche* merchant class, and, as Stoumen's film notes, there is a certain common mood between the fleshtints of Rubens and the reddish-pink suntan of a *Playboy* pin-up. It even reveals a certain affinity between the Venus of Willendorf and, though only in her most *outré* poses, the fleshy oozings-out of Jayne Mansfield. So far as the middle- and low-brow audience is concerned, the film usefully insists on the human elements of painting; and since this public is unused to 'reading' pictorial compositions (a knack which they are hardly helped to acquire by the tiny size of most reproductions) the camera's movements across the surface of a painting, turning it into a film sequence, helpfully by-pass all questions of 'aesthetic mystique' to rivet attention, for once, on a lately rather neglected aspect of painting, its simple, direct yet subtle presentation of human experience as nuanced by the artist's vision, and on the significance of the details (as compared to form *per se*) and their relationship. In its best passages the film possesses a certain sociological awareness as well as that honest, sensitive vulgarity which seems to me the most sympathetic of aesthetic vices.

In contradistinction to *Sicilia Ellenica*, the counterpointing of a work of art by its background is creatively utilized by Georges Franju in his *Notre Dame, Cathédrale de Paris*. By careful choice of detail and composition, it brings sensitively to the colour and Dyaliscope screen the shapes, rhythms, volumes and weights of the building, and takes as its key Le Corbusier's evocation of the days 'when the cathedrals were white'. But now they are black; the heavy copper bells are green with the slow decomposition of age, their iron hinges are ravaged by the ingrowing fires of rust, blurred gargoyles scowl impotently at the city around. The cathedral will never be white again, except when it snows, and then, among the Christmas roofscape, pigeons die of cold, while, below, the faithful still utter that prayer, so rarely answered, for 'Peace in our time, O Lord'. The seats are empty, the space between the walls is curiously sullen. . . .

Some of the most interesting art films are those whose subject, like *Les Charmes de l'Existence*, is artistically defective, limited or naïve. This is no reflection on the cinema medium as such. The older visual media, when translating literary subjects are no less 'approximative' in their effects, and no less hospitable to the second rate, while words can no more than labour clumsily after most painterly effects. Jacques Kuppissonnoff's *Apparences* presents eighteenth-century mechanical dolls in glowing colours such that they reacquire their pristine glitter, which, often touchingly, co-exists with disfigurements and chips. Charles and Ray Eames' *Toccata for Toy Trains* quite transcends a simple presentation of its material, and becomes a fantasy world of its own, an Elysian Fields of old toy trains which have acquired, 'posthumously', the autonomy, the seriousness, of real ones, and go sprinting, glinting, cavorting, dashing along to Elmer Bernstein's spiritedly brassy music. Some have their passengers painted stiffly on the windows, others, of humble wood, with their drivers-cabs magically empty, some humbled by rust, one limps along on a damaged wheel, going 'halting into heaven'. By a technical *tour de force*, the camera treats these trains as if they were real trains; the resultant shallow depth-of-focus blurs much of the backgrounds (also toy) into a hazy glow of coloured patches, so enhancing the effect of nostalgic enchantment. Thus 'interpreted', or, rather, liberated, the toys (which introductory comments carefully distinguish from scale models, a modern, spiritual dullard's fad) reveal themselves as a collective 'vision' of trains, interpretations of 'essence of train', by adults, for childhood—neither, exactly, 'primitive' art nor 'child' art, but something, beautifully, suspended between the two.

The icons, the 'cathedral', of a modern age are the subject of William Klein's *Broadway By Light*. The neon signs garnishing the Great White Way are seen, first, as opportunities for abstract designs; but, gradually the bulbs' blinking and flickering suggests the movements, the sensibilities of living things. A big green loopy sign resembles a sprawling dragon, its bulbs like scales. The winking bulbs form a multicoloured blood-stream, as of some gigantic organism which must die, like a ghost, each dawn. Occasionally we glimpse a human form in this Sahara of strident light, a dark silhouette as cowed and alienated as on another planet. And perhaps this is 'another' planet, or at least an inhuman one: that of automated commerce . . . a last lavendar-green light has the same tone as the green of dawn, and the sun's flare finally spearheads through the 'o' of 'Pop Up'.

Part Two

THE HAREM GAME

8 · Pleading an Aesthetic Excuse

It is a professional deformity which sees films in order to have an opinion about them. And it is an eccentric minority who judge films by their realism or by their chances of what is optimistically called 'immortality'.

For the masses, the cinema is dreams and nightmares, or it is nothing. It is an alternative life, experience freed from the tyranny of that 'old devil consequences', from the limitation of having only one life to live. One's favourite films are one's unlived lives, one's hopes, fears, libido. They constitute a magic mirror, their shadowy forms are woven from one's shadow selves, one's limbo loves. The cinema is a theatre of cruelty, a land of cockayne, cloud cuckoo land, Parnassus, where passions are always young and in their prime, like the Gods. Wishes are horses and beggars can ride. Cuts and dissolves melt space and time. We live dangerously in safety. *We* are the immortal Gods watching the screen characters live their anguished lifetime-in-90-minutes lives. Our immunity sets us free to participate 'in the round'. Art doesn't really make the artist immortal, but it makes the audience *feel* immortal.

A moth-eaten dogma has it that a director is 'the' creative personality of a film. But even in cases when this is so, the audience participates by identifying with and caring about the characters. We share their feelings, if we like them, or project our repressed desires into them, if they're villains, or hope against hope if, like us, they're made of mingled shades of moral grey.

Awareness of the film as a work of art, and of the director behind it, is already the result of 'alienation', of intellectual abstraction, of *inattention*. Yes, of course, behind Marlene is Sternberg. But it's with Marlene that we feel. To live one's unlived life is to live through and with the screen characters. The rest is culture, and while it might interest us in other contexts, doesn't concern us here and now.

It's often presumed that the star system was a cynical mogul's fabrication foisted on to the public by sheer weight of dollars. Nothing could be further from the truth. It is directly descended from the nineteenth-century theatre and was equally prominent among preachers on the revivalist circuits from the 1880's down to Billy Graham. When film producers, fearing that stardom meant astronomical salaries, refused to name Florence Lawrence, the public countered by writing to 'The Biograph Girl'. As Edgar Morin relates, fan-mail arrived from all over the world addressed to the *characters* of French silent serials—Nick Carter, Fantomas. We have already seen how one brief glimpse of an extra looking longingly at Lillian Gish in *The Birth of a Nation*, or two words by Mae West, elicited a deluge of letters.

Alastair Cooke remarked, the majority of popular stars combine striking good looks (on the screen) with 'certain typical whimsicalities or personal traits of humour, temper, sarcasm—some single quality that is entertaining because it is effective to dramatize. Most movie-goers seem to prefer this compromise (between mere beauty and deep psychology) as a steady diet, probably because it offers superior beauty than anything they are personally familiar with, but is at the same time linked up—by the chosen personality characteristics—with a life they know. Thus Jean Arthur's husky downrightness and loyalty, Claudette Colbert's tongue-in-cheek, Carole Lombard's air of honest-to-goodness exasperation, Ginger Rogers' natural acceptance of hard facts. . . .'

In a sense the star is to the public as the sumptuous women of Tintoretto and Veronese were to the *nouveau-riche* of Renaissance Italy, or as the langorous females favoured by the Pre-Raphaelites: in Edgar Morin's words, 'Movie glamour bears witness to the presence of the ideal at the heart of the real . . . the archetypal beauty of the star acquires the hieratic quality of the mask. . . . The star's ideal beauty reveals an ideal soul.' Movie glamour is part of the artistic urge which tends, not towards the real, but towards the ideal. It is the Platonism of *l'homme moyen sensuel*, for whom 'heaven' is more Garden of Eden than a cloudy realm of sexless angels.

There are stars without superior beauty—Wallace Beery, Marie Dressler—for glamour is, perhaps, just one over-used facet of the life-force which stars assert as the classical Gods asserted (with

Charlton Heston for Mars, Jerry Lewis for Dionysus . . .). Glamour without this streak of life-force can never make a star. Of all Rank's charmschool girls only those who broke the mould made the grade—Diana Dors (by being brash, vulgar and working-class), Jean Simmons (by the glint of intensity, of Celtic feyness, in her well-balanced middle-class *persona*), Belinda Lee (after being liberated by an Italian love affair), and Honor Blackman (after donning black leather, high-boots, and topical fetishists' rig). The physical and the psychological interweave: 'Invariably what made them stars' observes Arthur Mayer, 'was some physical attribute or personal mannerism'—he cites, 'John Bunny's jovial bulk, Mary Pickford's golden curls and sweet smile, Maurice Costello's urbanity, Clara Kimball Young's yearning eyes.' We might add: Alan Ladd's deadpan, Bogart's paralysed upper lip and pebble voice, Veronica Lake's peekaboo wave—far from being just gimmicks, they are more even than iconographic emblems: fans take them as metaphors for personality-traits, as lyrical assertions of character. To see such traits as being, by the literary standards asserted by Henry James, psychologically crude, is only half the story. The well-loved characters of Dickens and Conan Doyle, or for that matter of Fielding, Richardson and Racine, are no more complex; Dickens endowed his characters with 'catch phrases' corresponding to a visual medium's visual 'tags'. And what makes an 'unrealistic' star seem, to an audience, realistic, is these feelings of theirs which his personality 'accommodates'. They are his resonance in them. Even when a star does happen to be a good actor, it is none the less in being *an object of the audience's projected feelings* that his stardom consists. The ingredient is some affirmative flashpoint with the audience's experience (the realistic aspect) and ideals (the idealistic aspect). If a star who can't act becomes a star, it is because the attitude which he automatically adopts towards his range of emotional material strikes at some emotional nerve-centre, some nexus of half-acknowledged memories, hopes, hesitations, fears. Stars, like poets, are unacknowledged legislators of the world—fans, and others, imbibe, imitate, their mannerisms, personalities, and implied ethos. More accurately, perhaps, the stars are a reflection in which the public studies and adjusts its own image of itself. The individual adopts those stars, and those aspects of those stars, which he feels suit him. The same is true of poets—which is why neither group are legislators at all, or rather: the artist proposes, the audience disposes.

'What happened to the human face in painting?' inquired Roy Mc-

Mullen recently in *Réalités*, and answered that it has been ousted by a network of 'stylistic' characteristics. The other half of the answer is that it found a home from home in the audio-visual media, which are first and foremost media of personality, like the theatre, from which the cinema is, ontologically, derived. People go to the movies to look not 'at', but 'through' the pictures, at the faces and the events. A few films are primarily visual, in that the spectator, to appreciate its full meaning, must respond to image or sequence as a plastic entity, but in most films the image is merely a transparency, and sometimes is as irrelevant to the basically theatrical idiom as the grooves on a phonograph record are to the music. Who ever went to the movies to count the number of cuts? Most cuts are invisible, just as bar-lines in music are inaudible: the notes of the melody are the faces.

The actor is as central to most movies as the actor to a play when it's on the stage.

The intelligentsia's disdain of the star is motivated by the fact that the public's demands on a star's personality tend to limit the range of his performances. (There are exceptions: T. S. Eliot was a Marie Lloyd fan, and her range was as narrow as Kim Novak's—or as Mr. Micawber's and Sherlock Holmes's.) Second, intellectuals like to identify with creative artists, and current dogma has it that stars are witless things who do only what they're told by the director. This contention is often quite false: Lillian Gish contributed as much as any of her directors, Mae West and Burt Lancaster are famous for directing their directors. In any case, the director works through his actors, just as a painter works through his paintings, and it is the work of art to which we should first respond. An older tradition of film criticism talked about Bette Davis films (rather than Aldrich, Sherman, Rapper films); James Agate and *La Revue du Cinema* (the grandfather of *Cahiers du Cinema*) criticized in terms of stars as much as of directors; and it's a pity that such criticism in terms of stars has been left to the ladies of *Films in Review*, or degenerated into half-facetious cults by solemn intellectuals gigglingly off-duty. (Which perhaps explains why *slapstick* is criticized in terms of stars—but not 'serious' films.)

The social history of a nation can be written in terms of its film stars (or indeed of almost anything, but film stars are in some respects better even than newspapers). It's not my intention here to trace the shift from the little-girlishness of Mary Pickford to the Lolita syndrome of Sue Lyon, or from the innocence of Lillian Gish to the bland toughness of Kim Novak; or from eager-beavers like Harold Lloyd and Douglas Fairbanks to nervy young rat-racers like Jack Lemmon; or from the portly young father-figure of the 'teen-years, through the exotic erotic idols of the 20's, the reassuring middle-class figures of the late 30's (Crosby), the bitter deadpan of the late 40's (Ladd, Murphy) to the passionate young rebels of the 50's. Even cartoon figures mirror mores, as we shall see in considering American screen comedy. But our first concern here is with the artistic contribution made by a star to the film *as an aesthetic object.*

For convenience, let us divide stars into the 'plain' and the 'sacred monster'. Plainest of the plain is perhaps William Holden, who said of himself that he was no artist, in the grandiose sense of the word, but he was an efficient and honest 'journalist of the emotions'. This attitude to his acting reflects the very quality that gives it its resonance to the audience's experience. He's not especially good-looking, not especially courageous, not especially cynical, not especially anything; he's the ordinary, self-reliant American, wavering between the meanness and pain of the Billy Wilder world and the reluctant heroics of *The Bridge on the River Kwai.* He's conspicuously devoid of the optimism of the middle-class eager-beaver, but he slides more easily into a middle-class world than say, Burt Lancaster (whose mere presence always implies a proletarian origin). To him there still clings a little of the tough individuality of the Gary Cooper hero; he *can* play in Westerns; yet a tense awareness of his own limitations prefigures the softer, nervier, more anxious 'little men' of Tashlin's heroes. Holden's very plainness is the secret not merely of his popularity, but of his authenticity as a screen personality.

Gary Cooper and Frank Sinatra personify two great currents of American culture. One can hardly imagine a film in which they could co-star; Cooper's Western virtues seem hard to key in with Sinatra's jaunty cynicism. Coop, grave, slow, decisive, rode in from the open spaces; he is a rustic, a small town man; and even when Mr. Deeds Went to Town his straightforward goodness had the city slickers and the intellectuals (a Goldwaterite combination?) driving him almost to a suicidal silence. Coop worries, with dignity; the sudden, bleak, black rage of fear, never dwelt on, but briefly glimpsed, gives much of its strength to his portrayal of Mr. Deeds, as to that of the sheriff in *High Noon* (and its absence is the weakness of Wyler's *The Westerner*).

Coop dreads, and punches; Sinatra shrugs, or drugs, or drinks, or takes a tranquillizer, or another girl, or a plane. Coop is rural, small-town, middle-class, inner-directed. Sinatra's cocky grin has the tough derisiveness of an alley cat, a gritty sensitivity, nerves as taut as his cheekbones. His easy assurance goes with a forlorn vulnerability. His bitchy petulance is that of the cosmopolitan orphan. His best films are all from his 'middle period' of the 50's, notably *Meet Danny Wilson*, *Pal Joey*, *Man with the Golden Arm* which came nearest to the sadness needed to complete his artistic personality. (Similarly, I wish Coop had been directed by Clouzot or Clément, who wouldn't have been afraid of plunging us into the 'black' band of his spectrum.) The same qualities inform Sinatra's singing—his voice is brassy and warm, can open up in a rhapsodic boost, jaunt along cagily, wrench out the sudden dramatic punch, the jab of pathos. However ingenuous the lyrics, he goes along with them, wholeheartedly, in hope. He sings a tourist's panegyric about Granada, and we know that he knows that Granada, like every other town in this over-trotted globe, is just a nightclub with broads, but his warm, even ebullience amounts to a reckless defiance of disenchantment, the raw half-tones easily sidle up to jubilation. But once, just once, he should make a film as uncompromising as *Jeanne Eagels*.

At the other extreme, some stars exist to shock and outrage the audience. The sacred monster's every gesture, every response, challenges the assumed, the expected, the 'right'. He (or she) may be aloofly wrapped in mystery like Garbo, or aggressively tormented, like Brando; either way, the audience is swung between hopeless adoration and noisy contempt, and passionate identification co-exists with something like fascinated hatred. Garbo and Dietrich with their strange accents came from vague foreign lands which are really the 'nowhere' of a late romanticism—indeed, the *femme fatale* is a romantic obsession, burgeoining in Keats' *La Belle Dame Sans Merci*, blossoming in Swinburne and d'Annunzio, whose poems inspire the great Italian divas, who in turn inspire their American adaptations (Theda Bara), and so on through Nazimova, Negri and Baclanova (who import the French interest in Slav *femme fatales*) down to the last romantic vamps of the 30's (Garbo, Dietrich). More often than we realize, Hollywood 'vulgarity' is simply the direct heir of high literary fashion. By the 1950's there are no romantic nowheres that haven't been flown over by the U.S.A.A.F. and Kim Novak, like Dean and Brando, is 'neurotic' so as to be unpredictable, fascinating, exotic. If the silent vamps, male and female, mirror the *dreams* of the kid next door, Novak, Dean and Brando, in an age dominated by psychological realism (not to say self-consciousness taken by popular pseudo-Freudianism to the point of hypochondria) reflects his *conflicts*. Their exoticism is only a pretext, for intensifying, lifting to the level of acting-out, conflicts in which the spectator feels he can recognize his own impulses, inhibitions and sufferings. With Valentino, the 20's audience escaped a brash, bustling world. Brando doesn't don Arab costume, and his name has intimations of immigrant vulgarity rather than of Latin languor. His inarticulacy signals his resistance to the rationalist, optimist, conformist, utilitarian, anti-emotional tendencies of middle-class Anglo-Saxondom. His struggles to speak, his fluttering eyelashes, his evident sensuality, his unreasonableness and male integrity-in-immaturity, subvert the middle-class ideal of the man well and unemotionally adjusted to routine action rather than passionately responsiveness to experience: in short, a ghost in a machine.

Or we may contrast two suffragettes—for the 30's, Katharine Hepburn, who was as hated in many popular halls as she was liked by the carriage trade. To see why, we can safely forget all her 'ladylike' films, like George Stevens' *Quality Street*, and concentrate on Gregory La Cava's *Stage Door*, where an astute storyline deliberately endows her with every trait which audiences (and particularly male audiences) of the time might have found most exasperating. She is (*a*) a topdog—stinking rich with unearned wealth, amidst a boarding-house-full of struggling actresses, (*b*) coolly and positively scornful of their envy, (*c*) bossy, (*d*) a self-righteous suffragette (spoiling a girl's affair with a sugar-daddy by trying to punish him for 'deceiving' her), (*e*) an ambitious and talentless career-girl, (*f*) intellectual, (*g*) arty. She gets another girl's part and indirectly causes her suicide, and feels just enough genuine remorse (no more) to make herself into a successful actress. Throughout the film she proves a verbal match for Ginger Rogers—the tough, bitter, proletarian blonde who is 'our' principal identification figure. One hardly needs the confirmation of La Cava's *Gabriel Over the White House* to detect the tightwing message of *Stage Door*. 'If you're over-privileged, don't apologize—you probably deserve to be: for unto those that hath guts shall be given and from those that hath not it shall be taken away.'

Katharine Hepburn also occupies a particular place in the evolution of the American woman. Amicably battling with Spencer Tracy in one comedy after another, she shows a specifically modern emancipation; but in *The African Queen* she is also the Puritan missionary of pioneer days—in fact if you substitute a covered wagon for a steam-launch, and the desert for the river, and Indians for Germans, the film reveals itself as more original in setting than in human values. In *Suddenly Last Summer* she presents another facet of the forceful woman—Momism gone mad. Perhaps the most moving of her recent performances was in *Summer Madness*, directed by David Lean, a lyricist of life's lost opportunities. She was miscast as a plain, characterless spinster whom no one even notices, but what came through was the story of a woman being lonely because she is too self-assured (strangely enough Miss Hepburn later complained that during the shooting of the film she was lonely because everyone assumed that she was too much the 'great lady' to enjoy their social life). A woman's yearning for her own lost softness and helplessness underlies the later Joan Crawford films, from Michael Curtiz' *Mildred Pierce* (1945) to David Miller's *The Story of Esther Costello* (1957); she was always letting herself be wronged by sleek, soft, effeminate Zachary Scott, or by gigolo womanizer Rossanno Brazzi—Katie's lover in *Summer Madness*. It's amusing to imagine Joan Crawford in Lean's film. Her very vulgarity might have made it as moving, in a different way.

The Hepburn of the 30's prefigures Lauren Bacall, with her rangey physique, husky voice, and dry attack. But Bacall, paradoxically, was less controversial—perhaps because the domineering strength was softened by compensations of sultry sensuality (whereas Hepburn has something distinctly schoolmarmish). But a fan in J. P. Mayer's *British Cinemas and their Audiences* talks of Lauren Bacall's 'slithery virility' and it's possible to see in the 'good-bad girl' of the 40's (perfect specimen: Bacall in *The Big Sleep*) a first step towards what Edmund Bergler establishes as the current fashion of *Counterfeit Sex*, partly confirmed by the quite unusual number of American films in which the manly men are sexually passive and the females have to be the males too, a turnabout reaching a mannerist intensity in Wilder's *Some Like it Hot* (1959) and Minnelli's *Goodbye Charley* (1964).

In a word, many an American woman is Katherine Hepburn posing, for men, as Lauren Bacall. If these generalizations seem outrageous, there's no doubt that they are; nor, of course, can one go into all the rights and wrongs of nomism, 'bringing up father', and other peculiarly American forms of the battle of the sexes. Possibly it's worth suggesting that puritanism (Christian and agnostic), competitive individualism, and the middle-class traits referred to earlier, all serve to stiffen the ego's resistance to erotic feelings, which are intrinsically dangerous to the ego: men, being more volatile, become more inhibited, emotionally, if not physically, or at least feel less assured, than women.

B.B.'s erotic aggressiveness is female, Dionysiac and childish, thus revealing her as post-puritan, post-suffragette and post-*bourgeois*—where the attack of her potential American equivalent, Debbie Reynolds, is slightly more masculine, certainly Apollonic and Momist. (I haven't forgotten Tuesday Weld; but she's ersatz B.B., Hollywood's misconception of B.B., just as Theda Bara is hick America's idea of the Italian diva.) With B.B. the equality of the sexes is assumed, freed from its rationalist-puritan associations, and given a libertarian tinge. The search of the erotically emancipated female is for a male passionate but firm enough, not to subjugate, the spontaneous, and therefore childlike, female (a common misreading of Vadim's first film) but to steady her impulsiveness, and satisfy her need for a paternal love. Instead of 'bringing up father', she's looking for one, and the dramatic mainspring of Vadim's *Et Dieu Créa la Femme* (1956) is that the younger brother (Trintignant) who really loves her is an idealizing 'son' type, the elder brother (Marquand) who has all the male virtues is a moral traditionalist who despises her for being beddable, while the fatherly tycoon (Jurgens) can only offer her money instead of happiness.

Trintignant, disillusioned and hysterical, tries to assert himself by a destructive masculinity (the shooting); Jurgens, though wounded, protects him from the consequences, and, paradoxically, the slap which the young man deals B.B. is a kathartic renunciation of violence, an acceptance of responsibility towards, and rights over, her. The idea that B.B., here or in any other film, is a 'mere' sex-object, a Lolita for Humbert Humberts, is puritans' rubbish. The teenage girls who spontaneously adopted her style, did so for completely different reasons. We all know that today male teenagers find growing up harder than girls (in Victorian days it was the other way round), and 1960's teenage girls adopted the B.B. style to appeal to, and to help, their boy friends to father them. You always see a B.B. girl with a boy of her own age, because this modern paganism, without being 'beat'—it's too straightforward—shrugs its shoulders at money and prefers a hedonism of the heart. B.B. has never played a gold-digger, and Sue Lyon is the very antithesis of the B.B. ethos. It's precisely this that makes Autant-Lara's *En Cas de Malheur* so poignant; it's Gabin, representative of the responsible older generation, who's too cynical to believe that he's anything more than a sugar-daddy to B.B., and so does as much as her weaknesses to precipitate the tragedy.

It's a pity that Sinatra and B.B. never made their projected film together, for leaving aside all the boring in-jokes about 'the clan' Sinatra is not only an American hero. He is twentieth-century cosmopolitanism—first, as the ex-alleycat at the London Hilton, second, as the globetrotting nomad of an endless nightlife. He would be almost as much at home in a French film; it's interesting to speculate what he would have made of the Aznavour part in *Tirez Sur le Pianiste* (1960). Curiously, one finds in a bad film of his for Charles Vidor, *The Joker is Wild* (1958), parallel themes, of the entertainer versus the gangsters, the hero betraying his women. At which point one remembers that Truffaut's film is based on a novel by David Goodis. Sinatra's world interpenetrates Robert Mitchum's—the hardboiled-sensitivity of the one parallels the beefy cynicism of the other. For Richard Winnington, Mitchum in Jacques Tourneur's *Build My Gallows High* (1947) incarnated the joyless masochism of the all-American ratrace. But the Mitchum qualities which Winnington evoked by such phrases as 'the saddest and most laconic dick we have ever known . . . another bout of enervated passion. . . . Jeff is by now too tired to love so he . . . dials the police. Kathie's last act is to release Jeff from the ennui of breathing . . .' have another meaning for Mitchum's fan-following, which is essentially teenage, urban and proletarian. The eye takes these qualities in another sense too, as 'lazy, relaxed, cynical, tough, shrewd, bold enough to be bad but too easy-going to be vicious, solitary, none too happy, undismayed . . .' the eternal outsider. His very shamble has something pre-beatnik about it (though beatniks shucked off the need to be tough). When in the late 40's he served a prison sentence on a narcotics rap, the Press ran photographs of Mitchum in prison gear cleaning up dustbins, and his fanmail soared to an unprecedented level. Publicity which would have annihilated a conformist star only perfected his screen image.

As Mitchum and his public, matured, a new mellowness and humour came to inform the initial blend of barfly cynicism and slumbering violence that made him, in Dmytryk's *Crossfire* a disturbing incarnation of the average man's know-nothing anti-idealism, from which a tough human decency (very) tardily emerged. Most of his films have been bad, content to exploit rather than to explore his screen personality; but such exceptions as Robert Parrish's *The Wonderful Country* and Vincente Minnelli's *Home From the Hill* have delved into its core, of honest nonconformity, where a depressed cynicism is the tragic error of a wry lucidity.

In its day *Sequence* expressed a rather refined admiration for such sappy youngsters as Diana Dors, Audrey Hepburn and Micheline Presle. Otherwise its 'People We Like' were a collection of Aunt and Uncle figures like Claire Trevor, Mary Astor, Catherine Lacey, Barbara Bel Geddes, Ward Bond and George Cole. Since then Bette Davis and Joan Crawford have become the Auntie Fun figures of *Sight and Sound*. All very safe and tepid.

A younger Oxford generation virtually ignores actors and enjoys only the vicarious experience of being a film director—via such easy conformists as Hawks, Preminger, and Leo McCarey.

However, Andrew Sarris once began an interview with a sustained defence in intellectual depth of his *auteur* theory, and concluded by confessing that what really kept him coming to the cinema was its girls. Here is the beginning of wisdom. Here human relationships are re-endowed with the shock of desire which our shallow rationalists, who use Freud only to reinforce their Anglo-Saxon psychological hypochondria, are so anxious to disallow. Here, however shyly, the old Adam peeps out from behind the *pince-nez* of culture, and the bland, shining mask of 'objectivity' cracks to reveal a human expression.

9 · The True Confessions of Shy Eunuchs in the Brothels of Art

Louis Seguin and Roger Tailleur adorn their trenchant left-wing exegeses of films in *Positif* with declarations like, 'As lovely as ever, Cyd, whatever you're in, whoever you're with,' and, their colleague. Marcel Oms, dedicates an article to 'Kim, my darling torment. . . .,'

In *Cahiers du Cinema* the critic-director Pierre Kast punctuated an abstruse article on film theory with photographs of his star, Alexandra Stewart, which had no connection with his article except that their presence on the page made for a kind of platonic marriage of beauty and brains (like the fair Lopokova and John Maynard Keynes).

He also told Jane Fonda he'd love to direct her in a film, to which the insouciant American girl replied that she's always wanted to make a film with Truffaut and was it true that François was timid with women? Ah, the wound and the bow. . . .

In *Cahiers*, No. 42, Patrice G. Hovald declared outright, 'I love you, Ava, and nothing will stop me from saying it. What matter the story you're in, for what overwhelms me are the movements of your body in the screen's magic circle [which to be pedantic is a rectangle]. I hate you, Ava, and I'll never grow tired of telling you so.'

If this be slosh, at least it's honest slosh, and much more to the point than the affected impersonality which reduces so much film criticism to triteness.

All the more refreshing then is such para-critical play as the Surrealists' 'Irrational Enlargement' of Von Sternberg's *Shanghai Gesture*. A panel of critics, including Ado Kyrou and Robert Benayoun, answered such questions as: 'What was the menu at the dinner given by Mother Gin Sling?', 'Describe the exterior of the Casino', 'At what moment did you intervene in the film?' and, 'What is the sexual perversion of Poppy Smith?'

The answers to the last question were as follows:

'Squeezing an octopus between her stocking and her thigh.' 'Stretched out at full length on one of the gaming tables, she separates one pearl after another of her necklace.' 'She has no perversity, only a preternaturally acute sensuality.' 'Sodomy of a consciously masochistic character.' 'Masturbation without sexual object.'

This section was written in response to a friend's challenge to explain why in three different articles I declared as 'my all-time favourite film star' divinities as diverse as Clara Bow, Lillian Gish, and Jean Harlow. My answer is to add a fourth, a fifth, and a sixth: Maria Schell; the Hong Kong star, Li Li Hwa, whose only Occidental film is Frank Borzage's *China Doll*; and the hard edge sensuality of Cleo Laine (the most beautiful TV image of 1964 was a big C.U. with the camera slowly tilting up from her sumptuous lips to her ageless eyes).

In the last analysis, all film addicts play two games. The first is the game of *alter egos*. Mine is the Aznavour role in *Tirez sur le Pianiste* as it would be if Jerry Lewis were interpreting it. The second is that of *les harems imaginaires* (I have to quote it in French to rhyme with André Malraux's *Musées Imaginaires*). Its tenants are co-opted, not for beauty in the abstract, but for any quality one feels like celebrating. It may be sheer, brute erotic shock-impact. Or it may be a congenial emotional wave-band (Fellini's, for example, is that of infinite maternal indulgence in all its modalities, with a little diabolism by way of pepper and salt). Or it may be some private emotional nostalgia. . . .

The New Sentimentality is giving the Harem Game a new tinge. The new-type Sultan longs for the *anti*-odalisque whose role is less to meet his every wish than to provide him with experiences which make him a sadder, wiser, tougher man. Fellini is Old Sentimentality, a primitive. The new harems are altogether more arduous. There one comes to terms with all that's unlived-out in one's own nature. Jean-Paul Torok subscribes to the New Sentimentality when he writes of Barbara Steele in *Black Sunday*: 'When aesthetic admiration is absolutely fused with desire and terror, it "blacks out". . . . Where are your vaunted intelligence and your cultivated taste when everything in you freezes and is fascinated before the revelations of the utmost horror? Beneath the flowing robe of this young woman with so beautiful a countenance there appear, distinctly, the tatters of a skeleton. *Is she any the less desirable?*'

One remembers the beautiful plot idea rather wasted by the imbecile script of Siodmak's *Son of Dracula*. A young woman becomes a vampire so that she will be able to confer spiritual immortality on her lover. . . . Here we are at the fountainhead of all religious aspiration: 'better a living death than life followed by death'.

Everybody has nightmares, and every well-appointed harem has its witch-bitch, for the same reason that fairy stories have them. Fellini's *8½* has a sort of Laurel-and-Hardy pair, the fat one, La Saraghina, and the thin one, Barbara. With her lean and hungry look, she is nervous, insomniac, masochistic, and addicted to philosophy and father-figures; she's wryly observant of the Frenchwoman with the healing hands and she's terrified of the telepathic clown who smiles like death and truth, and who is to *8½* as Anton Walbrook is to *La Ronde*. What is Barbara here by everything that fascinates and frightens Fellini about secular *thought*. . . .

It's fitting perhaps that Barbara Steele reciprocally plays the harem game, and is putting the finishing touches to a novel about a girl who has to have three lovers, each for a different aspect of her character.

In general though one can only smile at the naïvety of those earnest souls who remind players of harem games that screen actresses aren't really what they're like on the screen. Philosophers can't endure the toothache patiently either, and in private life some poets use frightful language. In fact, a marked screen type almost presupposes its interior antithesis. Delicate Lillian Gish has a will of steel, everlasting ingenue Debbie Reynolds has been called 'an angel—with spurs', and Maria Schell's quick sweet smile, meant to appeal and placate, obviously means: 'I'm going full speed ahead anyway. . . .' This sort of ambiguity makes every real star as satisfyingly complex in herself as the film in which she appears. By the same logic, Theda Bara was an amiable stodge, and Marlene an intelligent, level-headed *hausfrau*, on whose streak of easygoing insolence her Svengali founded a religion. Screen victims (Pearl White, Lillian Gish, Screaming Lady Fay Wray, Lualdi, Lee Remick) only make good victims because their innate stubbornness and robustness enables them to keep on protesting like mad.

However, this rule-of-thumb that the 'real' person is the artist's negative soon breaks down—since both may be defence-mechanisms against unconscious urges. Much *personality* is only bone-structure, and has nothing to do with *character*, except in so far as its impressionable possessor reacts to other people's expectations. Ursula Andress can't possibly be as exotic as she looks. Honor Blackman virtually invented Cathy Gale, telling her scriptwriters to write her dialogue as if they were writing for a man (a favourite Howard Hawks principle, and more or less how he invented Lauren Bacall).

Speaking quite personally, I find most films with Garbo, Jeanne Moreau, and Annie Girardot very depressing. All three actresses suggest a passionate temperament rooted in some sort of auto-frustration. On the other hand, many an actress is forever debarred from screen stardom by her very sensitivity. Maggie Smith looms to be a case in point. Her blend of brimming feminine sensitivity, of superior intelligence, and something mockingly autonomous, is all too much of a tease, and worse, it's idiom is too upper-class for the film public. To this diffuseness of highly cultured responses, the masses prefer their stars to have a clarity of basic drive. In their different ways, Deborah Kerr, Audrey Hepburn and Katharine Hepburn combine a reminiscent sensitivity with some such clarity.

Fellini looks at the same syndrome from his angle in *8½*. Marcello's mistress Anouk, is a symbol of loyalty and order, and, like Claudia, she wears neat white linen. But her sisters are more complex and sinister, as if Anouk's sensitive intelligence bordered on a lack of passion a certain unfemininity, a *bourgeois* habit of aridity. The real ideal is Claudia, who blends neatness, true femininity, and true philosophy. She repeats: 'You can't love. . . . You can't love. . . . You can't love. . . .' This is the first film in which Fellini's 'angel' is unmistakably of the flesh, of *this* world, worldly-wise, without Christian overtone.

How much of this film's meaning is revealed by the girls' personalities! And what is *Hiroshima Mon Amour* without the personal 'style' of its lovers? Why, it's almost as boring as *Muriel*.

For cultured players of harem games, exoticism has a particular value. Again, though, human nature contributes its usual twists. Simone de Beauvoir remarked on her friends' dismissal of B.B.: 'She has a face like a housemaid!' She has, and that's the miracle. Any exotic can be unique; the real divinity is to be both housemaid and goddess, reality and liberation from reality. What perfection!

Nor was B.B.'s childishness a new phenomenon. After all, the 20's flapper celebrated emancipation by half-playing at being half-tom-boy, half-child. . . . Men had to be fatherly in those days. National Film Theatre audiences laugh incredulously when in Hitchcock's *Blackmail* (1929) the young copper taking his girl out for a big night at Joe Lyons' marble halls makes like the heavy father to her. Hitchcock was absolutely right. I can just, just remember pre-war adults behaving *exactly* so. What's startling about B.B. is not that she played the sexy child (so did Clara Bow), but that the men are so reluctant to accept any paternal responsibility towards her. So film fashions lead us back to our sociological issues. . . . And how exotic, how dazzling to us now, the women of the 20's and 30's, and 'teens! It's easy enough to analyze their mannerism and glances in terms of mutual influence or sociological resonance. Yes, Helen Twelvetrees in Tay Garnett's *Her Man* (1930) is a middle term between Dorothy Gish and Susan Hayward. And quite amazing is Louise Brooks' mixture in Genina's *Prix de Beauté* (1930) of sphinx, housewife, and flapper, all blended with that direct, quick, soft, vulnerable emotionalizing which seems to have died, on the screen, during the Second World War. By comparison, the 'Method' is so gritty, so laborious a search for spontaneity. . . .

One still finds such actresses—but where are the films they deserve? For Susannah York, *The Greengage Summer* was a shining spring, but since then she has had only one worthy—and grossly ignored—film, John Huston's *Freud*. Who can forget that glance of concerned horror with which Freud (Montgomery Clift) accepts, for the first time in human history, with full lucidity, the emotional abnormalities which now make for callow party chit-chat? That glance keys the film's superb rediscovery of so unfashionable a thing as moral dignity—the seriousness which adds such strength and depth to the proud warmth of Susannah York and the volatility of Susan Kohner. In Huston's film hero and heroines pool their resolution and their sophistication and prefigure what is almost a new humanism. Not since Lucia Bose in Bunuel's *Cela S'Appelle l'Aurore* has the screen offered such a portrait of feminine integrity.

The similar simplicity of total, unquestioned commitment, gives such beauty to Maria Schell's playing in the handful of films which redeem her career from middlebrow tearjerkery, notably, Daves' *The Hanging Tree*, and above all of course René Clement's *Gervaise*

(1956). But isn't the presence of this valiant pocket battleship of Teutonic monogamy a negation of the harem spirit?

Perhaps. And so we bid farewell to that happy land where 'good night' really means 'good night'. . . .

10 · The Road to Profundity and Seriousness leads through Superficiality and Irresponsibility

The Harem game is only one of the many games whereby one can use the cinema to explore oneself and one's friends, games which critics ignore, because they require participation in, surrender to, the film, because they are quietly Dionysiac, where critics, by nature, are ticket-inspectors, meter-readers and sanitary inspectors. They thus miss most of the fun of the fair.

The general public responds to stars, and critics like to differentiate themselves from the uneducated. The star communicates by a personal, even physical, language—face, gesture, build—the intellectual prefers to find implications, symbols, deep meanings. And being suspicious of vulgarity, he usually refuses to respond to stars who aren't 'good actors' (in the very conventional sense of the phrase); thus he accepts Bette Davis, but not Kim Novak, Brando but not Audie Murphy.

A fourth factor requires a little more explanation. To adapt a phrase of Pauline Kael's, the average educated American is, in his attitude to movies, a social worker at heart—a phrase which one may briefly, construe as meaning: rationalist, conformist, optimist, utilitarian and complacent.

In one form, which we may call Mrs. Miniverism, and which true highbrows (like the writer) energetically repudiate as middlebrow and suburban, an optimistic conformism prevails over 'reason'. The intellect is mistrusted, and 'reason' softened into what is felt to be 'reasonable', that is, a good 'adjustment' is held to be the sign of a good life (when it's as often the sign of a mildly schizophrenic one). Indeed the schizophrenic possibilities of this ethos are widely criticized by Hollywood via such screen characters as Blanche Dubois in Kazan's *A Streetcar Named Desire*, James Dean's mother in *Rebel*

Without a Cause, Shelley Winters in Kubrick's *Lolita* and Shirley Booth in Daniel Mann's *Hot Spell*, which like many Hal Wallis soap-operas is truer and more lucid than it has the reputation of being. (*A bas* Stevens, *vive* Wallis!?)

Another form of this ethos, if not actually Puritanical in the classic sense (as in Natalie Wood's father in *Rebel Without a Cause*), is permeated with an all but unexamined neo-platonism: the assumption that reason is 'higher' than emotion and 'the heart' than the flesh. A development of this is the easy intellectual acceptance of carefully isolated aspects of Freudian theory, with a view, not to easing the demands of an over-rationalized civilization on man, but of intensifying 'adjustment' to that civilization, in short, intensifying the processes of repression and 'alienation'. The middle-classes are the chief carriers of such a culture, and as, not Marx, but Margaret Mead, remarked, the U.S.A. is, culturally, a 'middle-class nation'.

But the cinema audience is largely proletarian; its view of life is influenced also by a more rebellious, more Nietzschean, scale of values, more cynical, and in a sense nihilist, but also hotter, less 'alienated' emotionally. The 'industrial hall' audience notoriously has a different morality from the 'small town' theatre; people who like Katie Hepburn don't usually like Bob Mitchum; and so on. But each 'culture' influences the other. Tenement housewives may have middle-class dreams; men of all classes identify relatively easily with the tough proletarian hero; in a sense, middle-class culture is feminine, proletarian culture is masculine, whence the antagonism-interplay of the young schoolmarm (Eva-Marie Saint) and the tough docker (Brando) is *On the Waterfront*.

Many stars cross class lines. Bing Crosby is everything about the middle-classes that the proletariat likes; easy, cosy, firm, relaxed. In top hat and tails, Fred Astaire is not at all the 'upper classes' but 'life as it ought to be, free of the cash-cramps'. His tap-dancing in top hotels is a capitalist society's equivalent of dwelling midst fields of asphodel.

In Europe the proletarian audience, citified though it may be, retains something of a pagan folk culture in its sexual attitudes; in the U.S.A. these seem to have been replaced by an obsession with toughness, perhaps because the European proletariat prefers class-consciousness to competitiveness whereas American culture blends the optimism of self-help with the cynicism of the rat-race, and, in eagerly conformizing sons of immigrants, saps spontaneous intimacies and tendernesses. Movies necessarily compromise between middle-class and proletarian attitudes—hence, to a large extent, the superficiality of most movies—but it's not difficult to disentangle the separate poles—Hepburn *v.* Bogart in Huston's *The African Queen*, schoolmarm and docker in Kazan's *On the Waterfront.* In films as diverse as Frankenheimer's *The Young Savages*, Brooks' *Deadline* and Cukor's *Pat and Mike* we can see the common American association of middle-class culture with schoolmarms and women, while the male prides himself on his fitness for surviving either in the Wild West or the city, blackboard, ashphalt, garment, etc., jungle. At its worst, this feminine idealism becomes complacent, wilfully blind to the fights that must be fought (*High Noon*, *Deadline*); at its worst, the male wastes his life in a brutal, nihilist, celibate individualism (*Shane*, *Marty* (1955), James Dean in *Giant*). Hence perhaps the fascination with the myth of the tender-hearted tramp—from Helen Twelvetrees in *Her Man* (1930) through early Ginger Rogers and Gloria Grahame to Marilyn in *Bus Stop* (1956) and Kim in *Kiss Me Stupid* (1964). She's free from schoolmarm puritanism, and she's tough enough *both* to take the sexual and emotional initiative *and* to give a lonely man's life the meaning of her kindness.

In so far as, to paraphrase Pauline Kael's remark, most Anglo-Saxon film critics are social workers at heart, that is, missionaries of 'liberal' sweetness-and-light, they themselves are on the defensive against the overt or covert vulgarity whereby movies delight their mass audience. Educational traditions make of them also—in their aesthetic reactions, at least—neo-Platonists. The commonest symptom of this is the *hypochondriac* use of Freudian concepts, that is, the substitution of a rationalist puritanism for a Christian one. Manicheanism switches from 'the body is evil' to 'subjective emotions may betray me into illogical immaturity; I must have only rational adult emotions and ignore the others' (a schizophrenic condition). One corollary of this is that intellectuals can bear musicals and Westerns and gangster pictures, but not soap-operas, which are felt to imply a surrender to middle-class Mom (actually crying at *Imitation of Life* would make one feel a helpless child in Momma's lap again). In fact many educated people weep at soap-operas but hate themselves for doing so—whence their tone of contempt or superior irony. Nor do they usually comment on the continuing, quiet, popularity of the male weepie, a favourite motif of Victorian melodrama, and at its most unobtrusively unabashed in John Ford's *She Wore a Yellow*

Ribbon (1949) and *The Sun Shines Bright* (1953). De Sica's *Umberto D* (1952) and Germi's *Man of Iron* (1955), can, like many Italian films, be assimilated to the genre. Actually the surrender to weepies, male or female, might be the beginning of maturity, if embraced wholeheartedly enough. But its rejection springs from the same root as the rejection of actor for director, of emotional immediacy for analysis: the ideological tension between middle-class puritan and the unregenerate masses.

11 · How Not to Enjoy the Movies

And if I've paraphrased Miss Kael it's for less flattering a reason than it may seem. Her article, *Fantasies of the Art House Audience*, found a suitable spiritual home in the pages of *Sight and Sound*, for it illustrates just how dim film criticism can become when the social worker *manqué* struggles to understand movies. Miss Kael is presumably a staunch anti-censorship liberal, but the woman-of-the-world style of her article ornaments her puritanism as uneasily as a moustache the Mona Lisa.

She begins with a pretence of briskly sweeping cant and cobwebs away and letting the fresh air in. 'For several decades now, educated people have been condescending towards the children, the shopgirls, all those with 'humdrum' or 'impoverished' lives—the mass audience—who turned to movies for 'ready-made' dreams. The educated might admit that they sometimes went to the movies designed for the infantile mass audience—the number of famous people who relax with detective fiction makes this admission easy—but presumably they were not 'taken in', they went to get away from the tension of their complex lives and work. But of course when they really want to enjoy movies as an art, they go to foreign films, or 'adult' or unusual experimental American films.

'I would like to suggest that the educated audience often uses "art" films in much the same self-indulgent way as the mass audience uses Hollywood product, finding wish-fulfilment in the form of cheap and easy congratulation on their sensitivities and their liberalism. Obviously many of my generalizations are subject to numerous exceptions and infinite qualifications; let's assume that I know this, and that I use large generalizations in order to be suggestive rather than definitive.'[1]

Which obviously applies to this piece too.

Miss Kael then goes on to examine some of the self-indulgent wish-fulfilment gratifications afforded by *Hiroshima Mon Amour, La Vérité, The Misfits, Twelve Angry Men, The Apartment, Ballad of a Soldier, The Cranes are Flying,* by Lo Duca's book *L'Erotisme Au Cinema,* by Saul Bass credits, by B.B. and by M.M.

Before showing how brisk, nice social worker's puritanism can ravage film criticism, let's look at just that area where its case seems strongest.

'Recently, at a cocktail party of artists and professors, I noticed displayed on a table right next to the pickled Jerusalem artichokes, two French publications . . . (including) . . . Lo Duca's new volume on *Eroticism in the Cinema.*[1] Both books are like more elegantly laid out issues of *Confidential* and all those nameless magazines which feature hideously outsized mammary glands . . . only these books are supposed to be chic—the latest intellectual camp. . . . What struck me about these books, which function as entertainment to what might be called highbrows, was that their chic seemed to consist largely in a degradation of the female image. The stars and starlets are displayed at their most grotesque . . . lascivious face, wet open mouth, gigantic drooping breasts. . . . She has no character, no individuality; she's blonde or brunette or redhead, as one might consume a martini, an old fashioned, or a gin and tonic.'

Yet Lo Duca's book includes a high proportion of stills from films by people like Pabst, Melville, Visconti, Becker, Antonioni and Mack Sennett; by Hitchcock, Sjoberg, Eisenstein, Méliès and Flaherty; by Carné, Ophuls, Lang and Bunuel; so it would seem as worth looking at as any collection of stills. Intermixed with these are about a quarter of inartistic stills from inartistic pictures. But what is so 'disreputable' about the collection is, of course, that it is a collection. The erotic ensemble paralyses people, they can't look at what is actually in the picture, the bare breasts and thighs intensify the meaning of the mere suggestions; the puritanical reader is overwhelmed by a vast, vague, semi-swoon of revulsion, the pages swim before his (or her) eyes.

This may sound like a facetious exaggeration, but it's strictly true. Lo Duca points out that many *bien-pensant* Paris critics described the book as a parade of outrageous nudity, where in fact the 330 illustrations include only 60 pairs of breasts, apart from coloured

[1] I'm presuming Miss Kael refers to the first of the three volumes, but *mutatis mutandis* my remarks apply equally to its two successors.

breasts, which of course aren't usually censorable on the European screen.

It's no odds to me, I've no reproach to make, if Miss Kael finds feminine sexuality hideous, grotesque, a degradation. But she then racks her brains to try and understand how artists and professors, of all people, could peruse and enjoy such ghastlinesses. She clearly has some vague but strong idea that intellectuals ought to be above the physical sphere. Anyway, she comes to the following conclusions:

1. Men feel that reading such books makes them appear virile.
2. Men enjoy seeing women degraded to a 'low, animal' level. It also makes them more potent than they usually are (as men don't find intelligent women physically attractive?).
3. Armies of homosexuals are chortling at this ridicule of their female rivals.

But life's so much simpler really. Here's a True Confession for our social worker's casebook. Years ago, when the book first appeared over here, some friends and the present writer, were giving a party for some other artists and professors. We invested in a copy of Lo Duca's book and put it near the potato crisps and the cider barrel (we were roughing it in those days, by golly). Apart from finding the book fun in an unedifying way, we put it out to say, 'This is Liberty Hall, you needn't mind your p's and q's, relax and enjoy yourself, nothing you say will be taken down in the backs of our minds and used against you.' The Duke of Wellington (I think) was once asked how he set about creating a friendly atmosphere among the ambassadors at peace conferences, and replied, 'Why sir, talk bawdy.'

Even allowing for the significant shifts in the sense of the word 'camp', one's imagination boggles somewhat at Miss Kael's fantasy about armies of homosexuals. I'd have thought it fairly common knowledge that the common or garden male enjoys watching on the screen people like B.B., Lollo, M.M., Carole Lombard, Arletty, Jennifer Jones and all the other 'hideous, grotesque, degraded' creatures. But Miss Kael can't tell a leer of homosexual derision from a smile of heterosexual admiration: well, it's proverbial that lady novelists can't create convincing male characters.

Miss Kael gets herself into analogous difficulties when discussing the highbrow interest in B.B. and M.M. I was never very taken by the latter myself, but having contributed a few thousand words to B.B.-ology and -olatry I feel myself entitled to defend myself against intimations of being a pathological silly-billy. Miss Kael wonders whether B.B. has any acting talent—fine as was her performance as B.B. in *La Vérité*, could she play anyone other than a quasi-B.B.?

But this question is dubiously relevant. Could Laurel and Hardy play anyone else but Stan and Ollie? I haven't the faintest idea. You might as well ask: Could A. E. Housman have composed poems in the style of say Hopkins, Keats, Dante? Presumably not, but he wrote the poems of A. E. Housman. To admire B.B.'s playing of B.B. is not to self-indulgently confuse sex-appeal with talent, it is to accept B.B.'s B.B. as a person. Let's suppose she can't act, then her playing is neo-realism; which is how directors like Flaherty, de Sica, etc., have given the screen many moving performances. However, if Miss Kael can't see B.B.'s playing in *En Cas de Malheur* as a *performance*, I can only suggest that it's she who can't see the acting talent for the sex appeal.

The basic question is whether B.B.'s screen personality is an interesting one. It seems to me so, first, for its intrinsic psychological complexity, second, as incarnating some key tensions of our time. It then follows that her private life is as legitimately interesting as, say, Lawrence of Arabia's, or Strindberg's, or that of any artist in whom the spectator feels he recognizes an *ami inconnu*. (Not that there would be the least disgrace in liking B.B. because she's one's dream girl, or one of one's dream girls, or just an entertaining personality that it's nice to be with.)

But because Miss Kael has missed the obvious and straightforward, but still feels she has to explain our interest, she proceeds, with commendable perseverance (and let's praise her for not settling for the bland sneers of so many English critics) to concoct a hypothesis which is not only highly implausible but simply tells us what Miss Kael's interest in B.B. would be if she were interested. She believes audiences want to *tidy her up*. 'The average American is a social worker at heart; he feels especially sympathetic towards these slovenly ladies because their slovenliness marks them as misfits in this orderly world.' She goes on: 'The same man who is enchanted with Monroe in the seduction scene of *Some Like it Hot*—crawling all over Tony Curtis while hanging out of her dress both fore and aft —expects his girl friend to be trim, slender and well-groomed.' Well, that's his problem, and I can't really speak from much personal experience of it, but again, I should feel that the most confirmed neatness-fetishist would be perfectly reasonable in relishing a change. All entertainment involves indulging nostalgias, which for one reason or other one can't or won't live out fully in one's own life —whether it's riding the range with Coop or being crawled over by the hanging gardens of Marilyn. Miss Kael is misled by over-simple definitions of wish-fulfilment into thinking that any discrepancy between what one wants in reality and what one wants on the screen makes one 'immature' or 'self-indulgent'. But you might as well argue that people who like horror movies end up by setting fire to their dear old mothers, or that people who go to church end up by going to heaven. It's just another permutation of the old puritan arguments about the cinema.

But now see what happens when you apply these principles to a film. Miss Kael is determined to debunk *Hiroshima Mon Amour*, on the principle that 'wish-fulfilment' is lazy and disreputable and 'self-indulgence' *infra dig*.

'The picture opened with those intertwined nude bodies—this could be symbolic of a true intermingling, but it irresistibly set off some lewd speculations about just *what* was going on.' Any such lewd speculations are, my dear, absolutely justified; but why that 'but'? or rather, why take refuge in symbolism? The couple are naked and intermeshed, like ying and yang, like the androgyne of Plato's myth, like a condition of primal unity, and hard at it too, which is why mysticism so often uses sexual imagery.

'Was it possibly an elaborate masochistic fantasy for intellectuals?' Certainly, the film is an elaborated fantasy, a fiction, intended for people who want to share, in a cinema, experiences they haven't actually had. Possibly it's masochistic; many films are, much art is, all guilt feelings, all morality, and much religion are masochistic. But we can see Miss Kael's little ploy; in her context, 'masochistic' means 'unhealthy', the term carries overtones of gruesome case histories in Kraft-Ebbing. People who are moved by Resnais' film are as immature as sex perverts. But a principal defect of obsessed interpretations like this is that they form so obvious a series. The shop-girl has her pin-up, the critic has her interpretation, but they're sisters under the skin. And Miss Kael spares no thought for the possibility that audiences are enjoying a katharsis.

'Surely, both sexes could identify with the girl's sexual desperation, her sensitivity and confusion.' Yes, of course. Here, though, Miss Kael's intention is to press home the attack; not only highbrow shop-girls, but 'tough' liberal and radical men are wallowing in voluptuous masochism, in fact they're transvestites too. But any normal man can identify with a wide range of feminine feelings, and regularly do, while watching, say *Gervaise*, *Broken Blossoms*, or *The Virgin Spring*. Communication between men and women would be vastly more difficult than it is if they couldn't. Indeed, an excellent reason for participating in works of art is that one's Godlike immunity facilitates one's feeling things through other's nerves. 'And had anyone dreamed up worse punishments for sexuality?' (than having one's lover killed and head shaved). Miss Kael's rhetorical question seems to hint that the whole story is an absurd, over-wrought guilt-fantasy. In fact, Riva isn't punished for sexuality, but for giving aid and comfort to the enemy. Miss Kael may mean that our masochistic unconscious minds misinterpret it all, which they doubtless do, since they misinterpret everything, including, say, ideas of patriotism and hubris. 'But this heroine not only had her head shaved, by people who didn't understand her love, and need of the German, but she went crazy and was locked in a cellar. You can't go much further in being misunderstood.' No? Is that a bet? In Bunuel's *El* the paranoiad diplomat sets about sewing up his innocent wife's vagina. Examples of poetic injustice in literature are just as abundant, from *Oedipus Rex* to Jarry's *Le Surmale*.

Any doubt that Miss Kael is trying to take us out of our vicarious participation with Riva is dissipated by the next sentence: 'And, at the risk of giving offence, is this not what sends so many people to analysis—the fear that they'll go crazy if they don't get love?'

But why should we take offence? Much suffering is undoubtedly due to a real or imagined lack of love, and fear of going crazy is quite common in suffering of this kind, or other kinds. But Miss Kael's hearty tone says: 'Pull yourselves together, you self-indulgent audience, real art (not this Resnais trash) would never tolerate your infantile self-pity. Mature sensible people wouldn't feel that they were suffering from lack of love. After all Riva has nothing to worry about really. She's only seen her lover shot and die in pain, and been humiliated and brutalized in front of the whole town, and renounced by her parents, but she doesn't really have anything to worry about.' As compared to decapitation, perhaps? What sympathy does Hamlet deserve, by such standards of mental health? or King Lear? And who's left as a culture heroine?—surely only Mrs. Miniver!

Miss Kael goes on: 'Everybody who has suffered sexual deprivations—and who hasn't—can identify with her and perhaps fantasise brutal parents and cellars. Even her insanity can be equated with those rough nights when a love affair fell apart or that nervous exhaustion at the end of the academic year that sends so many to the hospital or the psychiatric clinic.' Put like that, few sorts of suffering don't seem trivial; Hamlet and Lear only needed a good talking-to. I admire Miss Kael's tactful choice of example: 'that nervous exhaustion at the end of the academic year'. One has an image of so many professorial Flauberts, lying agonized on couches. For someone who despises highbrows' masochism, Miss Kael is adept at appealing to it.

Equally, the mention of rough nights with love affairs falling apart irresistibly evokes the moral, love is a matter of insomnia, not to worry, another affair will appear shortly, one friend or lover is as good as another, heartbreak is impossible (because the heart hardly exists?). 'This woman (beautifully as Emmanuele Riva interpreted her) was exposing one of the worst faults of intelligent modern woman; she was talking all her emotions out—as if bed were the place to demonstrate sensibility.' Would Miss Kael feel bed is the place to demonstrate insensibility? At any rate, she's finally remembered the kathartic process—in this context, not in the other, of course. In fact, many people find talking=confession=communion; Miss Kael seems to equate sexuality with gruntings. But let's just suppose that Riva talks too much at the wrong time and is physically frigid. Why would this make her uninteresting?

'It is unfortunate that what people take to be the most important things about themselves, the innermost truths and secrets—the real you and me—that we dish up when someone looks sympathetic—is very likely to be . . . drivelling nonsense . . . slop . . . why should anybody want it?' Looked at objectively, it is possibly arguable that all our thoughts are drivel and slop, but most of us sneak along, getting a dash of wish-fulfilment here, a kathartic fix there, a little ridiculous giving and taking of drivelling sympathy; and after all, that's all we've got, and it's the stuff of art as well.

'Few of us have seen our lovers killed by partisan bullets, but something kills love anyway—something always does—and it's probably highly gratifying for many people to identify with a heroine who isn't responsible; it is the insane world that has punished her for her sexual expression.' Without going into details over this assumption-ridden sentence, it's clearly just Calvinist dogma turned inside out. Not only are we not to grieve over bereavement and suffering, but we are to react as if we were being justly punished for our own shortcomings. Yet to assume that we are responsible for whatever happens to us is to live in fantasy realms of our own guilty omnipotence.

'But what has her sad story to do with Hiroshima and the Bomb?' Here the nuance is: a story about a mere individual's mere emotions must be pretty petty compared with 'real', 'big' issues that concern masses of people and get dated in history books. One is reminded of John Grierson's citation to the effect that Asquith's *Dance Pretty Lady* was trivial because it was only about a girl losing her virginity, to which a character of Wilfrid Fienburgh's political novel *No Love for Johnnie* provides us with a useful reply: 'Today I have been reading a draft proof of our policy statement for the next election. It is sound and constructive stuff. We promise a universal pension scheme, comprehensive education and an extension of the health service. And all this needs to be done. All this will no doubt make people happier or relieve their worries, and that is our aim. But I have read, today, the report of a sociological institute based on an investigation of sexual relationships in Glasgow. It seems that 15 per cent of women resent the sex act, 32 per cent endure it, 40 per cent like it occasionally and only 13 per cent really enjoy it. It would appear, then, that the most useful contribution we could make towards the greater happiness of humanity would be to replace our policy statement by a useful handbook on sex.'

Miss Kael again: 'Would not some other psycho-sexual story of deprivation (say, *Camille* or *Stella Dallas*) be just as relevant to the horrors of war if it were set in *Hiroshima*?' It might; it depends, Suppose two lovers are separated by the Bomb, and killed, but die, in their fantasy, 'together', this would be a story about the Bomb, even though, logically, the lovers might have died by plague or earthquake, or been run over by motor-cars. A reasonable way of making an anti-war film is be deprecating its effects. Of course other events could have similar effects.

What's really happened is that Miss Kael is shocked because Marguerite Duras has dared to put a 'serious' social problem like Hiroshima on the same level as Mon Amour and lewd trivialities like that. In fact it's just the lewd triviality that has kept the human race going at all.

It's no coincidence that Miss Kael chose *Hiroshima Mon Amour* (and that we relate it to harem games). The whole film is about Riva's refusal to remember what she *felt* in the cellar, her *refusal* of katharsis and therefore of the rebirth that might follow, her inability to 'see'

Hiroshima because she will never see 'Nevers'. It takes a Japanese lover to get this French girl to remember her grief for a dead German and so to find herself. Resnais' film, like this article, is about the acceptance of emotion.

Miss Kael's write-offs of—on the one hand—tears, katharsis, tragedy, and—on the other—lewdness and desire—is emotional obscurantism gone nutty. The human heart, for her, is a neatly ruled ledger, which ought to show a credit balance of optimism; all grief is to be promptly written off. The only conclusion one can draw from her article must be that her cultural ideal is not just 'rationalist puritanism' and 'Mrs. Miniverism', but a schizophrenic condition.

We rush to add that Miss Kael *in vivo* is doubtless a lively and charming body. She can be an excellent critic, when defending common sense against various extremisms, both political and aesthetic. The brisk and jolly tone of this particular (and nauseating) article of hers suggests she feels she's homing in on some common assumptions, and I'm afraid she is, which is why one bothers about it. But isn't it time we stopped accepting in film criticism an anti-emotionality, a phoney rationalism which we know to be not just harmful but absurd, in any other context? Isn't it time we plucked up our courage and allowed our hearts as well as our heads to go to the pictures?

Yes, of course educated people enjoy their films in just the same way as the mass audience, as well as in their own way, and so they should, for the latter without the former is just a collection of intellectual formulae. Those who strain to purify themselves into moral computers inevitably conclude by missing all the intellectual points of *Hiroshima Mon Amour*.

It's interesting too that no one would dream of applying to literary forms the kind of indiscriminate blitz which, wreaked on the cinema, not only passes without comment, but is the orthodoxy, challenged only by the younger critics?

What it is that the cinema lacks? That greasy dull brown patina of cultural 'prestige' that has made so many works of art all but invisible? Perhaps it lacks, above all, that thick screen of 'busy', intricate, but often tautologous, intellectual detail which, in currently fashionable literary formula ('complexity', 'density', 'texture'), serve to protect the moral-emotional hypochondriac from the impact of straightforward emotion.

What happened to the human face in painting was that it suddenly, and curiously, seemed banal, as if artists had half-forgotten how to locate human experience in its whole human context: analysis was devastating, synthesis too onerous a task. The language of simplicity was inadequate for complexity, that of complexity inadequate for simplicity. The precision, even, of Lawrence's *Sons and Lovers* shades off into an imprecise Messianism. But the 'pop' arts (with middlebrow literary strata) retained the old idioms, and maybe today's real *avant-garde* is the drive to unify that dimension, and those idioms, with the daring thoughtfulness of all that was best in the old *avant-gardes.*

Much 'pop' art is, from this viewpoint, an opportunist perversion, or a nihilistic parody, of this reconciliation, being as crude in its humanist nuances as the worst of the 'pop' media which it loots.

12 · Through a Star Darkly

What then have 'the stars' to tell us about our experience?

Adolescence found an emblem in James Dean, and another in a star whose personality we now explore simply because the 'academic' reaction was to see her as an incarnation of candyfloss glamour: Kim Novak. In Preminger's *The Man With the Golden Arm* she plays the 'dance hall hostess' (read: prostitute) who becomes Frank Sinatra's angel of mercy, the cruel-to-be-kind young mother-figure who deprives him of dope and puts him through the cold-turkey cure. She blends a soft body with a butch suspicion and a childlike potentiality for devotion. She is a specialist in bewildered, passive suffering—in George Sidney's *Jeanne Eagels* and *Pal Joey*, in Hitchcock's *Vertigo*. In Delbert Mann's *The Middle of the Night* her infidelity results from her inner confusions.

What is usually meant by innocence is a condition too pleasantly curable to be very interesting, and Kim's is something deeper and knottier; that of a nervous fear, a freezing of the soul, a virginity more sinister than anything the body can provide. In her most 'innocent' roles something in her glance implies previous lovers, to the number of n—whether n=0 or 100 seems all but immaterial. Rhapsodizes Michel Mourlet: 'Her large black eyes in her blonde's face reveal a depth of innocence which creates vertigo. . . .' Her innocence is not that of the 'sensitive plant', it's that of the tough backalley shrub that has yet to discover the tenderness for which it longs. This is the most moving innocence of all, which is just as well, since in today's cities it's the only sort left.

The reticent, but intense, torment implied in her slow, deliberate playing is combined with what is possibly Hollywood's most succulent physique. Her long mannequin's body bears breasts like meringues, and shoulders like a stevedore's. She has a back like a tulip and thighs like pythons. Her slim elongation, her electric eyes, make one think of an El Greco, but with a spirituality rooted only in the flesh. In her love scenes she shows a marshmallow melting, a slow, deliberate avidity, a ruthless self-giving which hardly dares trust, is therefore as painful as despair, and inspires Mourlet's: 'She is so fragile and passive . . . to make love to her must bring tears to one's eyes. . . .'

She has everything that's vulgar and *nouveau-riche* (but in an affluent age who isn't?), and she bears it in the most sympathetic way—that is, without apology, with a carefully calculated flamboyance, and with the hint of sadness inseparable from the use of fashion as poetry. Her inner shyness gives her display an orchidaceous quality. She is a flower wrapped in the cellophane of her own provocation.

But her china doll quality palpitates with nervous tensions. She is a frozen avalanche of feelings. Fragments of the snow queen's ice litter her heart. In Richard Quine's *Bell, Book and Candle* only one tiny tear reveals that her love for James Stewart has transmogrified her from witch to woman. In her candyfloss mask of a face, her eyes are tigerish. Her very deadpan is vehement. Even her passivity is a movement *inwards*, a retraction of being; the face preserves its smoothness while the mouth closes, like fingers into fist. It is this implacable loneliness which makes her surrender so touching, so total—a repudiation of her own depth. Her resonance as tragedienne is inseparable from her delectability as an erotic object (especially in *Vertigo* and *Pal Joey*, where her older rival, Rita Hayworth, forces her to renounce Sinatra by performing a striptease in front of him). And as she strips, she has, of course, to smile alluringly.

Her glamour is dazzle-camouflage for inner paralysis. Her 'style' —a quick hesitation followed by an almost laborious deliberateness —make of her both passive woman and vamp. Like Marilyn, she takes both traits to their extremes—but *both* traits, so that each renders the other as tantalizing as it is duplicitous, even, meaningless. Like Marilyn, she has a 'false' voice, a low whisper. But where Marilyn always breaks the dramatic tension by her deft, knowing, caricature of the 'dumb blonde', Kim remains the sumptuous puppet —and has *gravitas*.

She is of Marilyn's generation—which is also the generation of Brando and James Dean—the generation of the uprooted and the anxious, of psychological turbulence groping for words, of middle-class ideals and the city jungle, old and new morality, puritanism and fun morality, grey flannelry and beatnikery, interpenetrating and undermining one another. In their different sorts of loneliness, frozen Kim and dizzy Dean testify to the tensions, the confusions of identity characteristic of her time. In her enigmatic quality, Kim's is the swansong of the 'glum, deadpan' style which began in the early 40's and included such adherents as Alan Ladd, Veronica Lake, Gene Tierney and Audie Murphy. Its 'stonewalling' signified the impasse attained between the suburban cult whereby complacent optimism was *de rigeur*, and jungle toughness. The 'Method' was a reaction against both creeds, an attempt to rock-drill down through to the magma below. The 'Method' has bequeathed a new liveliness and warmth to America's younger generation, but its deeper possibilities, of an anti-conformist wisdom, have not prevailed. The comedians (like Jack Lemmon), and Kim's eternal hesitations, have proved truer after all.

Each glance of hers evoked the depths of pain which the Method endeavoured to explore. While Antonioni was still stumbling for an idiom, Kim, by her sheer presence, had brought the full lyrical weight of alienation to the screen.

The very perfection of style, in her 'classic' films (*Jeanne Eagels*, *Pal Joey*, *Vertigo*, *Middle of the Night* and Quine's *Strangers When We Meet* (1960), with George Sidney probably her most congenial director) leads to the current artistic crisis in her career. As her confidence and competence as an actress have increased, her magic has dimmed. She is in a transitional period, as awkward as that endured by Marlene in the early 40's. I believe that Kim's is essentially a tragic art (even in comedies, like Garbo's), that her creative essence is a struggle against some confusing hectic environment, and the inner turmoil it brings—whether it be some *Shanghai Express*, with spies and counter-spies, or a woman's prison in dire need of reform, or the John O'Hara country.

The reader will possibly ask himself whether all this lyricism about her isn't a delirium of interpretation, an intellectual's infatuation, quite unconnected with Hollywood's view of her, as crude as Harry Cohn's comment (to her face): 'You're only a lump of meat.' After writing this passage some time ago, I was both disturbed, and comforted, to come across Ezra F. Goodman's *The 50-Year Decline and Fall of Hollywood* (essential reading for anyone interested in the mass media) and to see how the comments made by George Sidney, Richard Quine and other Hollywood personalities suggested the responses described here.

Meanwhile, Elizabeth Taylor has become one of the most popular screen personalities, and, again, for good reason. In her teenage roles, during the late 40's, there seemed in her little more than plush glamour and a spiritual mediocrity, rendered only more banal by a trace of nervous pride and a sharp primness. But Richard Brooks' *Cat on a Hot Tin Roof* (1958) revealed a new nervous energy, doubtless distilled by the dissatisfactions of her private life. Currently her resonance for the masses is as the incarnation of middle-class femininity triumphantly capitulating to a post-Kinsey understanding of sexuality. Think of her roles: *Cat on a Hot Tin Roof* (a benevolent sexpot with a sulking husband), *Suddenly Last Summer* (a reputed nympho with a homosexual husband), *Butterfield 8* (a high-class call-girl—in the Kim country, here), and *Cleopatra* (the female tycoon in her Executive Bedroom). Through Liz Taylor, Golders Green bears the shock of Freud.

More paradoxical still was another critically unsung star, Jennifer Jones, lately too rarely on the screen. How aptly her very name combines ordinariness and gracefulness! She rose to stardom by playing St. Bernadette as simperingly as only Catholic lumpenhagiography and the Anglo-Saxon middle-classes could endure, and went on to writhe with animal lust as the half-breed 'devil's gal' of *Duel in the Sun*. More perhaps than any other star this apparently bland personality reveals a paradox of the American woman. In repose, her face suggests the complacent, slightly empty, idealism of middle-class America. Yet an oddly dry quality suggests a little sourness, a very carefully controlled egoism. The nervous movements of her beautiful mouth betray an intense dissatisfaction, and in King Vidor's *Ruby Gentry*, matched against Charlton Heston, she becomes demonic, a veritable Niagara of the revengeful eroticism which her own selfishness has frustrated.

Because she is so authentic in roles as diverse as Dieterle's *Love Letters*, Vidor's *Ruby Gentry* (1952), Johnson's *The Man in the Grey Flannel Suit* (1955) and Henry King's *Tender is the Night* (1961), her central presence makes each of these films an exploration of undertones in the other. The four heroines are the same girl's four possible existences in typical sectors of American society. Each film takes to its logical consequences the results of the development of the different impulses found in any American girl. Thus the group of films affords the European an insight into the American soul which, all things considered, few novelists can rival, least of all those lightweights like Salinger who become the cult-pets of European highbrows. These films together make 'the great American novel' superfluous.

Part Three

THE AESTHETICS OF HUMAN INTEREST

13 · People Look at People

We suggested, in our chapter on the stars, that academic criticism often finds itself trying to attribute to stylistic features in themselves (cutting, camera-angles, etc.) artistic effects whose origin is simpler and more obvious. It is in the spectator's sharing of, and concern for, the experience of *these* characters in *these* predicaments. It is a simple empathy-sympathy—and no more uncritical than is our sympathy for friends and acquaintances in real life.

Thus the spectator's response is largely to human experience. Undoubtedly this experience is nuanced by, affected by, 'seen through' all the 'secondary characteristics' of style—cutting, camera-angle and movements, and so on. But, in the dramatic films which are now the mainstream of the cinema, it is the function of these characteristics to relate themselves to, to build up, to add to, this 'resonance'. This resonance can be discussed only in moral-emotional terms. Its frame of reference is to a body of overt and covert feelings, assumptions, value-judgements, which an artist expects his spectators to share, through which he can appeal to them. Not only can he express his feelings to them, he can express their feelings for them, stimulate questions, affirmations, negations.

Certainly, every spectator is a unique individual, who will react in his own way to a film and in no one else's. None the less, culture, in the broader sense, exists in order to create just such a 'field' of agreements, to which the film-maker, the poet, the painter, and, more mysteriously perhaps, the abstract painter and the composer, can appeal.

If we avoid here any discussion of how 'visual music' can refer to our emotions and ideas, it is because it would lead us to a discussion of basic musical aesthetic. But our chase has another end in view.

Some films are 'abstract' (like *Begone Dull Care*; rhythmic cutting may create effects which are felt by the spectator as distinctly 'musical'). Our remarks here are intended to apply to the 'dramatic', the story-telling cinema, which has, for obvious reasons, been its mainstream, both as an art form and as a phenomenon in mass culture.

This moral-emotional-intellectual stratum identifies with the whole interplay of culture and human nature. It is probably this stratum which certain critics mean when they speak of 'literary content' as distinct from 'style'. To qualify it as 'literary' is particularly misleading, because it also underlies other arts. After all, music, and abstract painting, though consisting largely, if not entirely, of 'style-without-literary-content', are authentic 'humanist' activities, not just stylistic games. And this stratum underlies not only the 'arts' but the entire texture of political thought, of everyday living, and so on. One might call it 'human content', provided that one remembers that it is created out of style as well as out of the patterns of the story.

Currently the various academic approaches to art show two main approaches. The first is a way of, as it were, 'frisking' a film for various characteristics which are taken to be 'touchstones' of artistic quality. Thus the spectator tends to look for certain evidences of stylistic nuance (sensitive acting, camera-movements, etc.), and, if he doesn't find them, to refuse to lend his feelings to the characters and their story in the film. Another reaction is to take the characters and their story for granted, to concentrate thought on 'deep meanings', general ideas, significances of one sort or another. We parallel the first course in considering the role of style in the cinema, the second in our discussion of stars, where we discussed certain 'sociological resonances' at the expense, perhaps, of thinking about *these* characters in *this* predicament. This section aims to repair this omission, and indicate how diverse aesthetic elements dovetail.

Even here, current academic criteria lead to a continued 'sideslip' of interest. In a lecture to the British Society of Aesthetics, Barbara Hardy quoted the case of the student of literature who, too well drilled in exegesis asked, in all earnestness, 'What is *the meaning* of the handkerchief which Oliver gives Fagin?' Everything is a symbol for something, nothing is part of the ordinary flow of living in the 'outside', 'non-significant', physical world. Often characters too dissolve in a haze of abstract generalization.

Our criticism, here, is not of the presence of 'extra' meanings, whether of stylistic nuance, or of symbolic extension, but of a curious devaluation of the obvious, mainstream components of art—a devaluation which reveals itself also in a kind of non-response to works of art which are neither subtle stylistically (or are subtle in unexpected and therefore unnoticed ways), nor rich in 'deep' meanings, or general ideas.

However, the general public focuses primarily on the personal story, and cares first and foremost for the main, 'unsubtle' experiences, the obvious, 'superficial' issues. This is not to say that general ideas are of no interest to him. But he doesn't seek them out; usually they have to manifest themselves as part of the personal problems of the characters, or be heavily emphasized, if they are to become, for him, part of his experience. From his point of view, no quality of nuance or symbolism can save a dreary personal story. But a sharp personal story with neither 'nuance' nor 'significance' will be lived through wholeheartedly, and, in consequence, more 'profoundly' than the 'profound' story.

The university graduate in literature, as a result of his special and prolonged cultural training, may go so far as to refuse to respond to any story which doesn't seem to satisfy the various criteria which he has been taught are distinctions between 'good' and 'bad' art. If a film has no 'significance', if its psychology is fairly straightforward, and if the emotions depicted are rather basic and familiar, he will be unable to take it seriously. Its lack of 'texture' kills it. He can't get involved or concerned. The film doesn't dissolve into the hallucinatory reality of its action. He may feel that such a film can't feel 'real' to anyone at all.

It is true that many popular films are well below the level of sophistication which their audiences can handle. But here we must add a caveat. The emotional response to a purely 'personal' story is no less genuine than the response to a 'meaning', and no less complex or profound. Worse, what academics accept as a 'deep' meaning is often only a generalization educed from the personal story. It adds nothing to its texture, and as a 'meaning', i.e. stated concisely, is often banal, silly or false. Only its context, the personal story, gives it what life or meaning it has. Thus the 'deep' meaning is very often 'parasitic'. It is *less* profound than a 'merely superficial' story.

Similarly, the fact that emotions depicted in a film are unsubtle does not mean that they are unreal. Many critics seem amazingly loath to allow that films which bore them can and do stir the ordinary spectator in a deep and generous way. They sometimes write as if the various entertainment media were one gigantic hoax of which the public was victim. Yet it seems curious to allow to modern publicity methods a potency far greater than that which one denies to entertainments. It seems odder that such writers so crudely oscillate between the view of the public as hoaxed and bored, and the view of the public as helplessly hypnotized and influenced by, the mass media.

Without going into all the ins and outs of these very complicated subjects, we would make the suggestion that, from the viewpoint of the larger public, there isn't a great deal of difference, in the quantity and quality of emotion aroused, between many merely popular films, and many of those which the most stringent critic will call an enduring classic. Academic aesthetics are so concerned with proving that certain films are better than others, that they sideslip, as it were, into the proposition that films which aren't *la crème de la crème* aren't even milk. They try to attribute the whole effect of the exceptional film entirely to the subtleties which make it more interesting to them than the stylistically more 'superficial' film meant for Mr. and Mrs. Bloggs, who haven't enjoyed the advantages of a three-year, full-time, examination-forced course of study in English literature, and simply respond, as people, to people. But maybe the exceptional film has a great deal of common ground with the relatively 'simple' film. And vice versa.

In the same way, apologists for 'sweetness-and-light' often inform us that only 'great art' is 'universal' in appeal. But so is melodrama. Indeed, the crude unconscious fantasies embodied in *Dracula* are incomparably wider in appeal, and for that matter more relevant to the ordinary problems of living, than the complex cultural configurations constructed by, say, Joyce or Eliot.

Similarly, it is often said that 'great art' 'lasts' and is 'immortal'. This may be so, although 'immortal' is arguably an exaggeration, and even Shakespeare doesn't mean to today's audiences what it meant to Shakespeare's. Shakespeare is dead, long live Shakespeare. But the fact that a film won't be 'alive' in 2067 doesn't mean that it isn't alive now. We need, surely as well as a 'discriminatory' aesthetic, an aesthetic which doesn't have to pretend that works of art which are merely mortal aren't at this moment alive.

Thus it seems important that one should, without denying or dismissing the superior subtlety of some films, find an aesthetic which can take into account the 'non-subtle' wavebands of middle- and lowbrow art and folk art. This section comprises approaches towards that aesthetic.

14 · Tales versus Novels

The Biblical story of Samson and Delilah is told so briefly that no publisher would accept it as even the synopsis of a novel. As an inevitable consequence of its brevity, the characterization is sketchy and vague, the 'motivation' nil, the whole lacking in convincing detail, or indeed, any detail at all.

The same synopsis, in the hands of three different novelists, could not but acquire three different themes, three different sets of characters, three different sequences of psychological cause-and-effect; three different 'contents'. Yet it is its sketchy, 'contentless' form that has intrigued generation upon generation of readers.

For the 'tale', bare as it is, intrigues, and communicates, by its structure of paradoxes. An (a) *weak* woman conquers a (a1) *strong* man. He (b) *knows* she is an enemy, but (b1) *acquieses.* His (a2) *strength* lies in his (a3) *weakest* part (his hair). When at his (a4) *weakest* (blind), he proves (a5) *strongest*, annihilating all his (b2) *enemies*, his (b3) *loved enemy* and (b4) *himself.* The 'eloquence' of the story is in its tension of paradoxes.

The 'tale', a genre distinct from the novel (and far from obsolescent, even though the novel evolved from it) conforms to the comments of Aristotle in his *Poetics*. 'There are therefore necessarily six elements in every tragedy, which give it its quality; and they are the Fable, Character, Language, Thought, *Mise-en-Scène* and Melody. . . . The chief of these is the plotting of the incidents . . . the fable ought to have been so plotted that if one heard the bare facts, the chain of circumstances would make one shudder and pity. This would happen to anyone who heard the fable of the *Oedipus*' (or of *Samson and Delilah*). Similarly, writes La Charrière, for the reading public of the fourth century A.D., 'whether pagan or Christian, no *Life* of a sage or saint could possess an *edifying* quality unless it had first the quality of *amazement* and conformed to the laws of the aretological genre, laws as strict and binding as the literary conventions which apply today as, for example, in the detective story'.

Myths, fairy tales and folk art generally conform to the same aesthetic. The tales of the Round Table, of Aladdin's Magic Lamp, of the Magic Tinderbox, the tales of Greek myths and Norse Gods are sequences of vivid, powerful situations and paradoxes.

Similarly with characterization. From *Sir Gawayne and the Green Knight* through the tale of Patient Griselda in Chaucer's *The Canterbury Tales,* through Mary Shelley's *Frankenstein* down to, say, Joseph Heller's *Catch 22,* many authors have sought, similarly, the 'striking fable', using either exaggeration or the bold, haunting idea. The 'poetry' is in the paradoxes of the plot.

Jean Cocteau's comment in *Opium* reminds us of the prevalence of this aesthetic in our oral culture, and of its incessant infiltrations into 'high culture'. 'I have come to know Eisenstein. I had seen aright. He invented the murder steps at the last moment. Those steps became part of Russian history. Alexandre Dumas and Eisenstein are the only true historians. . . . Tragic events have the power of those little obscene anecdotes, anonymous anecdotes which are perfected from one mouth to another and finish as the typical stories of a race. Jewish stories or Marseilles stories.' Some other modern 'tales': Dr. Crippen, the Angels of Mons, the Wreck of the Mary Deare, Casey Jones, Frankie and Johnny, Stephen Ward. . . .

In such tales, detailed characterization, where it exists at all, is of secondary interest. But even where authors and spectators are interested in character, such characters, by current academic standards, are 'two-dimensional'. Ulysses, Gawayne, most of Chaucer's pilgrims, Sir Epicure Mammon, Sir Toby Belch, Tom Jones, Mr. Micawber and Sherlock Holmes are, essentially, 'bas-reliefs', rather than 3-dimensional in the modern sense. Sharply realistic details exist in, for example, Defoe's *Robinson Crusoe* and Richardson's *Clarissa Harlowe,* but those exegeses which seek to establish a continuous 'stream' of subtleties smack of special pleading. These early novels are just as limited, just as complex, as L'il Abner or James Bond. 'The popular imagination . . .' writes Louis James of nineteenth-century proletarian tastes, 'is interested in character conceived on a simple, well-defined place, which exists independently of a complex literary form. All popular heroes have been subjects of prolonged story cycles, whether *Odysseus*, King Arthur, Sexton Blake or *The Archers*, the successful English radio serial.'

To the aesthetic of the 'tale' academic culture has, by and large, turned a blind eye. As recently as my grammar school days, English masters instructed us all in the necessity for realistic and deep characterization, logically consistent behaviour, penetrating studies of motive, and that proliferation of vivid detail suggested by Henry James's phrase, 'density of specification'. We were besought to insist upon the 'texture of lived experience', and many of the exegeses we studied had strained to detect such 'density' in such improbable places as folk ballads, or Chaucer's tale of Patient Griselda. Yet it was curious that, rich and complex as was the showpiece of the 'complexity' school, *Hamlet*, each critic struggled to isolate its hero's 'real' motives, to simplify, to synopsize, him into a figure almost as systematic and simple as another famous procrastinator, L'il Abner. For, as Erich Auerbach remarked in his study of the development of European literary realism, 'To write history is so difficult that most historians are forced to make concessions to the technique of legend.'

Nowadays, of course, the 'tale' aesthetic has taken on a new vigour. Science fiction offers a particularly clear example of popular art's inheritance from folk art. A science fiction story may be written in a merely competent style, with scarcely adequate characterization, and yet fascinate and haunt the reader because of the inventiveness with which the author has developed his central 'extrapolation' (or integrated his cluster of them). The ideas have an eloquence apart from the 'density of detail' ('style'). The plays of Ionescou depend, to a great extent, on their qualities of 'tale'. And though the 'texture of lived experience' remains important, the study of motivation through literature has, and it's high time, been overtaken by psychology, sociology, and various other branches of the 'humanities'.

The quality of the tale of Samson and Delilah lies in its paradoxes. Similarly, complexity in 'tale' characterization, where it is present, arises not from meticulously stated detail, but from contradictory traits which build up the tension of paradox. The Frankenstein Monster is *brutal* but *pathetic*; he's a *creature* who masters his *creator*; he's brute *material* capable of a lofty *idealism* that turning *sour* makes him a *devil*—but a *sympathetic* one. Sherlock Holmes is, overtly, far less complex than the Monster. (Mainly: his acumen assorts oddly with such weaknesses as morphine-taking, his non-emotionality with his violin-playing.) But his very *extremism* is, judged by ordinary human preoccupations, if not actually a paradox, a challenge, a shock. It haunts.

Ours is a 'realistic' age, which means, in effect, that we like our fantasies to be readily identifiable as such, and to be realistic in their details (requirements now being challenged by the literature of the absurd). Outside such overt fantasies (e.g. *King Kong*) 'extremism' stops short of the (to us) outrageous implausibilities of, say, Chaucer's Patient Griselda story, which, ontologically, is half-way between a 'realistic tale' and the Byzantine fairy-story on which it is based (and, it may be added, a very awkward half-way indeed).

Similarly, a film story which is, essentially, a 'good tale', may be mistakenly dismissed as a 'bad novel'.

15 · Paradox cut Paradox

The Wicked Lady: a female highwayman. *It's Great to Be Young*: schoolboys on strike. In *The Bridge on the River Kwai*, the inflexible Briton becomes a quisling, the academic becomes a callous man of action, and the egoistic American dies doing his duty, obeying some moral pressure as impalpable as it is irresistible. All three heroes are traitors to themselves.

None of these films takes the easiest path to their surprise. The 'obvious' solution to the paradoxes of *The Wicked Lady* is, 'Oh, make her a bit of a tomboy, say she's always lived poor and rough.' But no; she's ladylike too, and far from having lived rough, has lived 'stuffy'. In such films the tensions are held together within a 'melodramatic' framework. In *Kwai* it is not the English Colonel's idealism that changes, but the object of his idealism. A slow change of situation turns *him* round. The limits and paradoxes of character are explored almost without introversion or 'detail', but by the 'demonstrative intermeshing' of character and circumstance.

Many vulgar films have the eloquence of multiple paradox. Thus, in Poe's *The Fall of the House of Usher*, as adapted by Richard Matheson for Roger Corman's film, a sensitive brother is so devoted to his invalid sister that he buries her before she's dead. What he thinks are the sounds of the evil ghost in her coffin are the living woman's futile struggles to escape. His mistake comes half-true; for burial alive renders her mad, malicious, an evil spirit. His—deserved—reward for his too-devoted care is—she strangles him (a reversal of 'invalid' weakness . . .).

Regularly, terrible fates from tiny errors grow. Give an inch, fate takes a mile. Fate is your own little slips writ large. Many a film is built on the crescendo of an original surprise, on a series of patterns like the inversions of a musical phrase in a symphony. The bitter bit, sudden reversals of fortune, sins coming home to rest, getting more than you bargained for, being beaten at your own game, losing what you love too much—all these, and many other dramatic ironies or 'reversals of expectation'—form the emotional substructure of most tales. It is by constantly inverting the basic situation that the 'simple, striking' idea can come to lift so heavy, so complex and ambivalent a load of feelings.

Often the pattern, or parts of it, is consciously noticed by the audience. Often it is unnoticed. Discussing his novel *Les Enfants Terribles* in *Opium*, Jean Cocteau remarks: 'I did not know that the book began with a white ball, ended with a black ball, and that Dargelos sent both of them. The premeditated look of instinctive equilibrium.' Generally the underlying symmetries are not felt as such, but form the 'skeleton' of a set of clashes, contracts, sharp reversals, plausible surprises, etc., on which the audience concentrates. But the 'structure' gives the film its cumulative effect.

Forms of paradox-within-consistency seems in some ways well fitted to the dynamic ambivalence of human nature, its warp and woof of opposing instincts. In other words, the violent vulgarity of a a 'bad taste' film may be profounder than a shallow rationalistic concern for 'psychological consistency'.

Throughout Thorold Dickinson's Victorian thriller, *Gaslight*, Anton Walbrook suavely bullies his sweet, ailing, submissive wife (Diana Wynyard). There is a little crescendo of humiliations disguised as 'fatherly kindness'. He humiliates her, first, in private, then before the servants, then in public at a concert. He decides to kill her dog (death introducing a deeper tone, but not yet, directed at *her*). Then we realize that he is deliberately using her fear of madness to drive her mad (a typical 'paradox'). At last we understand he is a murderer trying to have his inconvenient wife certified insane. But even when a detective opens her eyes to her husband's true nature and motives, she cannot cease being submissive: 'After all, he is my husband.' He is overpowered by the police, and tied to a chair. Left alone with his wife, he commands her to cut him free. Obediently she advances towards him with a knife. But an abrupt change comes over her, and instead she goes as if to plunge it into his heart. A close-up shows his face bursting out into sweat and we are almost sure she has actually stabbed him. But no. He bursts free, with terrified strength, from his bonds. Will he attack her? No, his fear has driven him mad, inoffensively so, for he is in a world of illusion, beyond fear. . . .

These quick dramatic reversals at the climax bring out what earlier were 'undercurrents' in the characterization. To be as submissive and unsuspecting as she was, not to recognize her husband's bullying for what it was, the wife had to be a bit of a ninny, or, in modern terms, paralysed by some unconscious guilt on which he plays. This comes to a peak when she knows that he is deliberately destroying her, but can't betray him—a Dostoievskian loyalty-masochism. Here the audience does see her as slightly 'mad', though it is a madness with which they have no difficulty in sympathizing. The very 'excess' of her loyalty hints at an instability—which in turn makes plausible her sudden reversal into sadism. When *he's* helpless, she bullies him—and he effectively suffers the fate he meant for her. This double reversal is plausible only because the film, sensitively played and directed, has hinted at the chinks in his armour through such details as the suppressed excitement (hysteria) that seethes in his voice in his moments of affected rage, and his cynical flirtation with a tough Cockney maid who stands up for herself, surprisingly effectively, against the 'despot'. All these 'premonitions' of reversal—the wife's excessive docility, the husband's rage and affair—are so plotted as, until the end, to make the reversal for which we desperately long less likely than ever. But, once the reversal has happened, it feels right. The 'undertow' suddenly emerges in response to changed circumstances. The wife's frightening violence is really a 'straight line' continuation of her eerie passivity.

In a sense, the film is perfectly conventional melodrama. The husband's motivations are straightforward crookery, the wife's responses are those of a stereotype Victorian wife. Yet, for most of its length, the film shows nothing more than a husband bullying his wife. The opening murder has warned us that 'something is up' (though we don't know the husband's the murderer), so that the audience doesn't ask for the husband's psychological 'motive' in bullying his wife. The 'mysteriousness' of the unsolved murder creates a mood in which his behaviour is acceptably arbitrary. The fact of a murder places the audience squarely in a land where the most pathological behaviour needs no explanation. None the less, if we cut out the detective theme, and just showed the domestic scenes, we would find ourselves investigating a Strindbergian aspect of human nature. The melodrama is in a sense, 'obscurantist', in re-routing this investigation to conventional 'circuits'. Despite this, the film arouses excitement, participation, concern, by the paradoxes of its 'human interest'.

The film goes to some trouble to introduce lighter scenes. For example, a detective meets the wife in a street-garden, and strikes up an acquaintance with her by playing on her repressed but intense longing for children. Such scenes lighten the atmosphere. But by re-asserting the wife's 'undertow' of normality, and her desires for happiness, they also 'tighten the screw'. Her tragedy is not that of a neurotic, but that of a normal woman who is being bullied into neurosis. We touch on a lowbrow characteristic; any kink, any paradox, of behaviour is easily understood and accepted provided that it is put within a framework of conventional ideas and provided that it is fairly directly related to deep, straight emotional drives—love, cruelty, loyalty, fear, greed, altruism, revenge, envy, etc. In other words, the lowbrow audience, by and large, accepts pathological behaviour as normal when it is presented as the outcome of a conflict between strong, normal drives, or between a passionate temperament and unfavourable circumstances. They may lose interest when the artist presents neurosis but omits to establish its roots in an essential, instinctual normality. In a general way, we may say that the lowbrow insists on a psychological *classicism*. He is interested only in those exceptions which illustrate a general rule. From another angle, he will mobilize his sympathies only when the eccentric is shown as having common ground with his own interests—'normality'. This normality need not be asserted by the script. The acting of Brando, Dean, Bardot, Kirk Douglas, Bette Davis and many other stars is in itself a powerful reassertion of a basic biological passion and vigour, and, given such an actor, the script can emphasize abnormality almost to its heart's content.

When Claude Chabrol and Eric Rohmer noticed some of the moral symmetries and patterns in Hitchcock's films, the general highbrow English reaction was to dismiss their exegeses as over-subtle, eccentric, brilliant-but-slightly-mad, and so on. Maybe their insistence on two particular patterns—the transference of guilt, and the severe justice of some metaphysical moral fate—was questionable, but in principle they are quite right. Indeed the patterns they detect in Hitchcock's films appear in very many others. The 'transference of guilt', for example, appears in *Gaslight*—the saintly wife has her terrible split-second paroxysm, and in that split second she effectively does unto her husband as he would have done unto her. Another common pattern arises when a film's hero and villain are 'moral anagrams' of each other, as we shall see in more detail in our analysis of an American Western.

Over the last decade or so, the ordinary run of entertainment films have steadily been availing themselves of the moral sophistication long enjoyed by novelists and by the 'art' film. The old 'soot-and-whitewash' polarity inherited from Victorian ideas has all but disappeared. American films, notably, still observe careful 'structures' of moral sympathy, structures which, at their best, are neither simple nor naïve, and have a genuine relevance to the complexities of living. They not infrequently have the effect of cramping those subjects which, for one reason or another, require the spectator to look at human nature in an amoral, or morally sophisticated, way, without, or before, passing any judgement at all, or to altogether separate attitudes to a character's traits from attitudes to a character as a whole. In American films, characters are too readily 'subsumed by' their dominant moral traits for such purposes, which currently are culturally central. The European cinema (even, now, the British) has greater fluidity, and it seems to me that the root cause is not the 'imbecility' of Hollywood, but more deeply-rooted American attitudes.

It may for this reason be all the more interesting to look at the structure of 'character anagrams'—the anagram being a form of paradox—in an American Western, which is fairly typical in having (*a*) a villain-hero polarity and (*b*) a careful moral hierarchy—that is, in being at a transition stage between the complacency of 'soot-and-whitewash' and a morally more fluid complexity and self-questioning. Both tensions are, I suggest, perceptible in the film, to the average uneducated spectator. Not that he sees, or even feels that the hero and the villain are 'brothers under the skin'. He feels that they are poles apart, even despite the common traits which give the film its hidden unity. But Mr. and Mrs. Bloggs sense the moral questioning through notable *parts* of the moral pattern—e.g. the 'guilty' past of hero and heroine, and the very intricacy of the intrigue between characters who 'shade' from one end of the moral spectrum to the other. Such partial similarities, coupled with violent conflicts, give the film the morally tense, enigmatic, bitter, air, characteristic of American films of the period. The film is Nicholas Ray's *Johnny Guitar* (1950), written by Philip Yordan whom we have already noticed as a minor, but competent, *auteur*.

16 · Theme and Variations

Our first glimpse of Johnny (Sterling Hayden) shows us a sad, forlorn fellow, riding slowly, aimlessly, along a dusty trail. He is conspicuously gunless, and unable to intervene in a stagecoach hold-up nearby. He accepts his helplessness with a philosophical detachment—resignation? cynicism? both? He strolls into an opulent gambling-house and humbly asks for a job. Its owner appears—an adventuress named Vienna (Joan Crawford), who is clad in what is virtually a masculine rig-out (black shirt, trousers, boots and guns) and behaves in a hard, bossy way. Her customers include a tough, brawling gang of outlaws— Black Bart (Ernest Borgnine), their boss, the Dancin' Kid (Scott Brady) and a teenager, Turkey (Ben Cooper). Black Bart hates everybody and is always on the look-out for someone whom he can bully. The Dancin' Kid is Vienna's prospective lover, while Turkey boyishly adores her. The hero makes a startling entry into this tough company—with a blue cup of coffee in one hand, a cigarette in another, no guns and a meek, smiling manner. When the others try to pick a quarrel with him, he asks mildly, 'What more can a man want than a cup of coffee and a smoke?' Black Bart sees a likely victim in this thoroughly castrated fellow (jobless, gunless, sexless) and sets about getting him drunk by plying him with whiskies and ordering the hero to consume them—which the latter obediently does.

The theme-song (sung over the credits), the casting (Sterling Hayden usually plays unromantic toughies), the actor's personality and the hero's calm self-possession keep reminding us that Johnny Guitar is the film hero and hinting that he'll come out all right in the end. Still, the audience is mystified and full of curiosity as to what, if anything, the hero's motives can be for his strange mildness and gunlessness. They fear he will take his line of conduct to the point of being thoroughly craven. They wonder whether they despise him, and are mildly mystified to find that they don't. Of course, it isn't long before he and Black Bart swap punches and, in a man-to-man fist-fight, the latter is shown up as a blubbering coward, though still so spiteful and treacherous as to be very dangerous.

Here then we have the thoroughly conventional contrast between the pacifistic but tough hero, and the bellicose but weak villain. All the same, the film has introduced it with a very unsettling 'excess'. One line of dialogue establishes a social-philosophical reason, of sorts, for Johnny's inoffensiveness. Why did he give up carrying a gun? 'Because I'm not the fastest draw west of the Pecos.' In other words, 'if I threaten nobody by disarming myself, I shall provoke no one and live, whereas if I carry guns I shall lose my immunity and meet my match eventually.' The audience thinks of his gunlessness as a deliberate, reasoned-out point of view. Later in the film this position is shown to be just a pretence, or, at most, a subsidiary reason. Still, for the moment, the encounter between Black Bart and Johnny has the quality of a collision of points of view, of ways of life. Throughout the film, Johnny is, vaguely, peace-loving modern man, the man with the grey flannel gunlessness. More specifically, he refuses to be aggressive, or warlike, for sensible, though unidealistic, reasons.

A few minutes later, in another scene, this interpretation is sharply contradicted. Turkey is showing off his marksmanship to Vienna; suddenly Johnny snatches up a gun, outshoots, humiliates and wounds him—indeed, only a sternly shouted warning from Vienna stops him killing the boy. Immediately after his violent impulse, Johnny is suitably contrite, or at least ashamed. This incident paraphrases, and leads into an exposition of, why Johnny and Vienna ended a previous love affair years ago. He is really Johnny Logan, who was not just a crack gun fighter, but actually gun-crazy, an instinctive killer. In a sense, he was, and, under pressure of jealousy, is, blacker than Black Bart: for whereas Black Bart is satisfied with bluster and humiliation, Johnny immediately snatches up a gun, without warning, to kill. Of course, he doesn't forfeit our sympathy: in the first place, he has renounced killing, his current pacifism is an expiation of his previous bloodthirstiness; in the second, he struggles against his psychological taint; in the third, even when unarmed, he is courageous.

Vienna's black, mannish, villain's clothes express one level of her character. Here is your American matriarch, woman as owner and boss, wearing not only the pants but the six-shooters. She and the hero have exchanged roles. She is tough and mannish to a fault, he is passive and inoffensive to a fault. But just as his outburst with Turkey reveals the turbulent virility beneath, so it isn't long before she too reveals that her masculinity represses an 'excessive' playing of the female role. Their debate over their past love-affair, and whose fault it was that they parted, provides a great deal of additional information about their 'present' characters. Although retrospective, their quick, sharp accusations and retorts set up a suspense of moral sympathies and a suspense of 'hope' about their chances of resuming their love affair and finding happiness. The heroine leaves us in no doubt about her past: during the conversation she wears a scarlet dress, and when explaining how she rose to become a woman of property, she cries, 'For each brick, each plank, each beam of this place, I——' He cuts in sadly: 'Don't. . . .'

The general impression we get from the conversation is that for their parting he must take most of the blame. Their past relationship is a 'complement' of their present one. Then he was emotionally hard, she was vulnerable and womanly. Now, emotionally, he is 'subject' to her, having no guns and no job. His 'castration' is really a moral penance. His 'civilized' point of view is really guilt, 'imposed' on him by a woman—or rather, by his harshness towards her in the past, leading up to her present re-rejection of him.

Later in the film, when she and Johnny seem to be coming together again, she changes to a white, full, feminine dress which might be a wedding dress, even a kind of virginity. She is seized by the townsfolk, who truss her up in it to lynch her, but saved by Johnny. She finally reverts to her masculine clothes for the film's climax, a gunfight between herself and the film's principal villain, another matriarch, Emma (Mercedes McCambridge). So there are really three Viennas—Vienna the bad (wo)man in black, Vienna the scarlet (Scarlett) woman, and virginal Vienna, made to be martyred.

Emma, a 'pioneer' type, wears a plain, full-skirted dress and has a raucous, corncrake voice. She is in Vienna's age-bracket, is plump and plain, but very susceptible to the charms of the Dancin' Kid, who, however, resolutely prefers Vienna. Emma is a spinster-cum-harpy, hating the Dancin' Kid and Vienna both, and constantly urging the decent but weak sheriff to arrest them: finally she does persuade him to lynch her rival. Apparently homely, feminine, ascetic and virtuous, she is really more dominating and destructive than Vienna. Vienna is a mannish matriarch and ex-prostitute, but love restores the wedding-dress woman she is at heart. She has pacified a vicious killer (Johnny). On the other hand, Emma's love has turned to hate: the Dancin' Kid 'makes her feel like a woman, and she don't like it, so she wants to hang him'. She doesn't get much sympathy for her frustration, for her personality assures us that her 'love' was never very generous anyway. And whereas Vienna's influence is pacificatory, Emma turns peaceful citizens (sheriff and posse) into vicious killers (lynch law).

When Vienna is seized by the posse, Emma gleefully takes potshots at the gambling-house chandelier (Prohibition-style) and watches the place burn down. It is these flames which, after Vienna has been rescued from the posse, set fire to the train of her white dress. For the lynching, the posse wear ultra-respectable black (having just come from a funeral). And after Vienna has been nearly hanged in her white dress, she is nearly burnt alive in it. Black slacks are certainly more practical in the land of gunfire and fire.

The lynching also retrospectively 'palliates' Johnny's vicious attack on Turkey. Emma's posse find Turkey hiding in Vienna's saloon (very much a son-and-mother situation). They half-promise to pardon him if he frames Vienna. He appeals to her. It's his life or hers, he's only a boy, what should he do. The appeal to Vienna's maternal instinct is of couree thoroughly treacherous. She answers curtly, 'Save yourself.' Emma double-crosses Turkey and persuades the reluctant posse to hang them both. Turkey is hanged, but just as the noose lifts Vienna out of the saddle, Johnny, who has been hiding nearby, cuts her down with a knife, snatches her up on his horse, and rides away. When Vienna asks him why he didn't save Turkey first, he points out that he had to choose between saving him or saving her (he hadn't a gun, only a knife to cut the noose—another 'inversion' of his being unarmed). His calculation is chilly but reasonable. And it's justice: Johnny's choice ('which shall I save?') is an inversion of the choice which Turkey treacherously shifted to Vienna. But, also, Johnny has now done, with every sort of justification, what he nearly did at the beginning, that is, get rid of Turkey and keep Vienna for himself.

The most emphatic antagonisms in the film are between Black Bart and Johnny Guitar, and between Emma Small and Vienna. Black Bart and Emma are both plumper, less attractive and more vicious than their opposite numbers. Emma is a frustrated spinster and a defeated gunslinger, whereas Vienna has lived out her desire to a fault (the scarlet dress, the badman kit). Johnny Guitar and the Dancin' Kid both have 'musical' names, as if to stress their decorative, i.e. sexual, appeal. Both are very dangerous—we have no doubt that the lithe Dancin' Kid would make short work of Black Bart. Both are rivals for Vienna, both are gunslingers. But the obvious dramatic conflict, between Johnny and the Dancin' Kid, is by-passed until near the end, when their gunfight is stopped by Vienna, who sets them both to helping her prepare breakfast instead, a nice housewifely-matriarchal touch. The Dancin' Kid is then accidentally shot by Emma, who appropriately mistakes him for Johnny Guitar. The emotional expectation of a gunfight, set up in the audience as Johnny and the Dancin' Kid bicker, is disappointed, but 'shifted' over into the climactic fight between the two gun-totin' Mommas.

So Johnny Guitar is 'patterned' not only by Black Bart, but also by the Dancin' Kid. And his encounter with Turkey has another undertone. For at this point both are 'subservient' to Vienna—Turkey because he is only a teenager, Johnny because he is a saddle-tramp. Turkey is the 'good' boy, Johnny is the vicious boy who has rejected his mother, made her a prostitute and now seeks reinstatement. In a limited sense, Turkey and Johnny are two 'sons', competing for 'mother'. But, of course, Johnny is older than Turkey, more experienced and formidable, and has had a previous love affair with Vienna. So, in a way, he is a father-figure to Turkey, just as Vienna is a mother-figure. According to Freud, authority-figures, in melodramas as in dreams, tend to be parental figures, so that the Sheriff is another weak father-figure, constantly being egged on by Emma, the 'housewifely mother'.

Vienna even has a father-figure; one of the employees at her gambling house is Old Tom (John Carradine), a lonely old man who dies trying to save Vienna. There is a fourth member of the gang, Cory (Royal Dano), not unlike Old Tom in being self-effacing and unaggressive. At every opportunity he buries himself in a good book —an 'intellectual', thoughtful streak recalling Johnny's 'musical' name. He shows the risks of being thoughtful and quiet by getting himself treacherously shot by Black Bart.

We have presented these patterns in terms of similarities—but only so as to show that these patterns do exist. None the less, the first impression they give is that of strong contrasts. The similarity is there to establish the tension of the dissimilarity. We don't feel Black Bart and Johnny Guitar, or Vienna and Emma, or Emma and Black Bart, as being 'the same, but different'—quite the reverse, it's a case of 'similar poles repel'. Our patterns of similarities are also patterns of differences. . . .

17 · The Emotional Flow

Although *Johnny Guitar* is shaped around a very forceful 'goodies-baddies' polarity, the pattern of emotional shocks and paradoxes is both involved and nuanced. It must be said that the plot is unusually complicated, so much that some of the conflicts are worked through very rapidly, in an almost schematic way, and only half-involve the spectator. This is not a negative criticism, for, being half-serious, they act as a streak of 'comedy-thriller', inculcating a satirical attitude towards the characters. Black Bart, for example, is the butt of a great many laughs, like Cory and, to a lesser extent, the Dancin' Kid.

The dramatis personae fall into three main groups: (1) the gang of outlaws; (2) the townsfolk; (3) the people who live at the gambling house (notably Vienna and Johnny). We might say that the gang groups four 'outlaw' attitudes; the townsfolk are 'respectability', with both its good aspects (the posses are decent at heart, though weak) and its bad one (Emma is frustrated and vindictive); while the denizens of the gambling house are outcasts but not outlaws—individuality with all its faults—and they are the most generous individuals in the film.

Each of the groups is split within itself. Johnny is Vienna's ally in some ways but her antagonist in others. Emma is constantly bullying the posse. The gang, as befitting lawless characters, mostly hate one another, and are constantly bickering. The egghead is less aggressive, but resolutely ignores them, preferring to lose himself in a good book, so perhaps he's just as egoistic. Even so, the discussion is far from schematic—the three groups are unified by 'overlapping' characters, e.g. Turkey (who in some ways is attached to Vienna, in others to the gang) or the Sheriff (who tries to stand up for Vienna and Johnny against Emma).

Each of the principal characters is split within himself. In a sense, each character is a group of characters. There are three Viennas—black Vienna, scarlet Vienna, white Vienna. Each is a different aspect of the same woman, just as Black Bart 'is' a different aspect of Johnny Guitar. Just as each group of characters is a set of variations on a common theme, so each character is a set of variations on a common theme. Very simple melodramas characteristically have the equation, 'one person = one attitude', but a film like *Johnny Guitar*, though, really, a melodrama, has left this primitive level of meaning far behind, it has a lively and stimulating chop and change of emotional permutations.

The emotional pattern is further variegated by the 'infrastructure' of audience response. At first we feel sorry for Turkey, admire his pluck and dislike the hero for humiliating him. We are mildly surprised to find this nice lad is in cahoots with Black Bart and the Dancin' Kid. We hope, we're sure, that he'll reform and save himself. But later the very vulnerability which we pitied betrays the heroine—we may still feel pity for him, but have to admit that his being hanged is poetic justice. The character-trait persists, but, as circumstances 'test' and reveal it, so our attitudes to it change. The audience's feelings towards the characters are like 'invisible' characters in the drama.

All this may seem to be getting us into very deep waters. But in fact scriptwriters swim happily about them every day. When adapting a novel for the screen, one often combines two characters—a 'group of characters'—into one person. Or one abolishes a character, but, feeling one particular aspect of his attitudes is important, transfers the relevant dialogue to another character. Or one may make two hitherto 'unrelated' characters 'accomplices', which one can do only if they have some common interest or attitude, i.e. are 'variations on a theme'. Or one may write in a character so that his 'attitude' will bring to the audience a new range of emotions. Any writer, often quite consciously, whether he is writing a film, a novel or a play, will invent a character whose job is to symbolize a particular response to the problem which comprises the film's theme. Literature abounds in friends, servants, confidantes, etc., whose function is to act as emotional counterpoint to the heroes. Juliet—virginal romantic passion—has an earthily Rabelaisian Nurse, Horatio provides a commonsense 'norm' helping us to orientate ourselves towards the more brilliant but unstable Hamlet, Arthur Seaton has Bert. In talking to them, the hero is revealing himself to the audience. But, simply by being there, they also tend to attract to themselves the role of contradicting or counterpointing the hero, becoming another bundle of feelings appropriate to the film's circumstances. Racine and Corneille, with their exceptionally rigorous approach, tended to keep the 'confidant' very close to the principal character's viewpoint. Even so, the confidant often, unobtrusively, moves into opposition and expresses forebodings, awe, and other forms of 'resistance'. In the Greek drama, the 'satellite' characters often become the voice of common sense, of 'the average conscience'—like the 'chorus'.

Thus one can almost see Hamlet/Horatio as a kind of 'twin' character—as well as being, in other ways, 'opposites', like Juliet and her Nurse. A hero's 'twin' may act as counsellor, or as tempter—suggesting to the hero ideas which are only vaguely and weakly formulated in his mind. In a sense Iago is Othello's 'opposite'—but he is also Othello's tempter, his still small voice; thus, he 'is' the concealed suspicions *in* Othello; indeed, he can influence Othello only because there is something in Othello to which his arguments appeal. Without Iago-in-Othello, there'd be no play, because Othello would be quicker to suspect Iago than to suspect Desdemona. Iago and Othello are opposites *because* they are twins, just as 'close' as Hamlet and Horatio.

However, the fact that the first pair of characters are enemies while the second pair are allies is, of course, an important difference between the pairs. The dramatic relationship (friendship, hostility) represents, in a sense, another 'bundle of feelings', another 'invisible character'. Looking at it from another angle, we can say that a hero who is hesitating between two alternative feelings (shall I trust her or murder her?) is a psychologically more sophisticated version of an argument between two characters each of whom stands for a different attitude. This sounds rather abstruse, but in fact it is a thoroughly practical proposition. An author may create a second character so that the hero can argue with him—when the second character is, up to a point, the hero's alter ego. Or the author may invent a character whose job it is to 'split the difference' between dramatic opposites. For example, given the situation of a good man and a bad man hiding out in the hills together, it is often very convenient to have a third party whose 'vote' carries the day, who can calm down their quarrels, or start them up, or work in different senses at different times. Or one might decide to do without this 'casting vote' and have goodie and baddie argue things out and come to some sort of decision. Or one may have a third person who is open to persuasion and wobbles between the hero and the villain.

Often the hero of the play is a wobbler—like Othello—and the entire play is the saga of his wobbling. Such a character—who splits the difference, has a casting voice, or wobbles—is from one point of view 'transitional' between the other two. But he may also stand for something very positive himself. For example, given our hero and villain hiding out in the hills, the 'transitional' character might be a wise, humorous old prospector, whose canniness both men respect. Or simply by being divided within himself, the 'transitional' character, as a storm centre of a conflict, can stand for the very important and positive *fact* of a conflict. If we distinguish drama from melodrama by the extent to which the former presents conflicts introvertedly while the latter presents them extrovertedly (the 'gearing' of character and circumstances), then it will often be found that in drama the 'transitional' characters are the principal characters, whereas in melodrama they tend to be in the 'middle distance'.

One might produce an inside-out version of *Johnny Guitar*—with one outlaw (instead of the gang) and a group of three women (instead of the three Viennas). The eldest woman wears Vienna's black clothes, another a scarlet dress, the youngest a white dress. Their professions and attitudes, of course, would correspond to these clothes. Or one might have only the black and white Vienna, and the bundle of feelings associated with the scarlet dress might be paraphrased by some dramatic issue or situation. The man they all love might be a combination of Black Bart, the Dancin' Kid and Turkey. He was once as likeable as Turkey, but was hardened when humiliated by the eldest woman's lover; and then betrayed her, becoming as seductive and dangerous as the Dancin' Kid, and humiliating the second woman; but some weakness of character, guilt and drink, say, brings him to the level of vicious, weak bluster reminiscent of Black Bart.

Such a film would no longer 'be' a version of *Johnny Guitar*. In making these changes we have substantially changed the bundles of feelings evoked by the film. None the less, we are working in the same 'key'. Our example is extreme, but the principle is exactly the same as the sort of alteration a scenarist makes to a novel. In a sense, one can't alter anything in a story without turning it into a different story. One can substantially alter the emotional content of a film simply by altering the background music—for example, by replacing a syrupy, consolatory orchestral score by a dry, curt, ironic guitar motif. Again we come to the same formulation: 'style' is just as emotional, just as fundamental, just as much a part of the film's 'content' and 'soul' as the characters, the psychology and the events in the plot. In fact our 'reversal' of *Johnny Guitar* might be nearer the emotional tones of the existing film than many a film is to the emotional tones of the story on whose narrative it is based—where the characters are retained, but their unhappiness softened, the whole thing made more upbeat, etc.

Given a 'striking idea' an experienced craftsman can, very rapidly indeed, develop a complete story, simply by contract-and-repetition —our pattern of similarities and dissimilarities. The 'core' of *The Wicked Lady* is—the wicked lady (Margaret Lockwood). She attracts her natural complements: a meek and good lady (Pat Roc), a victim male (Griffith Jones), an even tougher male (James Mason) and so on. These very symmetrical characters are thrown out of all-too-predictable symmetry by further surprises—it's the toughest male who is killed by the heroine, it's the one she killed for who kills her, etc. It is by throwing the symmetries out of any obvious symmetry that the film creates its 'imbalance', that is, the 'disharmonies' which the 'harmonies' exist to resolve.

One can imagine a version of *Johnny Guitar* in which Vienna is played by Margaret Lockwood, and a version of *The Wicked Lady* in which the wicked lady is played by Joan Crawford. In fact, the changes of personality would necessitate a considerable number of supplementary changes—in dialogue, in the performance of the other actors, in camera-angle, etc. Still, the general resemblance between the wicked lady and Vienna reminds us that the striking idea is itself a complicated balance of feelings, which can be developed in an immense number of different ways. James Mason's highwayman might be replaced by a highwayman with a pathological streak like Sterling Hayden's. Oddly enough, *The Wicked Lady* does give us a young lad, rather like Turkey, the stagecoach guard whom the wicked lady shoots and then, mothers as he dies—it's as if Vienna had had to shoot Turkey to save her own life, which is the opposite of what happens, Turkey sacrificing Vienna to save his.

There is, after all, only a tiny number of dramatic situations (thirty-six is a well-known estimate), although clearly it depends on what one defines as a situation. Most situations are really 'bundles of situations'—i.e., each confrontation between two specific characters can be considered as a sexual situation of some sort, a social situation, a moral situation, etc. If one took these arguments far enough, one could probably demonstrate that every plot is a second-cousin-twice-removed of every other plot. Yet—at the same time—in the sense that a change of music or of actor makes a film substantially different from an otherwise exactly similar film—no two films have more than a general, vague resemblance!

Though *The Wicked Lady* and *Johnny Guitar* work from a similar core—the wicked lady and Vienna—and have some storyline resemblances, we certainly don't think of them as 'variations on a theme'. There are too many differences. In *The Wicked Lady* none of the characters enjoys violence for its own sake; conventional sexual polarities are retained; and so on. A theme is not the 'soul' of a film; its 'soul' is its whole atmosphere, including *audience* response.

People and places are atmospheres—bundles of feelings—too. Often the last scene is set in the same locale as the first (or as the first 'crystallization' of the dramatic issues). Yet the atmosphere of the place has been transformed by all the events that have taken place since. Once, it was a happy house, now the characters are gloomy. There is a sense of 'return' to the place, but there is also a sense of 'no return'. The memory may add a particular tone of desolation, of irony, of melancholy. The place functions like the recapitulation, in a symphony, of a musical phrase, but in a sadder cadence. Feelings snowball round it, just as they snowball round the *human* characters. It creates a pattern, is part of the orchestration of feelings, of the very structure of a film. Its function as a symbol is far less important than its function as a 'motif', recalling the feelings it picks up as it goes on.

Similarly with 'props'—or any object involved in the action. A gives B a ring, swearing eternal love; B tires of him and gives it to C; C . . . and so on, back to B, who is now ninety years old and just hoards it in a box of trinkets. At each appearance, the ring is 'the same, transformed'. There is no pattern of cause-and-effect; the idea is communicated by the simplest and crudest intellectual process, the 'association of ideas'.

Thus settings and objects are used as rolling stones to gather emotional moss. Points of style may function in the same way, like the repeated movement in *Le Diable Au Corps* which we quoted earlier.[1]

[1] Possibly academic criticism tends to overemphasize the importance of a specific meaning to a symbol and underemphasize the role of a symbol in creating, resuming and transforming a whole 'atmosphere', a use more complex than a specific 'deep meaning' can ever be.

To say that 'atmosphere is soul' is a way of saying that the story is not there to explain the characters—the characters are there to provide the story, and the story is there to provide the atmosphere. The profundity is in the superficialities—including those meanings which the film exists to stimulate it, and exist only in, the spectator's response. Whether the ideal or the average spectator is another series of problems. . . . Centrally though the audience's feelings 'snowball' with the principal characters. The hero and the heroine are the 'themes', like those of a symphony. But a theme is less than a symphony, nor is a symphony there to express the theme. . . .

18 · Meaning and Motif

In our previous chapter we suggested that in 'dramatic' films of the 'mainstream' kind, the real theme of the film is the bunch of feelings embodied by, or centrally associated with, those characters who are the centre of focus for the spectator identifications; and that this theme undergoes diverse variations, by a character's own changes of attitude, by context, and by the surrounding characters.[1]

To minimize confusion we may call the 'theme' in this 'musical' sense a 'principal motif', and 'deep/symbolical/underlying meaning' a 'deep meaning', and use 'general meaning' for any topic, generalization, abstraction, etc., whether it is presented on the surface of the film or has to be 'interpreted out' (a process giving the feeling of 'depth').[2]

It is often presumed that it is the various layers of underlying 'deep meaning' which give richness and resonance to a merely 'personal' story. Hence phrases like: 'This isn't just the story of a man who . . .' (because we wouldn't be very interested in the story of a mere individual, would we?), 'it's much deeper . . .' and then follows some moral, psychological, sociological or philosophical generalization, some sort of archetype of wide applicability. There is

[1] This isn't to say that such films may not include irrelevancies, second themes none too well linked with the first, and so on. But in so far as there is a structure in a film, it's usually determined by a 'superficial' pattern like this.

[2] A 'general meaning' may be one of a film's motifs—as when the characters themselves are obviously involved in some moral dilemma. The *auteur* who wants his general meaning to be understood by the general, non-exegetical public usually has to present it as a motif (e.g. a problem for the hero), a sensible procedure which some academically-trained artists seem to find unbearably direct, even 'vulgar'; as soon as they've thought of a general meaning, they like to bury it under the surface, like a dog with a bone, for the spectator to enjoy disinterring it again.

often also a slide to the assumption, either that films feel 'real' because of their 'deep meaning', or, which is more plausible, because their motifs-and-variations build up to a satisfying exposition-and-exploration of a deep general meaning.[1]

My suggestion is that most of the weight and complexity of a film comes from the motifs, and that a deep general meaning, where there is one, is, at its most important, subsidiary to the motif, and, more often, an excrescence, a 'cadenza', a flourish that calls forth our applause, that even a superficial general meaning (a specific problem for the hero) is only a motif, and that most of the complexity comes from our participation with, and attitudes to, the characters as 'mere' individuals.

Even where the *auteur* had a deep general meaning in mind, the spectator's primary concern, from which he deduces the other, is his superficial participation. It is true that the spectator may be quite conscious of a general meaning, so conscious that it may even determine a positive or negative reaction to the superficial action. The general public, as well as critics, may dismiss or dislike a film because it rejects its implied values. But even here the development of the deep meaning has had to be posed in terms of a motif (except where the *auteur* resorts to overt moralizing). I should further suggest that it is excessively 'cerebral' (i.e. a reduction of art to philosophy) to claim redeemingly 'deep' meanings for a film which isn't interesting on the superficial level—and that the critic who rejects a film's complex surface because of an ideological undertone (it's his right) is none the less avoiding, refusing the complexity of the film.

Let us look at two films with these questions in mind. Before becoming a director, Claude Chabrol had, as a critic, been a prominent and devout admirer of Hitchcock, interpreting his work as that of a severe Catholic moralist. From internal evidence, he seems to have set out to embody such general ideas in his own films. What general meanings would it be reasonable to see in Chabrol's second film, *Les Cousins* (1959), his most substantial success, with critics and public alike?

1. For Chabrol himself, it is a study in 'good versus evil' and in the true complexity of this eternal antagonism (it is as if an essential

[1] This is probably true of those critics who are only interested in general meanings, and not really in personal stories, and who immediately think of the latter only in terms of the former—of which 'the artist's vision' is a current favourite. Of course a critic may maintain both *loci* of interest.

Manicheanism were giving up a soot-and-whitewash attitude to characters and problems and asserting a moral 'chiaroscuro'—in response, perhaps, to the same tensions that engendered existentialism). The film suggests that it concerns a 'good' cousin and a 'Satanic' one. But as the action proceeds. . . .

Other noticeable themes include:

2. A hardy perennial: a provincial youth sets out to vindicate himself *vis-à-vis* the Parisian *beau monde*, which corrupts and destroys him.

3. The long-standing opposition of Paris and the provinces.

4. Youth's new autonomy from the adult world—and from morality? It is a 'Vadimian' film.

5. The destruction of all that is best in traditional *bourgeois* attitudes by a new, slick (and crypto-Fascist?) affluence. It is about the 'OAS generation'. This gave rise to assertion that it was;

6. an apologia for those French youths with Fascist sympathies, or at least indulges Fascist nostalgias to a pernicious extent.

From these deep meanings, and there may well be others, the spectator can choose any one or all. He might combine them by some such formulation as: 'There is a real opposition of life-styles between all that is best in *bourgeois* morality and the moral nonchalence of Paris. None the less the former has the defects of its virtues, which are its 'tragic flaw'. So tragedy is a result, not of moral polarities, but of secret affinities-in-evil. . . .'

Yet any theme which the spectator sees in the film he sees *through* the human story, the story of the people as people, and its emotional overlap with his own experience of life.[1] A secondary satisfaction comes from the presentation of this 'meaning' in personal, human terms, as, reciprocally, in the linking of these human terms with general principles. But in no sense is the personal story only a 'metaphor' for deep meaning(s), whether considered singly or together. Indeed much of the superficial, dramatic meaning, is altogether irrelevant to the deep meaning.

Let us look at Chabrol's film in more detail. Charles (Gerard Blain) the country cousin, comes to live with Paul (Jean-Claude Brialy) in the latter's super-luxurious apartment, the last word in

[1] Of itself a 'sociological' relevance is no richer than a 'moral' one. But tactfully handled it may well make a film popular, since many members of the audience are responding to the sociological phenomenon, and their own intense feelings find relief and release in the film.

slick chic. Charles's character is soon established, not only by his appearance and manner, but by his first actions. On arrival, he sits down to write a letter home beginning, 'Ma petite maman. . . .' When, later, he falls in love with Florence (Juliette Mayniel), a girl from Paul's set, he wants to tell her his feelings about her in poetry. But he is too shy to speak it, so he recites it mentally to himself while she 'listens', and finds it beautiful because she knows what his feelings for her are. Everything about his personal style says that he believes implicitly in sensitivity, in integrity, in diligence, in everything that is best in the *bourgeois* qualities.

Paul is debonair, hedonist, opportunist and unscrupulous and has the easy amiability of superficiality. He is egoistic and sadistic and in every way reverses the '*bourgeois* virtues'. He refines his sadism into a teasing and amusing charm and expertly deploys his charm to get what he wants. He is outrageous and irresistible—but he is not malicious and he is certainly not a 'villain'. His friends like him and he is an excellent companion. Paul's first chat with Charles includes a complicitous: 'Between you and me, our parents are so many c——ts.' Charles grins, for he is man-of-the-world enough not to be shocked; but he still writes that letter home to his mother.

Charles also has a great deal of charm, poise and tact. Florence falls in love with him at first sight; at the party he moves towards her with self-assurance, smoothly monopolizing her against competition. If Paul's charm derives from his playfully frank egoism, Charles's derives from his kindness and sensitivity. In the game for Flo, his hand is as good as Paul's—much better, for she loves him.

Both cousins are slightly 'lost'. Charles writes to his mother, but we never see her. He is alone, the flat and the clique belong to Paul, and constitute a forceful continuous attack on his values. There is a ritzy Americanism about this opulent world, where Henri Decae's photography throws up little stars of light from the glossy coachwork of fast cars and the women's necklaces. The apartment is smart enough to be sinister, and its real owner, Paul's Oncle Henri, makes his money through a racket of some sort. On the walls is a collection of pistols—the virility of inflicting death. Paul, by way of a jest, terrifies a Jewish friend by waking him from sleep with cries of, 'Get up! Gestapo!' and flashing a torch in his eyes. But he hardly realizes the cruelty of his joke, and his victim forgives him. There is a certain innocence in his *insouciance*, and an underlying insecurity in his sadism. At a party, he dresses up as a Nazi officer. Fancy dress in films often expresses either what the characters would like to be, or what they really are without knowing it; and Paul's Nazi officer is dying alone in the snows of Stalingrad, vainly calling for his mother to comfort him.

But Charles has a décor of his own: the bookshop. Prominent among the titles in the window are, *Le Chateau de ma Mere* and *Les Sentiers de la Gloire*. The friendly bookseller is quick to recognize Charles as a serious, hardworking student; he himself is contemptuous of detective stories, of frivolity and women. But the last time we see him, after Charles has lost Flo and failed his examination, he urges Charles to begin work again, harder than ever, and he has the air of a brutal, sweating taskmaster, even Mephistophelean. His cynicism is unobtrusive, even virtuous, but it is there, and it is nasty. He tells Charles that diligence is the path to worldly success and security and that then Florence will be Charles': 'I know that sort of girl! with my money I could buy ten like her!' He has never seen Flo and she is, in fact, indifferent to money. The efforts of a rich Milanese industrialist to find himself a good-time-girl among the playgirls of Paul's set only result in his being mocked. But Charles seems to believe the bookseller's remark.

Paul has, not a taskmaster, but a parasite, Clovis, who steals his money (Paul knows but doesn't mind) and makes a little on the side by bringing the industrialist to their party. Clovis is a sycophant and creeper; he is a frustrated homosexual and has a violent hatred of almost everybody, but particularly women. He snarls viciously at Paul's ex-mistress when she asks for the money to procure an abortion. He resembles Satan the tempter as he talks Flo into feeling Paul's flesh and betraying Charles—his demonic intensity is inspired not only by his jealousy of Paul for being attractive to Flo but also by his jealousy of Flo for being attractive to Paul. His brilliant embittered loquacity about their flesh contrasts with Charles's unspoken poetry about—souls.

At the first party, Charles takes Flo from under Paul's nose. Paul, who can do what he likes with most of the girls in his set—with the possible exception of the Lesbian in the heavy raincoat—retaliates, with all sorts of tricks—whisking off Flo in his car to separate her from Charles, 'accidentally' removing the receiver when Charles waits for a call from Flo, and, at last, spurred on by Clovis, seducing her while she is waiting for Charles. But after Paul has seduced Flo, Charles gives up. Clovis's jealous gloating over the flesh has its counterpart in his sulking, and gradually his jealousy runs away with him. One evening, while he is studying, Flo, having quarrelled with Paul, comes to him and tries to tell him that she is free for him, that she is repentant and anxious to be accepted by him. But he has become dishonest. He forgets that his motive in working like a demon was to win Flo back from Paul. But the means have become an end in themselves. He rejects her. Success in the examination has become his collection of pistols. Only he is in deadly earnest.

He gives himself away in one of the neatest examples of screen dialogue outside a Prévert film. Over breakfast (served by Flo) Charles tells Paul, 'It's only four days to your exam.' We sense his unspoken thought, 'Because of your frivolous life, you'll fail, I who have worked hard, will pass.' It's true this statement contains a warning to work, but there is an unmistakable *schadenfraude* in it. Paul replies pleasantly: 'Three days to *my* exams, dear boy. I sit a day before you.' His negligent precision shows his superiority to Charles; and Charles's mistake is a self-centred one, in his childish way he thinks everybody sits their exam on the day he sits. Paul has the whole situation casually clear in his mind. Paul 'plays' the egoism and cruelty which in Charles is concealed, is almost morbidly ingrown. We are not surprised when, having overworked, he fails his exam—and Paul passes.

We don't know why, finally, Flo leaves Paul. My guess (based on a certain sensitivity in her, a capacity to respond to Charles's purity) is that she realizes that in his love there is no depth, no permanence. (He and Clovis had taunted her with the dull, mediocre permanence of middle-class domesticity which was all Charles could offer someone of her sexual experience and avidity.) But Charles's love defeats itself. For with his old-fashioned jealousy he seems to accept that Flo 'belongs' to Paul, because they have gone to bed; and later, when she comes to him, he rejects her, as if she were now soiled beyond redemption. After his failure in the exam, he plods the streets, and catches sight of Flo in a restaurant with Clovis and a callous-looking business-man. She is sinking to the status of a *poule de luxe*. Charles had only to walk into the restaurant, tell her to get up from the table and follow him, and, surely, she would have done. She casts at him a look full of shame and appeal, but, egocentric in his despair, he turns away.

Humiliated by his failure in the exam (though he would have another chance a year later) and by his (entirely self-inflicted) loss of

Flo, he tears up his identity card and throws it into the Seine as a brightly-lit pleasure-boat glides by—crossing a dark, heavy barge which is his own feelings. He has sentenced himself to death. Maybe he blames Paul for degrading Flo (maybe not, she had in fact already slept around). He takes one of Paul's pistols from the wall, inserts one round and holds it to Paul's sleeping head. 'You have a chance in six . . . I have one in five.' He pulls the trigger, and Paul, with his customary luck, lives. The symbolic act brings Charles to his senses, i.e., satisfies him. He 'cheats'—sensibly—and does not attempt suicide. The next morning Paul, playfully, points the gun at him and pulls the trigger. Their combined malice claims its victim—both are victims, for Paul, brokenly, paces the room, also coming to his senses—his senses of guilt.

Undoubtedly Charles is the finer, the more sensitive of the cousins; we want him to win Flo, in this sense the film is unambiguously 'for' Charles and 'against' Paul. We feel that in different circumstances Paul's 'play' would easily have become a happy Nazism. But in these particular circumstances, the virtual murderer is Charles. Since only an accident saves Paul, Charles's accidental execution is, by a poetic morality of intention, morally just.

Charles's home is surely a Christian one. In his grief, he tries to enter a church, which is closed. A continued coincidence? A coincidence, emblematic of this 'absurd' world? Or is it closed to him because he has murder in his heart, and is closed to Florence, and to God? Or because the visible, institutional church is fallible, corrupt, a *bourgeois* institution like his jealousy? Or because God is an illusion anyway and 'cannot' give grace when it is needed? I take the film's basic (and perhaps unconscious) theme as a struggle, not between virtue and vice, but a struggle for power. Paul is a showy disciple of garbled Nietzsche. For Charles power is hidden behind the 'virtue' of hard work. Indeed, two minor characters, both Italians, represent power in its naïvest forms. The Milanese industrialist thinks it's money. The Strong Man at the second party thinks its physique, for while bursting chains with his colossal muscles he bawls an operatic commentary at the top of his lungs. But real power is subtler. Clovis is perpetually penniless, sexually frustrated and sycophantic—the film's most impotent, he is also its nastiest, character. Charles, betrayed by his own weapons, resorts to Paul's, and, via Paul, kills Charles.

Behind the diverse forms of power looms that of virility. Paul, the too-ostentatious virility figure (in psychoanalytical characterology, a phallic narcissist), whose charm and beard are slightly diabolical, is *exceeded* in Satanic nastiness by Clovis, his apparent opposite—and accomplice. Both have a streak of homosexual sadism and form a 'binary character'. Clovis's presence locates Paul on the spectator's moral scale. Charles's excess—and binary—is the bookseller. His relationship with Flo is echoed by that between a younger boy, Rameau, and a girl whom Rameau insults in a fit of uncontrollable jealousy and for whom he commits suicide. Charles and Paul, without quite knowing it, complement, and love, each other. While Paul kills Charles his radiogram plays the *Liebestod* from *Tristan and Isolde*. The music occurred earlier, during the first party, as Paul dies in the snows of Stalingrad. It's not surprising that the film has two (reciprocal) paraphrases of Oedipal jealousy. Paul, calling vainly for his mother, sees Charles and Florence together, in the light of his torch; and Charles swots hard while, through the frosted glass of the bathroom, Paul and Flo showering together in the altogether, laugh and wrestle.

One may also see in the film the sort of religious meaning Chabrol and Rohmer attribute to Hitchcock. Thus the closure of the church is an Act of God to ensure that Charles will endure his martyrdom, assume guilt for the unconscious murders Paul is always playing at, recover his innocence (by repentance) and become a scapegoat for Paul, whose final remorseful condition may be a prelude to a state of grace. The sun-king is chastened.

Chabrol considers *Les Cousins* to be a positively anti-Christian film, though his previous Christianity, as evinced by *Le Beau Serge*, was hardly traditional in its attitude to sexual morality. *Les Cousins*, arguably, gains in intensity if one allows the two sets of meaning to 'oscillate' in one's mind. But this 'complex' of contradictory possibilities reminds us that it's not the deep meanings that dignify the personal story; at best they enrich it. Were it only an analysis of the various 'deep' meanings assigned to it, the film would be far too schematic to hold our interest for ninety minutes or so. Indeed most of these 'deep' meanings are rather banal, more like new old saws and rules of thumb than creative in any real sense.

But though much of a film's power and nuance lies on the superficial level, one may none the less entertain similar reservations towards the delight with which critics celebrate 'density of specification' for its own sake, taking it, sometimes, as synonymous with 'complexity'. It's often assumed that the more *information* a film provides about its characters, the more satisfying and complex it must be. My own suspicion is that such 'detail' (in novels, notably; the cinema is a sparer medium) is mere tautology, or 'noodling' (unstructured and irrelevant), and that strong construction is as important a quality, is a way of laying bare central conflicts from which a minimum of 'tautology' or asides distracts the spectator. *Some* complexity there must be. None the less, a film may provide very little information, a bare minimum of 'irrelevance', and sweep one up simply by the intensity of fundamental, dynamic conflicts. The films of Antonioni do so in one sense: neither 'analyzing' the characters' motives and context (scattering hints, certainly), nor stating the basic issues clearly, still less allowing them to distract us from the lyrical presentation of a 'superficial' mood. And what is perhaps Hitchcock's 'deepest' film works in an analagous way. Not that *Psycho* (1961) is restricted to the lyrical finesses of Antonioni, though one sequence (the car-drive) compares with them. But its pattern of atrocity and exposed libido allows only the minimum of 'asides', its bareness subsumes some central conflicts and ambiguities. Yet it has a resonance as authentic as that of music, the least informative of the arts. . . .[1]

[1] To relate it to music isn't to claim it as more than a minor masterpiece, a *petit-maître's* most striking film. My point is that the participation it compels, the barbed way in which it has lingered in so many spectator's minds, and the emotional 'shifts' (amounting to 'illumination') which it engineers, are not to be explained in terms of 'information provided', but arise from the 'structure of participation and concern' provided for the spectator.

19 · Inside Norman Bates

The camera climbs towards a window like any other window. Documentary-style, a subtitle states time and date; but it really means: Here and Now, at this moment, without warning, imperceptibly, destiny entered these lives. On a hot day, during their lunch-break, in an impersonal hotel bedroom, Marion Crane (Janet Leigh) and Sam Loomis (John Gavin) are half-naked and necking. The nightmare begins at noon. The heat, the bleached feel of the visuals, the half-naked-ness, the time, evoke an atmosphere of unsatiated sensuality (indeed, the heavy petting of so many of Hitchcock's American films, from *Notorious* to *North-by North-West*, suggests a frustrating coldness, even, intercourse with neither orgasm nor emotional relief). In a very matter-of-fact way the lovers are discussing the man's divorce and the money they need if they are to marry. The general situation —half-stripping at lunchtime and then talking about cash—is vaguely offensive; yet they seem decent people, we accept and care about them. This ambiguity pervades their whole relationship. In some way Sam seems petulant, weak, unworthy; in others, Marion seems prim, tough, less concerned with unconditional love than with—respectability? Are they in love or only convinced they are? At any rate, we're not especially anxious for them to get married. In default of the money, she is tempted to break off the affair, and we are sufficiently disquietened to watch with something between curiosity and concern, rather with an eagerness for them to get married and live 'happily ever after'.

Marion returns to the sane, shallow, superficial people of the office where she works. It's not long before sex and cash are intertwined again. A fat client makes a rather coarse and vulgar attempt to flirt with her, brandishing a fat bankroll in her face. The other office-girl, a plain and silly creature, is naïvely jealous of these gross attentions. 'I expect he saw my wedding ring.' Her self-consoling remarks rubs salt in Marion's wound. We agree with her feeling that she is too pretty, efficient, sincere in love, to deserve to be worse off than this other girl. The fat customer brags that he wouldn't miss the money if it were stolen, and Marion's boss absolutely insists on entrusting it to her. Such smug, imperceptive responses all round reinforce our feeling that Marion has as much right to this excess money as its actual owner. These pinpricks accumulate into a kind of obsession and reinforce the confusion between her respectability (or pride) and her love (or sensuality). The money seems to offer a solution to all these 'raw edges' of feeling. Her theft is (so to speak) an impulse born of converging obsessions, which suddenly click into place forming an irresistible urge. It is also a tribute to her daring, her strength of passion; there is an element of moral *hubris vis-à-vis*. There is also an element of *hubris vis-à-vis* her lover, as if in acting so boldly where he has been so weak she is taking over the initiative—and is not going to be thanked for her devotion. Soon she is driving hard away from the town, tormented not so much by conscience as by fear. We can't believe she'll get away with it, especially as criminals never do in American films. We hope she will, and there is still a get-out: the theft won't be noticed until Monday morning, she can always return the money. Will she go on to decide to return it, but lose it? will someone else steal it from her? will Sam betray her, by his weakness, somehow?

A big, brutal-looking motor-bike cop with dark glasses trails her, suspiciously. His menacing figure recalls the law-breakers of *The Wild One* and the motor-cyclists of *Orphée* who ran men down in the name, not of justice, but of a law above the law, the brutal Will of destiny. He is 'the law', but he has a special, *personal* brutality of his own. Is he really following her, or is she only imagining he is? The psychological pressures complicate and intensify. To shake him off, she exchanges her car at a garage run by a very obliging character, apparently the very antithesis of the cop. The cop is saying, 'I remind you of punishment: turn back!' the garagehand, 'I make crime pleasant and easy, go on.' She acquires a white car—the colour of her underwear in the necking scene, the colour of innocence and dissatisfied sensuality; but all her precautions are of no avail. The cop still tails her, a terrifying dark angel sent to give her a last chance. Or sent simply to torture her, to diminish her chances: for without him she has a week-end in which to repent. There is danger of, as it were, rape-by-justice. We sigh with relief when at last she shakes him off.

She is beyond the reach of the law—or fear—now. But—where is she? The rain pours down across the windscreen, blurring lights and creating a wavering landscape. She is in what in *Orphée* is called *la Zone*, the no-man's-land between reality and the nightmare. The cop was both danger and safety. It is almost as if he were sent, after all, not to turn her back, but to make her drive on. The theological notion of double predestination provides a clue, 'God sends sinners a chance to repent *in order that* by rejecting it, as he knows they will, they will damn themselves more thoroughly than ever.' But as she reasons with herself, she is beginning to realize the futility of her theft—Sam is too sensible to accept the money. . . .

The rain forces her into a motel, managed by Norman Bates (Anthony Perkins). Norman is an engagingly naïve country youth, very honest, unconcerned with making money, almost a symbol of rustic virtue and country contentment. The whole film hinges on his sensitivity and charm—we tend to like him whatever his faults. His friendliness is all the more reassuring in contrast with the sinister atmosphere (the stuffed birds of prey, the Victorian house just behind the motel, where his petulant, tyrannical old mother lives). He seems tainted by the atmosphere, but the over-obvious horror clichés shift our suspicions from Norman to the atmosphere; they camouflage the inevitably stilted presentation of his relationships with Mrs. Bates; they contrast with the slick, modern, informal style of the film as a whole. Mrs. Bates comes from Norman's childhood and it's fitting that she should exist in an aesthetic idiom now considered childish—she would feel quite at home in James Whale's *The Old Dark House*.

Marion calls Norman's bird-stuffing a rather morbid hobby and says Norman resembles the dead birds of prey. Hitchcock plays fair with his audience, even while misleading us. True, he lets us believe in Mrs. Bates—but so do Marion, and Norman. Maybe, as the psychiatrist says later, Norman was never entirely Norman, he faintly knew the truth about Mrs. Bates—but then again Mrs. Bates is very stilted, we only half-believe in her.

Norman cheerfully admits to his faults of character; he is a very reasonable, modest guy. Gradually Marion realizes that she is his superior, that, if unhappy, she is self-possessed, whereas his 'contented' acquiescence in looking after his domineering mother has something weak and helpless. His wisdom about money and the example of his servitude help to free her from the power of her impulse. She realizes that what she stole was not love but only money, an attempt to avoid her problems. Norman is almost a sacrificial victim whose tragic example frees her.

But he is not a hopeless case. We feel that she owes it to him to return the favour. We want him to be freed from his horrible mother, for he is a decent fellow. There is something dissatisfying in Marion's decision simply to return, alone, to the everyday, with its little degradations, its mutually exclusive choices—while leaving Norman here, unhelped. A sort of bewilderment percolates through the audience at this weird, premature 'happy ending'. We are, so to speak, in another 'zone'.

The film elaborately establishes Marion's search for a hiding-place for her cash. The search seems to turn her indifference to Norman into as entrenched cynicism for he isn't the sort of lad to steal it. As she undresses, Norman watches through the peephole. We laugh very uneasily at his avid voyeurism, but it does not quite put him in our bad books. For he has been lonely and dominated by his puritanical mother; and his spying on Marion represents a movement towards normality and freedom, which we want for his sake. This is almost a dissatisfying love-scene (like necking for lunch). The erotic overtones are juicy, and please us. And we are pleased to feel the story moving again.

The 'movement towards' Marion is intensified—with a vengeance —when Mrs. Bates with a knife upraised charges in and stabs her to death in the shower. The murder is too erotic not to enjoy, but too grisly to enjoy. Its ferocity and pornography are opposed, we are shocked into violent protest and horror, yet they force on the average spectator a rapid, hysteric, moral oscillation between protest and enjoyment. There is a Hays Code sort of moral in the air: 'Look what thieving necking girls get', but her fate is also ironically unjust: for she had just resolved to return the money.

If the Peeping Tom episode is a 'weak' yet eerie version of the hotel scene, the murder is a sarcastic exaggeration of it—her sensuality's satisfied now, all right. We feel guilty about enjoying this film, but we have to admit we're having our money's worth of fun and fear.

Mom would be a convenient scapegoat; but we are headed away from complacent hatred back into something subtler and far more uncomfortable by Norman's distress at her crime and his concern for her. In the next sequence, he begins mopping-up operations in the bathroom, the action of an exceptionally dutiful son. The presence of Marion's naked corpse is both erotic and extremely uncomfortable. The film offers us a 'first-person' experience answering the question which so often occurs to crime fans, 'Would I be able to get down to the practical details of clearing up the corpse and the blood'—a thought which appals many people more than that of the actual killing. The answer the film gives is, 'A sensitive and dutiful son like Norman can—therefore, so could you, if you really had to.' We watch Norman doing it, and the feeling that we could too is gratifying to the worse side of our nature, but upsets the other.

Although there is a quietly disturbing contrast between Norman's usual sensibility and his matter-of-fact practicality on this particular chore, we feel that in his way he was on the edge of being 'liberated' by his interest in Marion, that she slew Marion so as to keep him, and that in covering up for Mom, Norman is turning the other cheek, manifesting the equanimity and charity of a saint. The spectator's moral purity is being outflanked at both ends—by morbid, pornographic interest, and by a sympathetic pity for charming Norman.

Not that indignation and disgust are lulled asleep. On the contrary. For example, there is a very precise mix between a C.U. of the plughole down which our saintly voyeur is swabbing the blood, and a C.U. of Marion's open eye staring at us as if to say, 'What about my feelings? Why don't you interview the dead?' She's peeping back at us from beyond the grave, from down the drain, with protest and indignation, eternal and colossal—or surprise and fear—or just nothing. This visual rhyme is not just a piece of sadistic wit but a little essay in metaphor; it never does to interpret visual effects too definitely, but, e.g. the plughole is like an eye-socket, the eye ('Window of the soul' as they say) is just a mushroom out of a black hole. There is a sense of total nothingness and if the 'joke' provides a little hysteria which relieves the horror faintly it insinuates a subtler unease: we must be mad to be laughing at a joke like this.

Norman chews candy as he watches the white car sink beneath the very black surface of the swamp behind the house. As the film uses psychoanalytical ideas it's appropriate to use them on the film—the bathroom scene, very glossy and white, and devoted to the theme of cleanliness, is followed by a scene in which everything disappears into a black sticky cesspool. Norman has pulled the chain.

When the car sticks instead of sinking, we are alarmed, but when at last it disappears we heave a sigh of relief. Thank goodness! Norman is a good boy (despite the candy), it would be wrong to punish him, Marion's a corpse, it's no use crying over spilt blood, bury her quick, tidy up, get her out of the way! But when Norman tosses in the thick wad of cash, which he thinks is just an old newspaper, a cry of shock and regret is wrested from the audience. That valuable money, what a waste! Norman's saintly indifference to Mammon hurts us. We want to forget Marion probably because her murder shook us up so much. But the money had become 'what she died for, what she hid', that is, virtually a substitute identity. Its derisive disappearance creates hysteria as again the narrative seems to 'end'.

Sam Loomis discusses Marion's disappearance with her sister Lila (Vera Miles). The visuals are grey and scruffy. The setting is Sam's wife's ironmongery store where callous chit-chat about insecticides is overheard and pitchfork prongs are visually prominent. The drab everyday is full of trivial or latent cruelty. The meeting of lover and sister is hostile, but their disputes are ironically complacent compared with the terrible truth. Lila seems more sensible, more adult than Marion, and perhaps more righteous—but also worried, subdued. A private detective, Arbogast (Martin Balsam) insists on introducing himself, and tells them that Marion has absconded with the money. They refuse to believe him. They detest his coarse, obnoxious approach—so do we, and, like Sam and Lila, feel he must be up to some dirty game. His cynicism doesn't fit Marion's case—although, in a sense, it is justified.

As he tracks Marion down to Norman's mansion we half-want him to fail—for Norman's sake, and because he may be up to some cynical scheme of his own. . . . Just before he confronts Norman we realize that he is completely, admirably honest. In the battle of wits between Norman and Arbogast we sympathize with them both—Marion *must* be avenged, Arbogast is tough enough to uncover the truth; and yet Norman's motives are selfless, and perhaps Mrs. Bates will be more than even Arbogast bargains for. As he climbs the stairs towards the old lady's room, we realize clearly that his pushful cynicism, hitherto his strength, is now his weakness. He is formidable, and physically is probably Mom's match, but he is too naïve to be looking for whatever he'll find—and Mrs. Bates comes tearing out of her room with the superspeed of the superstrong insane and with repeated jabs of her knife sends him tumbling backwards down the stairs, dead, just like that. Is Mom invincible?

Another car sinks into the swamp, the narrative 'ends' at another nihilistic moment.

The whole plot, which has twice ended so disastrously, starts again, as Sam and Lila come to investigate the disappearance of the investigator who came to investigate the disappearance of. . . . Probably by now most spectators have guessed that Mom=Norman. But we can't be sure, in such a film. The only thing we can be certain of is the imminence of violent death—again. What matters is not whether we know, but whether Sam and Lila find out—or get killed. They might. Heroes and heroines do, in this film. And if they do find out, what will happen to Norman—saintly accomplice of two—at least—crimes. . . ?

The determined, but prosaic and therefore perilously naïve, couple call on the local sheriff (John McIntire) who explains that Norman is eccentric but harmless, that Mom has been dead and buried these ten years past, and so on. But we heard Norman persuade Mom to hide in the cellar and we saw Mom come tearing out of her room to kill Arbogast. The sheriff's clue is so wrapped up in complacency and ignorance that instead of clarifying our suspicions it confounds them further. The sheriff's suggestion opens up astounding new avenues of depravity: 'If Norman's mother is still alive, then who's the woman buried up there in Green Lawns Cemetery?'[1] If they believe what the sheriff says, they will never go to the old house, and then how can Marion and Arbogast be avenged? But *if* they go there. . . .

Sam keeps Norman talking while Lila sneaks into the house to explore; clearly the most dangerous game to play, especially with a possible Mom waiting for her. As we can't make up our mind whether the danger is coming from in front of her (Mom) or from behind her (Norman), we're no longer thinking very coherently, and as we can't make up our mind what we want to happen to Norman, we yield to a helpless hysteria.

Norman grows more anxious and angry as Sam brutally presses him; he struggles to keep his temper, to quieten his tormentor's suspicions, while keeping Mom from breaking out in himself (if you know) or (if you don't) bravely protecting his Mom or (if you're not

[1] Well might he ask.

sure) both or neither or which? The scene almost shifts our sympathies round—such is Norman's sincerity—to: 'brutal smug adulterer bullies sensitive kid into despair'. After all, whether Norman is weak or maniac or both, he probably believes in Mom, he is only trying to obviate another climax, another killing, he is frantically on the side of peace.

Lila explores the house. Amidst the tension there is an unexpected intellectual interest, and pathos. Norman's rooms are a picture of his mind and everyday life. There is the record-player with the classical L.P. (so out of place in this Gothicy house), there are the fluffy childhood toys which are presumably still played with. Norman is weaker-minded, more sensitive, than we thought, which makes him more pathetic (and more surprising—menacing?). Norman, mad with suspicion, rushes from the motel into the house as Lila takes refuge in the cellar—where, we know, Norman puts Mom in times of stress. And Mom does exist, there she is, horribly old, evil and withered, at a closer look she's dead and withered, but still grinning malevolently, she's a ghost, and when Lila turns, there's *another* Mom, grinning malevolently, very much alive, knife upraised. There aren't no Moms, there are two Moms, then the second disintegrates, the wig slides off, it's Norman. It's not simply the surprise that shocks; it's the intensity of terror and the obscenity of the disintegration. In rather the same way, when Mom came tearing out of her room at Arbogast, she had the notoriously terrible strength of the insane, and a visible virility quite obscene in an old lady; the explanation doesn't explain *that* away; it intensifies its impact because illusion and explanation co-exist.

We are relieved to hear that everything is going to be comfortably explained for us by the police psychologist (Simon Oakland). As soon as we see him we begin to dislike his brash, callous, know-all manner, he puts our backs up as Arbogast did. We expect the clichés: poor mixed-up kid, it was all the fault of stern, possessive, puritanical Mom. But gradually we realize he's not saying this at all. It was Norman who was jealous, who imagined that his (for all we know) normal Mom was a promiscuous Mom and murdered and embalmed her and then imagined she was a jealous puritanical Mom and then lived out two false characters—nice normal Norman and nasty Mom. So much for rustic contentment. Norman was never, we gather, entirely Norman, i.e. even when he was being charming and we felt sorry for him, he knew deep down what he was doing.

The psychologist's explanation takes away our explanation: what we thought was 'deep', the 'solution', is merely the topmost level of nastiness. He restores terror, guilt, injustice. Up till now Mom's gruesome appearance has been in accord with her character: 'Well, if she's dead, she asked for it, look at how she messed up her tender and devoted son.' Now all this is reversed, the cocoanut-faced corpse was once a sunny, apple-cheeked mother. The boy has literally turned her into his fantasy of her.

But if the psychologist, brutal and cynical, is the most intimate of private eyes, the joker is still to come. All we've had has been an intellectual, rational explanation. Now we see Norman sitting against a blank, white, hygienic wall. He is in full-face close-up, his madness is rammed into the cinema. Briefly our entire world is his face, the thoughts behind it, *his* world. We have little else with which to identify. An utter flatness, whiteness, simplicity, in short, eternity. He is cackling to himself, in Mummy's mummy's voice. She is jubilant because she is outwitting them all, pretending to be a sweet old lady who won't even hurt a fly. Mom has just killed Norman and disguised himself as him.

The Chinese sage wrote: 'Now I do not know whether I was then a man dreaming I was a butterfly or whether I am now a butterfly dreaming I am a man.' With Norman it's flies. His ricocheting self-punishment is so total that—well, we can hardly pity him, for there's no one left there to pity. And he or she or it seems to think it is escaping punishment, which is very immoral of him or her or it; but a nausea *like* compassion makes itself felt. We are too thoroughly satisfied to hate.

The appearance of Mom's face under the madman's, and then of a skull under Mom's, has a climatic brutality, but also simplifies, liberates us from the baffling maze of malevolent Nothings which our sensitive boy has become. Needless to say, it is a simplification on the most nihilistic level: are any of us realler than our skulls? There follows a shot of the police lifting Marion's car, wrapped in chains, from the swamp. There is no 'decent obscurity'. And Nothing to the nth degree has killed real people whom we sympathized with. But we too hoped the car would sink (just as we hoped Marion would get away with the cash). We too have been accomplices after the acts—futile acts.

People leave the cinema, chuckling incredulously, groggy, exhilarated yet hysterical, half-ready to believe that everybody in the world is as mad as Norman. A kathartic indulgence in pornographic murder is succeeded by an embarrassed humility, an unsentimental compassion towards insanity. The entire film is a prolonged practical joke in the worst of taste. If it weren't in bad taste, it would not be kathartic, embarrassing or compassionate.

It is not just a sick joke, it is also a very sad joke. Because it is outrageous, it exhilarates, but it is a very depressed film as well. The by-play with the money is strange and disturbing. It is produced as a weapon of seduction by a repulsive but normal male. Its victim resents the implied insult but yields to the money. The money, she felt, would enable her to find, all at once, respectability, sensuality, love. It becomes the last clue, a substitute-identity, an anti-soul. Marion who hoped to avoid choice, and sacrifice (the *hubris* of American optimism), is reduced to a nude body, a car, bankroll.

Everything piles up in the swamp—and is dredged up again. The film is not just a sick joke and a very sad joke, but a lavatory joke. It is a derisive misuse of the key-images of 'the American way of life': Momism (but it blames son), cash (and rural virtue), necking (and respectability), plumbing and smart cars. The reality to which Sam and Lila return is not a joyous one, but a drab shop of insecticides, pitchforks and—in addition—a vision of horror. The plot inevitably arouses in the spectator a feeling that Lila and Sam could eventually, possibly, consolingly, fall in love. But there is no hint of it in the final image. Each is still alone. This is the sanity that balances the diabolical nothing which is the human soul. Marion, striving for everything, lost everything. Only Norman has defied society and superficiality and found 'rest'. Only Norman has found himself, and lost himself.

Like many films, *Psycho's* aesthetic method is not that of providing enlightening information about its characters; it provides just enough to confuse us; it works by luring the audience into becoming the characters, sharing and living out their experiences within them in carefully determined patterns. The characters tend to be alone on the screen. Even the conversations are filmed mainly in alternating close-ups. The close-up both enlarges (intensifies) and isolates (blots out the rest of the world). While each character is speaking the spectator sees, feels, becomes him and only him. The next shot wrenches him into becoming the *antagonistic* character. Our sympathies alternate rapidly—our feelings are poured into so many moulds which are distended or smashed by contradictions, revelations, twists. Simple as the characters are, in principle, they are, because well acted, convincingly real. The atmosphere is hypnotic, the events so outrageous and managed with such brinkmanship of taste, the hints, allusions and subversive shifts of sympathy are managed with such sly tact, its constant emotional collisions are so quick, subtle and drastic, that the 'sketchiness' of the characters no more invalidates them than it invalidates the plays of Racine.

In its powerful vagueness, it works on the spectator not unlike music. It is planned, felt out, in terms of varied motifs, of emotional chords and dissonances, of patterns. Hitchcock has a very refined sense of sly or brash emotional discords, of how to modulate and combine them. The coarse customer, the cop, Arbogast and the psychologist are incarnations of the same force—unpleasant common sense. The trusting boss, the garageist, the local sheriff, Norman himself all agreeably further evil. The woman in the ironmonger's who is determined to kill insects painlessly is mirrored in Norman's final crone-voiced cackle that he won't even hurt a fly (is absurd squeamishness the hypocritical form of homicidal mania?). Norman, in conversation, unwittingly frees Marion of the compulsive theft which Sam inspired in her. But Sam bullies Norman like the cop bullied Marion.

Lila is a more reasonable, but 'joyless' double of Marion. Sam loses Marion to Norman but Norman is destroyed by Sam and Lila. Lila, in a sense, is Marion 'come back'—a parallel to the 'second Mom' in the basement. As Lila roams through Norman's rooms, she is almost the substitute mother, the young woman who is kind and normal and will therefore destroy him. Norman and Sam are both dark-haired, faintly resemble each other. Norman killed his mother because he thought she had a lover; and is destroyed by a young adulterer and his mistress's sister. The three penetrations to 'the truth about Norman'—Marion's, Arbogast's, the young couple's—are like three movements in music—the first two themes are contrasted (a sensual theme involving a girl, an unromantic theme involving Arbogast, the third combines them—a young couple who aren't quite romantically connected).

All these patterns, like inversions of certain emotional chords, result from the film's simplicity of form, but they are like haunting harmonies placed on a simple, yet eerie melodic line. The cutting has a quick, ragged, Stravinskyian rhythm.

The minor quirks and sins (adultery, a 'thing' about insecticides) of the normal world are the tips of the horns of the real reality, concealed beyond, or below, the 'zone'. In *Psycho* nothing that isn't disturbing or tainted ever happens, and to enjoy it (as most people do) is to stand convicted, and consciously convicted, of a lurking nostalgia for evil (i.e. of thoroughly enjoying it in fantasy). Norman's big mistake is that he let his fantasies enjoy him. The film is a practical joke: it convicts all the spectators of Original Sin. One does not so much watch, as participate in, it, as one might in a religious ritual involving the confession and a—well, one cannot say that absolution is granted. On the contrary, we have to take what comfort, or discomfort, we can from the implied complicity.

Hitchcock may have had a Jesuit education, but surely *Psycho* isn't a Christian film; it has a Dionysiac force and ruthlessness, one might call it a Greek tragi-comedy.

Part Four

THE ANGEL OF POETRY HOVERING

20 · Mute Poetry in the Commercial Cinema

So far as the masses are concerned, poetry, in its academically esteemed forms, labours under four main handicaps. Any one of them would alone be sufficient to kill interest, although they generally apply in combination and reinforce one another.

Thus poetry is, alas, first and most insistently (compulsorily) offered at school by missionaries of middle-class middlebrows sweetness and light, whose attitudes and values (*bourgeois* moral uplift and/or romanticism) are frequently ungraftable upon genuine working-class attitudes. It usually concerns 'symbolic' things (rainbows, daffodils) which have little real, intimate meaning for urban or indeed for rural youth. Worse, it eschews 'vulgar', i.e. interesting, subjects, in favour of middle-class feelings about what is 'refined' and 'beautiful'. Fourth, the intellectual complexity and cultural range of reference of genuinely 'modern' poetry handicap communication with untrained audiences. And conversely, academics often ignore or deprecate the popular mythology from which the mass media so often derive their intimacy of resonance with their audience.

'Poetry' is notoriously difficult to define plausibly and clearly. We are not using the word in the common literary sense, to mean verse with a certain intellectual and emotional texture, but in the looser, larger sense, whereby it is possible to speak of certain paintings, Surrealist texts or *objets trouvés* as 'poetic'. The implication is of some lyrical quality which is deep, intense, obscure in origin, and somehow over-and-above or below-and-beneath the obvious, logical 'dramatic' meaning. In fact, this 'overtone' exists out of art, in everyday life, in, for example, the melancholy exhilaration of a sunset, the eerie seductiveness of window dummies, the erotic delicacy of flowers. In art's special, 'meditative', circumstances, these atmospheres are easily and naturally brought to the fore. Poetry, in this sense, consists of the free, intensive, subtle exploitation of these irrationalities.

A famous example is the burglary sequence in *Du Rififi Chez Les Hommes* (Jules Dassin). A burglar alarm is stifled by coils of white sludge exuded from a fire extinguisher. The plaster of a ceiling is pierced from above by the tip of a fabric-muffled drill. An umbrella is poked down through the hole and opened outside-down, to catch falling flakes of plaster. The team of craftsmen work in a dreamlike wordlessness. The scene's realism is documentary and it was in fact used as an instructional manual by gangs of burglars in several countries, one of whom used its techniques to burgle the cinema where it was showing. But, the dramatic tension, the unaccustomed use of objects, the silence, also creates a strange 'Surrealist' atmosphere, over and above the dramatic sense of the scene.

Clearly there can be no hard-and-fast boundary between the 'dramatic' and the 'poetic'. As an example of such 'equivocation' we might glance at the common association of women, horse-riding and sexuality. In John Sturges' *By Love Possessed* Lana Turner rides a horse furioso, and before any plot has developed we know she is sexually frustrated. In *All the Fine Young Cannibals* Susan Kohner goes out horse-riding just before a quarrel with her sexually uninterested husband. In John Huston's *The Unforgiven* John Saxon talks about taming a shy mare and looks at Audrey Hepburn while he says it, which is generally felt to be ample justification for her brother (Burt Lancaster) promising to kill him if he ever talks that way again. In *The Big Sleep* Humphrey Bogart and Lauren Bacall talk about horse racing when everyone concerned, except the Hays Office, means the act of love—with a quite hilarious precision.[1]

An even more recondite symbol is the association of fresh cold water with sexual relief. It's not surprising if, in 'desert' films, water and women go together—in Mario Bava's *The Wonders of Aladdin* the sumptuous Amazons of the Persian desert lure parched Donald O'Connor towards them by pouring water on to the desert sands. In

[1] Obviously horse riding more often than not lacks these overtones. It may stand for social status. In Westerns the cowboy's love for his horse links with power, independence, even loneliness—Howard Hughes' *The Outlaw* would rather have his horse than Jane Russell, the traditional hero rides away from the sad heroine, the hero and his horse (Trigger, Silver) are a kind of joint being. Often the particular helplessness and inarticulacy of animals makes them metaphors for the purest and sincerest human feelings—so that Elizabeth Taylor has National Velvet and Lassie, Toomai has his elephants, Fay Wray has King Kong, and so on.

Arthur Lubin's *The Thief of Baghdad* Steve Reeves has just braved the magic Ordeal by Fire when he finds himself by a cool clear rivulet, which leads him to a luxurious palace whose attractive mistress tries to poison him. And in Terence Fisher's *The Stranglers of Bombay* Guy Rolfe finds himself pegged out in the Indian sun at noon while a villainous girl with an ostentatious bosom (bosoms would be more accurate) sits by him cruelly showing him the water which he isn't allowed to have.

Similar overtones apply even in temperate zones. In *La Ronde* timid student Daniel Gelin is sweltering with suppressed sexual desire for Simone Simon, and keeps sending her out to the kitchen to bring him a glass of cold, clear, fresh water.

The same association of ideas turns up in the popular myth that cold showers are a cure for sexual longings. Association of 'ideas' is a misleading phrase, really, for the remark isn't 'interpreted'—it's 'understood', or it communicates, because of the sensual shock, the contrast of physical sensation between 'hot' feelings and a cold douche. Here, cold water and warm feelings are antithetical. But in the 'desert' films, cold water and warm feelings are interchangeable —the hero (or the spectator) wants both the water and the women. The pleasantness of cold water makes it 'like' sexuality, instead of its opposite. In neither case is there an 'objective', 'intellectual', connection of ideas or sensations; everything is interpreted in the context of a very subjective thing like the urgency of desire.

These 'dramatic' meanings may be consciously understood by the spectator, or simply felt as 'mood' or 'atmosphere'; but in neither case are they interpreted or decoded in a matter-of-fact way. The general audience doesn't say to itself: 'Horse-riding . . . hmmm. . . . Freud says that in dreams it often stands for sexual intercourse. . . .' Apart perhaps from the educated fad, it hasn't read Freud, it might well think the whole idea ridiculous of it had, nor has it the intellectuals' habit of half-serious, half-satirical play with Freudian interpretations. The 'horse-riding' parallels depend on the lead given by the dramatic contexts (including an off-screen scandal involving Lana Turner), and are felt on the basis of a physical, kinaesthetic similarity. Horse-riding is a physical, exhilarating, rhythmic and legs-astride activity. In any event, the spectator never substitutes the new meaning for the obvious one; Lana Turner *is* riding a horse, the scene isn't just a 'symbol' for how she's feeling. The explanation doesn't explain anything away. The audience *feels* rather than *thinks out* the second meaning, which is not so much a *substitute* meaning as an *additional* one, not so much *deeper* as an *overtone*.

There is a subtler poetry in Marcel Carné's *Le Jour Se Lève* (scripted by the Surrealist poet Jacques Prévert), when Jacqueline Laurent enters a factory workshop, carrying a bunch of flowers, to be confronted by a burly welder (Jean Gabin) clad in a protective asbestos gear. Given this strong contrast, we know without thinking that a girl cradling a bunch of flowers is a bunch of flowers herself. To make the metaphor more conscious—say, by intercutting, as older textbooks recommend—would be too emphatic, indeed, cheapening. For in outline the metaphor, girl=bouquet, is banal. It is given life by the contrast (carrying the sense, industrialization versus the natural), and by nuances of style: the girl's face, her reserved, disturbing expression and presence. She is not *reduced* to a bunch of flowers. Their presence *enriches* hers, but in no way limits her, as, in itself, a 'like' clause might do. She 'is' as fresh as the flowers, but she is herself too, with all her dramatic possibilities. . . .

Thus, a specific metaphor would be an impoverishment. To put it another way, the metaphor, in novels, dramas, or films, is only one way of making us 'feel' girl and flowers on our mental 'screen' at the same time. A metaphor is a 'prop' which couldn't masquerade as part of the plot or scene, and so had to be introduced by the tacit word 'like'.

Because cinema visuals are intellectually clumsy (having no prepositions, conjunctions or grammar to speak of) the commercial cinema's natural tendency, at least in its present stage of development, is to disguise metaphors as props, décor, setting, plot-symbols, locale, and so on. This is so much part of the cinema's dramatic, not just grammar, but spelling, that one's choice of examples is bound to be arbitrary.

In Orson Welles's *The Lady from Shanghai*, Orson Welles and Rita Hayworth have a lovers' meeting in an aquarium in whose tanks silhouetted sharks and octopi are prominent. During an island picnic, shots of the graceful but enigmatic heroine are intercut with shots of high-stepping white birds and a writhing black snake. (The plasticity of the contrasts is important—'high-stepping white' versus 'black writhing'.) In Joseph Losey's *The Sleeping Tiger* the correct, yet chilly relationship between a psychiatrist (Alexander Knox) and his wife (Alexis Smith) is expressed by their smart, yet starkly lit, rooms.

The husband invites a young criminal (Dirk Bogarde) to stay with them. An abrupt cut from bare white walls takes us into a steady, stealthy tracking movement past rubber-plants, whose leaves, in close-up, evoke some steamy, slimy jungle, and, sure enough, our track concludes in a close-up of the trouble maker reading, sure enough, a volume with the sweltering title, *Sexual Behaviour in the Human Female*. The polar clinic is challenged by the tropic jungle.

Henry King's *Snows of Kilimanjaro* offers a rare example of a pretty recondite poetic symbol which is (just about) communicated to a fairly large majority of spectators—though its meaning will cross most people's minds briefly only, if at all. Its hero, a writer (Gregory Peck) looks back on his life as he lies dying and surveys the steady loss of his spiritual integrity. This theme is crystallized by a prologue, a symbolic story about a leopard found frozen in the snows of Mount Kilimanjaro—no one knows how or why he climbed so high. In retrospect, it becomes evident that the leopard is the hero, the snows in which his poetic fire was frozen those of the higher social strata. On several occasions the film compares good writing to hunting big-game; the writer's second mistress (Hildegard Neff) is nicknamed 'Frigid Liz, the semi-iceberg of the sub-tropics' (the same paradox as snow on a tropical volcano); she creates modernistic sculptures with holes (like craters) where their breasts ought to be; and she also has a laugh like the hyena laughing as the hero lies dying. Interestingly, the film begins with the 'parable' of the leopard, challenges the audience with it, offering it as a riddle. Instead of irritating, as obscurity sometimes does, it creates interest, a sense of anticipation—for the imagery is bold and striking, the anecdote has a certain toughness and romance in itself.

The cinema's relatively clumsy syntax and its exploitation of objects gives it an easy affinity of technique with Surrealism. Stanley Kramer's generally mediocre *The Pride and the Passion* has one sumptuous sequence. During the Napoleonic Wars a band of Spanish guerillas haul a gigantic cannon across the mountains. At one point they can avoid capture only by hiding the monstrous thing in a cathedral, and then under a float, which, festooned with pious images, is wheeled through the streets of a city during a religious festival.

This contrast has no precise sense. Are we supposed to reflect that cannons and cathedrals, war and love, however opposite they may seem, are natural bedfellows, since freedom is sacred and this is a clear case of 'Praise the Lord and Pass the Ammunition'? Is it that Christian sanctimony conceals in a hypocritical though necessary way the brute facts of military might: 'right may be right but it must have might too'? Should we concentrate on a psycho-analytical undertone—a cathedral is a cold, stone womb, a cannon is a phallus in a bad mood? At any rate, the contrast of objects with contrary emotional associations has a massive effect. Each of these 'meanings' is created by the spectator, in his own mind. It is, so to speak, his response to the 'problem', the disturbance posed by the film. As we have so often seen, much of a film's 'content' isn't in the film at all, but only in the spectator's mind. Whether the spectator 'solves' the 'problem' in the way the artist foresaw depends on their affinity of culture, experience and temperament. Sometimes, the artist doesn't really mind how the spectator solves it, or wants him not to solve it.

21 · A Little Dictionary of Poetic Motifs

Every generation of poets evolves its particular 'style, part of which is contributed by its vein of imagery. The poetry of the fiction film is no exception. There is a vast repertoire of vivid and valid symbols which spectators understand without thinking of them as poetry. Whether they are convincing or not often depends on the accompanying richness of detail.

Blindness. Terrible as this fate is felt to be, a sentimental style easily transforms it into something almost voluptuous, a kind of graceful helplessness (Chaplin's *City Lights*, 1931; Mark Robson's *Lights Out*, 1951). Because of our impulsive pity, a barking, aggressive blind person, brutally rejecting it, is not only admirable (for his courage, like Rochester) but frightening, almost magical (Anna Massey's witch-mother in Michael Powell's *Peeping Tom*). Blindness is, strangely enough, associated with the all-seeing eye. *The Informer* (Victor McLaglen) in John Ford's film is followed everywhere through the Dublin fog by a blind man with a tapping stick, who is his 'conscience'. In the fog, the blind can see. . . . The Peeping Tom, with his apparatus for seeing (camera, mirror) and his spiked tripod is 'seen through' by the blind woman.

Carnivals. Like the fair, it is a sudden explosion of caprice, of desire; it is fate, destiny, because it is visual fireworks of impulse and instincts. In fancy-dress the characters, consciously or unconsciously, reveal their 'real' selves, their hidden aspirations. The ingenue masquerades as a vamp, timid M. Hulot as a pirate. The tragic figure wanders through the revellers, who jestingly or carelessly buffet him—just as the clown is traditionally a tragic figure *because* any seriousness he can feel is mocked by his own comic mask.

Derelict houses. A life in ruins. Beaten up by, in symbol, his own conscience, Laurence Harvey in *Room at the Top* finds himself in a blitzed house. In *Rebel Without a Cause* the restless adolescent couple (James Dean, Natalie Wood) find a home of their own—an abandoned old house. Its elegance evokes the fragile beauty of their love, its dilapidation the 'half-finished' quality of adolescence. To underline the point, they make-believe that they are parents, who have put their troublesome children to bed and are alone 'downstairs'. . . .

Fairgrounds. 'In their attempts to define the character of a fair, literary sources repeatedly evoke the memory of Babel and Babylon alike. A seventeenth-century pamphlet describes the noise typical of a fair as "such a distracted noise that you would think Babylon not comparable to it" and, almost two hundred years later, a young English poet feels enthusiastic about "that Babylon of booths—the fair". The manner in which such Biblical images assert themselves unmistakably characterizes the fair as an enclave of anarchy in the sphere of entertainment. This accounts for its eternal attractiveness. People of all classes and ages enjoy losing themselves in a wilderness of glaring colours and shrill sounds, which is populated with monsters and abounding in bodily sensations—from violent shocks to tastes of incredible sweetness. For adults it is a regression into childhood days, in which games and serious affairs are identical, real and imagined things mingle, and anarchical desire aimlessly tests infinite possibilities. By means of this regression, the adult escapes a civilization which tends to overgrow and starve out the chaos of instincts—escapes it to restore that chaos upon which civilization nevertheless rests. The fair is not freedom, but anarchy entailing chaos.'[1]

Flowers. Suspect of sentimentality, and used more drily than in Wordsworth poems about daffodils. In *Duel in the Sun* the spot where the lovers died together is marked by the appearance of a flower known nowhere else—a cactus with a large red blossom. The cactus is the villainous hero, the passionate red flower is the heroine. The lovers' souls are mingled in death; here is the folk image of the briar-and-the-rose growing from the lovers' graves and intermingling.

Mechanical music. Especially in European films, musical boxes,

[1] Siegfried Kracauer, *From Caligari to Hitler*, Dennis Dobson, 1947.

pianolas, barrel-organs, and horn phonographs are used in a sense opposite to what we might expect from 'mechanism'—to express nostalgia, delicacy, a lost innocence. The fascination they have for children, together with their 'period' feel, outweighs any adult diffidence about their banal 'pop' tunes and canned quality. As so often, the popular poetic sense of a symbol is derived its meaning for children. The music comes from long ago and faraway, the popular tunes of yesterday have the charm of memory.

But the sweet, unstopping blandness of musical boxes associates them also with crime. In Jean Renoir's *La Règle du Jeu* an aristocrat expresses his basic spontaneity of soul by enthusing over the latest acquisition to his collection of musical boxes: a huge, elaborate Dutch street organ. But its sound acts as background to an attempted crime passionel, as, again, in Hitchcock's *Strangers on a Train* the carousel organ plays, 'And the band played on . . .' as a brutal strangling takes place.

Barrel-organ and fairground-organ have lived down their unsavoury social origins; the jukebox has yet to do so. Vadim's *Et Dieu Créa la Femme* (1956) is possibly the first film in which its coloured lights, its baroque streamlining, its loud and unstoppable thumping, are used affectionately rather than to create a vulgar atmosphere. Still, close-ups of the machinery choosing and manipulating a disc tend to suggest something slightly ominous, an anthropomorphic indifference—here is a robot in embryo. . . .

Mirrors. At critical moments, a character inspects himself in a mirror. 'Is this really me, who is that stranger, am I becoming someone else. . . ?' Characters who hate themselves smash mirrors. Inspecting his reflection is an extrovert's form of introversion.

As our hero sees himself in the mirror, the laws of logic are broken. He is in two places at once. The 'seer seen' creates uneasiness, or dreaminess. Hence the supernatural often appears via mirrors. Combing her hair, the heroine sees the werewolf loom in the mirror. Vampires have no reflection. In *Dead of Night* a mirror with its own room begins to take over the room in which the heroine lives.

A mirror is a latent doppelganger. *The Dark Mirror* tells the story of identical twins, one good, one evil. Mirrors tell the truth, but in a menacing way: 'Magic mirror on the wall. . . .' Cocteau's *Orphée* follows his Princess through mirrors into a mysterious land. . . .

Paintings and posters. The portrait of Dorian Gray is a 'magic mirror'—it absorbs his spiritual ugliness while he remains the fairest of them all. In Godard's *A Bout de Souffle* Jean Seberg pretends to be happy and *insouciant*, but, pinned to the wall, just behind her head, life-size photographs of herself looking sad and thoughtful give the game away.

In *L'Avventura* Gabriele Ferzetti wanders moodily through a party in a luxurious mansion. He pauses to look at a painting, which, 'Old Masterish' in style, shows a plump young woman arrogantly presenting one of her breasts to the mouth of a sad, bearded patriarch. A slim, quietly depraved looking girl, also looking at the portrait, turns and smiles provocatively at the hero. The plump girl and the old man 'balance' the slim girl and Ferzetti, in the prime of life. Dramatically, there are no parallels—or are there. . . ? Vague as it may seem, this scene has so pointed an impact as to draw quiet gasps from any audience.

Often, paintings and posters *attack* the characters. A laughing clown points his finger mercilessly at Anny Ondra in Hitchcock's *Blackmail*, as, knife in hand, she edges back from the corpse. . . .

Railway stations are drab fairgrounds. From the platform the rails stretch away. Even when the terminal is a bustle of arrivals and departures, the mood is one of routine, separateness, greyness. Hence they recall the renunciation of passion: Lean's *Brief Encounter*, de Sica's *Indiscretion*.

Shop windows. In Fritz Lang's *M* the child murderer (Peter Lorre) sees his next victim gazing into a shop window full of toys. He pauses by the next window, and his reflection is hemmed in by a display of serried knives. In yet another window, the movements of an attention-catching spiral and an arrow have a mesmeric, mechanical quality, like the psychological pressure pounding inside his head.

Photographed as reflected in the shop window, your character is transparent to what he is gazing at—his desires and obsessions are more solid and real than he himself. . . .

Many people enjoy window-shopping as much as the Romantic poet enjoyed communing with Nature. Shop windows are the realms of the coveted, the fairyland of desire, the magic casements of toys, clothes, plaster mannequins, a Surrealistic jumble of bric-a-brac. Audrey Hepburn has *Breakfast at Tiffany's*.

Statues. Statues are people waiting for their turn to come alive—as in the Pygmalion myth. In *One Touch of Venus* shop-assistant Robert Walker falls in love with a statue window-model of Venus. His love brings her alive (as Ava Gardner). In Jean Delannoy's *Les Jeux Sont Faits*, from a story by Sartre, and in Powell and Pressburger's *A Matter of Life and Death* (both 1946) the temporarily dead walk among the motionless living—in eternity the living are the statues. Corpses are statues—in Milestone's *All Quiet on the Western Front* the dead soldier in the shell-hole stares, stares and stares. . . . In *Blackmail* the blackmailer and his pursuers seem tiny as flies as they run past the huge impassive face of an Egyptian Pharaoh in the British Museum. In the same director's *North-by-North-West* Cary Grant and Eva-Marie Saint are tiny as flies as they hang from the huge serene, moonlit faces of American national heroes, carved in the rockface. 'As flies to wanton boys are we to the Gods. . . .' In Clouzot's *Le Salaire de la Peur*, Bernard Blier pathetically succumbs to jealous fears about his wife's infidelity, while, in the foreground, the cold, sensual, expressionless face of a female singer waiting to rehearse seems that of a vulgar sphinx.

Tape-recorders. A mechanical contrivance, a substitute for the voice; depersonalized man. The dead speak to the living; it is a mechanical ghost. It is a liar—murderers use it to establish their alibi. It enables us all to be one another's Big Brothers. Played backwards, or too fast, the voice becomes a shrill, absurd gabble, a mocking parody of words and feelings (*La Notte*). In *La Dolce Vita* the intellectuals play one another beautiful tapes of the thunder, the birds, running water—longing for the simplicity of nature, which they appreciate only when it has a 'frame' around it, when it is merely traces of itself. . . .

Trains. Steam locomotives are rich with emotional associations—their whistles are cries of anger, joy, malevolence, jubilation, or, on the prairie, forlorn and lonely, or, in the blues, the consoling thought of escape. Sometimes they smash by like the characters' passions, emotion gone berserk, on the rails of ineluctable consequences. Sometimes they are invitations to suicide: 'throw yourself under me' scowls the steam monster, growing in size as it approaches. In *L'Avventura* a train rattles by as Monica Vitti and Gabriele Ferzetti make love, then diminuendoes away into the rocky landscape, like the failure of their passion to transform reality.

Under the sea. Lea Massari in *L'Avventura* tries to alleviate boredom by pretending she has been attacked by a shark. At the end of *La Dolce Vita* a flabby deep sea monster with jelly-fish in its mouth symbolizes the soul of the sweet-lifers—or their impending despair. Jacques-Yves Cousteau's *Épaves* (1945) most vividly crystallizes the poetry of the undersea realm. Wrecked hulks resemble eerie cathedrals through which the swimmer flies, gliding in three dimensions as if he were a great, leisurely bird. Weird fish and corals seem as bizarre as another planet. Skin-diving is the twentieth-century's version of romantic 'Nature' poetry, with a similar sense of 'escape' from people and routine. The erotic sense of floating-'flying' is taken up in a passionate underwater embrace in Robert Webb's *Beneath the Ten-Mile Reef* (1953).

L'Avventura is, in a sense, less a story than a succession of poetic atmospheres, with no clear 'dramatic' or 'psychological' meanings. The helicopter (a sinister, gigantic insect), the sharks, the starlet bursting out of her dress, the church-bells which Gabriele and Monica tweak with sad whimsy, the breast-obsessed paintings of the nervous adolescent (curiously reminiscent of Tony Perkins, the ultimate Momist of *Psycho*), the stark rocky island on which the sea beats spitefully, the 'dead' church, the despairing—suicidal?—intellectuals, the endless corridors down which the characters rush in a kind of green anguish, the visual sense of being exposed to infinity between sky and flat landscapes. . . . Each of these images is echoed in *La Dolce Vita*: the helicopter from which a statue of Jesus is ludicrously slung, the quietly nihilistic intellectual whimsically playing jazz in church (tweaking the bells), Anita, Our Lady of the Pin-Ups, incarnation of a society's pagan obsession, the soggy dead fish parallelling the sharks, the sea drowning the angel's words, the intellectual's suicide, the hero's surrender to commerce and vulgarity, the sense of endless travelling and perpetual waiting. . . .

Round the edges of the conventional thriller melodrama in Hitchcock's *North-by North-West* appear images reminiscent of *L'Avven-*

tura: the long train-journey, inexplicable disappearances, the suddenly sinister crop-spraying biplane which catches the hero alone and exposed at a country cross roads, the lost lovers hanging from the huge dead faces of American Presidents who 'don't care' (alienation . . .). In the U.N.O. building, glassy edifice of idealism, intellectual Cary Grant sees a good man slickly knifed in the back, as, in Antonioni's *La Notte*, behind the bland glass cage of a clinic, an idealist lies dying. Is there not even a similarity between Eva-Marie Saint, apparently nymphomaniac, later so cold and reserved—and the nymphomaniac in the clinic of *La Notte*, succeeded by Monica Vitti, offering and withdrawing herself. . . . In Hitchcock's entertainment melodrama, death-by-cancer becomes death-by-murder, loneliness becomes a spy story, uneasiness becomes terror, the ambiguity of human feeling is simplified into the 'either-or' of suspense. In Marcel Camus' *Orfeu Negro*, the silent glass curtain-walling of a modern office-building contrasts with the colour, noise and shouts of the natives' carnival. The harmony of affluent modernity is the anti-fair, a delicate, but steely edifice of anti-passion, a world cold as Kafka's. . . .

22 · Poetry without Papers

In such poetry there is no intellectual protocol, no received 'tone of voice', no sense of sensitive loftiness. In Hitchcock's *To Catch a Thief* a cigarette is stubbed out in the yolk of fried egg—hinting at the burning out of an eye, but with a tactile sickliness of its own. In his *The Lady Vanishes* a nun reveals that she is not what she seems, her cloven hoof is her high heels, while the patient in her care is really her prisoner, bound and gagged by the bandages. Poetry gears in with melodrama, with narrative, with action, as in the old myths. Its lyricism has not yet become autonomous. Similarly, the pop 'lyric' is still conjoined with music, in the way that 'high culture' has all but lost, or is still rediscovering.

For the most part, poetry is derived from 'obvious' symbols—those of everyday experience, such as window-shopping, or listening to tape-recorders, or looking at the moon, whose poetic spell hasn't been destroyed by its rhyming with 'June' and 'croon'. How could it be, when it has been a literary motif for several thousand years? Just as in literature the 'stock' image can be revivified by sensitive words and ideas, so, in the cinema, the cliché can be brought alive again by sensitive art-direction (as in Murnau's *Sunrise*) or lighting (as in Frank Borzage's *Moonrise*) or photography or by associated imagery (the theme of sun and moon in *Orfeu Negro*, Brahms and whisky in *Les Amants*). Such poetry retains the epic poems' 'narrative' relationship with the world. Its interest is less in intellectual subtlety or complexity than in passionate attitudes and intense experiences. Subtleties arise out of the paradoxical encounter of profound, simple elements (the cathedral and the cannon). On the other hand in much poetry written with a highly 'cultured' frame of reference the simplicities are reached through a 'pointillisme' of subtleties—and so become indecipherable by all but the expert few. Often, as with the Aristotelian emphasis on the fable—the mass media retain older techniques which our academics have not recognized.

In its primitive stage, poetic myth is closely bound up with religion. If the universe is made 'poetic' by means of myths about sun and moon goddesses, it is not to 'prettify' it, but to attempt to explain it. Such poetry, in intention, is documentary and philosophic. In the popular cinema, documentary films, heavily influenced by middle-class middlebrow ideas of poetic 'sweetness and light', try for a lyrical 'poetry' to which mass audiences are healthily insensible. Disney's *Real Life Adventures* restrict themselves to a complacent sentimentality which narrowly fails to banish all wonder and beauty from such films as *Water Birds* and *The Living Desert*. Such 'underwater' films as *Épaves* illustrate the 'superimposition' of documentary and poetry interest. The *Rites of Spring* episode in Disney's *Fantasia* has a certain mythic grandeur. The sun as an inchoate mass whirling and blazing through space; the spectacular convulsions and metamorphoses of the earth's crust before the appearance of any living thing; life's slow crawl from the single cell on the seabed ooze to complicated animals crawling on the shore (a time-lapse 'tracking shot' of poetic compression); the affection of dinosaur mothers for their pups; the earliest mammals scuttling about beneath the legs of the giant reptiles they are destined to supplant; the inexorable and anguished extinction of entire species—here, documentary, spectacle and drama blend into a vision of philosophical grandeur, lowbrow, certainly, but not invalid.

Yet this 'factual' episode is closely related to the least serious of cinematic genres—the monster fantasy (*King Kong*, *The Beast from 20,000 Fathoms*, *The Lost World*). The dream meets fact—creating the myth. . . . Science-fiction at its most poignant is the poetry of scientific possibility, i.e. the exaggeration of technology into its 'poetic' meaning . . . hence fantasy and horror films so often have a rich vein of poetry—poetry in narrative form, that is, myth.

The older forms of myth are still valid currency. Superstitions of many kinds afford convenient rendezvous for poetic fantasy and the proto-scientific myth. Ludicrous as it may seem, many people still believe, or half-believe, in ghosts, in poltergeists, in dark forces with which it is as well not to meddle—and, by emotional extension, in their Transylvanian kin. Films about black magic have surprisingly little to surmount in the way of audience scepticism. It's a safe bet that more English people are frightened of cemeteries, or believe that the dead are watching us, than know the meaning of such exotic initials as 'F.A.O.' or 'U.N.E.S.C.O.'

The 'dream sequence' is characteristically the realm of libidinous delirium. In Victor Fleming's *Dr. Jekyll and Mr. Hyde* (1941) women's bodies suddenly turn to sand, and flow away as if scattered by a driving wind.

In all these ways the ordinary commercial cinema maintains something at least of the fullness of the primal myth, blending, in various permutations, fact, drama, the 'Surreal', dream, magic and the supernatural powers at their play. Perhaps we too readily assume the mass media's lack of, and antagonism towards, poetry. . . .

23 · A Great Defect

An over-eagerness to penetrate to the allegorical layer of a film may lead to distortion of that very layer. Jean Cocteau's *Orphée* (1950) affords a striking example.

Orphée (Jean Marais) a celebrated poet, defiantly visits a café patronized by the hostile writers of the *avant-garde*. An old friend gives him two pieces of advice. 'Your greatest defect is that you know just how far to go too far,' and: 'Astonish us.' Orphée catches sight of the Princess (Maria Casarès), a beautiful patroness of the *avant-garde*, trying to prevent a drunken young poet, Cégèste (Edouard Dhermite), from scattering his papers about. A fight develops, and her chauffeur, Heurtebise (François Perier), phones for the police. Cégèste is knocked over by two uniformed motor-cyclists who drive on without stopping.

The Princess orders Orphée to help her carry the injured man into her Rolls-Royce. After Heurtebise has driven them some way into a strangely deserted part of the countryside, Orphée realizes that Cégèste is dead. The Princess is stonily unperturbed, and greets the two motor-cyclists as if they were her agents. She takes Orphée to an eerie and dilapidated chalet; two Chinese servants appear as if from nowhere and serve him with champagne. While he drinks, the Princess resuscitates Cégèste, who recognizes her as 'his death' and enters her service. Orphée catches a glimpse of the Princess leading Cégèste and her aides through a mirror—which ripples like water—but when he tries to follow the mirror is—just a mirror.

He comes to, apparently lost in a sandy landscape, but is hailed by Heurtebise, who, presumably on the Princess's orders, drives Orphée home. There, his wife, Eurydice (Marie Déa) is discussing the sudden disappearance of the two poets, with the Commissioner of Police and with Aglaonice (Juliette Gréco) leader of a League of Women, a friend of the *avant-garde*, and an old enemy of Orphée. Heurtebise parks the Rolls in Orphée's garage and, after pacifying the Commissioner, Orphée begins listening to cryptic lines of poetry coming over the car-radio. He refuses Eurydice any explanation of his disappearance—when she tries to tell him she is pregnant, he refuses to listen. Instead she confides in Heurtebise, who tries to reassure her of Orphée's love.

Night after night the ghostly Princess appears in Orphée's room and watches him sleep . . . as if Orpheus had charmed even his Death. . . .

A journalist friend of Aglaonice publicly accuses Orphée of being implicated in Cégèste's death; but Orphée, utterly indifferent to his wife's pleas and the counsel of Heurtebise, now spends all his time in the car, whose messages have mostly degenerated to meaningless series of numbers. Although Orphée has forbidden her to see Aglaonice, Eurydice resolves to appeal to her. Heurtebise refuses her the use of his car, and, when she ventures out on her bicycle, he vainly tries to drag Orphée away from the radio. Just outside the house, she is run over by the motor-cyclists. Heurtebise carries the injured woman to her bedroom, where he confronts the Princess and her new, still clumsy, aide, Cégèste. Heurtebise is insubordinate, querying her orders, and again tries to warn Orphée, without success. Cégèste broadcasts the messages which keep Orphée in the garage, while the Princess 'strangles' Eurydice and leads her to the underworld. But she forgets one of the rubber gloves which enable her to penetrate mirrors. Heurtebise remains behind and tells Orphée that by following him to the next world there is a chance of reclaiming Eurydice. Orphée follows, not simply because of his love of Eurydice, but also in the hope of finding the Princess.

Heurtebise explains: 'Mirrors are the doors through which death comes and goes . . . watch yourself in a mirror as you age, and you will see death at work, like a swarm of bees in a glass hive.' Beyond the mirror, they traverse a No-Man's-Land, resembling a ruined city. 'Life dies little by little. This is the twilight zone. It is made of the memories of men and the debris of their habits.' The two men appear before an underworld tribunal, not as the accused, but as witnesses. The Princess is on trial for having killed Eurydice, without orders. Her crime is 'Initiative', and her motive, she confesses, love of Orphée. She and Orphée declare their undying love for each other.

Orphée, being a poet, is allowed to reclaim Eurydice, but on condition that he never looks at her again; if he dies, he will lose her. Heurtebise is allowed to return with them to ease them into their new ways during the awkward 'honeymoon' period of living back-to-back. During a tragi-farcical scene of hide-and-seek, Orphée's exasperation mounts. At last Eurydice is convinced that he hates her, and tries to kill herself by creeping into his bedroom and startling him into seeing her: her plan is frustrated by a sudden power-cut.

The next morning, however, Orphée glimpses her in the driving-mirror of the fatal car. Simultaneously, Aglaonice and her friends (the Bacchantes), determined to avenge Cégèste, burst into Orphée's house; Heurtebise throws him a revolver, for self-defence, but Orphée is accidentally shot in a tussle and dies. The Bacchantes scatter, and the police are held at bay by the two motor-cyclists who carry off Orphée's body.

Beyond the Zone, the Princess waits impatiently ('Strange, I almost have a sense of time . . .'), while Orphée and Heurtebise traverse the Zone, this time with the greatest difficulty, for they are going where they have no right to go. The Princess asks Orphée if he will accept any ill-treatment she cares to inflict on him, and then orders Cégèste and Heurtebise to 'kill' him. The death of a dead soul is rebirth. . . .

Orphée awakes beside Eurydice. She remembers having had a bad dream, he feels he has been inspired.

Cégèste watches as the Princess and Heurtebise, guilty of disobeying their totalitarian superiors, are marched off to face a terrible punishment. . . .

Cocteau's remark, via Heurtebise, 'You seek too hard to understand, Sir. That is a great defect,' is of a piece with his many pleas to critics to believe, not to interpret. All the same, he might have saved his breath to cool his porridge, for much critical effort has been devoted to establishing 'deep' meanings. For example—the Princess is Death, Heurtebise and Cégèste are angels of death, the Zone is one of the outer circles of Hell, and so on. (But why is Death a seductive woman, and not, say, an old woman, or an old man? or a skeleton? What does an 'angel of death' symbolize? what does 'Hell' symbolize? The explanation explains nothing.) One might see the Princess as a black angel, a guardian devil, trying to pervert Orphée from a healthy domestic life with Eurydice. Or, if the film is an allegory about the poet and poetry, the Princess is a false muse, a black goddess, a 'negative' of the white variety worshipped by Robert Graves.

In a Jungian interpretation, the Princess might be the 'terrible mother', the witch, menacing the child with an alluring possessiveness, also incestuous. A Freudian interpretation might suggest that the notion of 'Death' symbolizes the punishment for incestuous wishes towards the mother, who is alleged to be responsible; and the land of Death is the land of repressed desire, where nightmares come true. This can point to the overtones of incest and homosexuality which many critics have noticed in Cocteau's work, and which he has hardly bothered to conceal. John Minchinton drew some interesting parallels between the film and the Greek Orphic religion (which, despite its name, had no real links with the Orpheus of myth, but was certainly a death-centred religion, ascetic and puritanical). Jean-Jacques Khim discovered some astonishing parallels between Cocteau's film and the Thibetan Book of the Dead.

Writing from a Roman Catholic viewpoint, Henri Agel complains that the underworld is not really Hellish enough, and accuses the film of a Manichean loathing of the flesh. Certainly one could make a terrifying film about the nuptials of Death in *The Seventh Seal* and the Princess in *Orphée*. But from this angle Cocteau's film lacks the high-voltage tragic protest of Bergman's, and the mutual love of Orphée and the Princess contradicts this interpretation. Death in this film is not particularly physical death—which takes some of the force from Henri Agel's remark. The film contains many personal motifs. 'Astonish us,' was said to Cocteau by Diaghilev in 1913; and Cocteau certainly knows just how far to go too far. One of the lines which Cégèste broadcasts, 'L'oiseau chante avec les doigts,' was sent to Cocteau in a letter by the poet Apollinaire in 1917. The Bacchantes are said to recall the Surrealists, who detest Cocteau and all his works, all the more because outsiders so consistently miscall *Le Sang d'un Poète* a Surrealist film. The champagne offered by Chinese servants in the house of death probably symbolizes opium; in his journal of that name Cocteau describes one of the symptoms of opium-craving as 'champagne in the veins'.

The film bears a general resemblance to Cocteau's relatively clumsy one-act tragi-farce of the same name. There, Orphée is obsessed, not by the radio in a Rolls, but by a horse, which nods its head in response to letters on an ouijah-board. Heurtebise is not a servant of death, but a glazier, constantly appearing to mend Eurydice's windows, which are, so to speak, the anti-mirrors in which, as Cocteau says: 'One sees oneself age and death approach.' (There is a trace to Heurtebise's original profession here: he and Orphée pass a glazier crying his wares in the Zone.) Death, who enters and leaves by mirrors, and uses rubber gloves, is a beautiful woman in a ball gown. Her aides, Azrael and Raphael, are white-masked surgeons. Orphée and Death neither meet nor fall in love. Eurydice, intending to poison her rival, the horse, is herself tricked and poisoned by Aglaonice. Orphée brings her back from the underworld on the same conditions. After he has been stoned, the Commissioner, who is an absurd dunderhead, instead of, as in the film, sympathetic, interrogates Heurtebise. Orphée's head then appears on the top of a bust and answers most of the questions, giving his name as 'Cocteau'. A last scene shows Orphée and Eurydice enjoying lunch together in Paradise.

Heurtebise is a recurrent figure in the Cocteau mythology. In *Le Sang d'un Poète* the character of this name is a muscular Negro with wings. Cocteau's poem 'L'Ange Heurtebise' includes the lines:

Angel Heurtebise, with brutality
Incredible, leap on me. Please
Jump not so hard,
Bestial boy, flower of great
Stature.

And the name means: 'breaking against the kiss'. The same poem features Cégèste as a secondary angel.

In view of this enigmatic personal mythology it is hopeless to attach 'philosophical' meanings to the film. As with *Marienbad* many interpretations *nearly* fit, but none really fits. (Indeed, the idea of an 'interpretation' which 'explains' everything is itself a myth.) Cocteau declares that 'the film sets out to be nothing but the paraphrase of a Classical Greek myth' (though what are Heurtebise, Cégèste doing there?). The film's 'meaning' is, of course, as nebulous as the 'meaning' of the Greek myth (which has never been agreed on). The film is not a message hidden in some obscure code, but simply, a story, a battery of emotional provocations. Enriching as they are, the interpretations mentioned above all have one limitation; they are too simple, they fail to take into account the fact that, far from symbolizing some vague abstraction or other, each character is torn between opposite desires. One can speak of themes, but not of symbols.

Cocteau sees three themes in the film. First, the successive deaths and counter-deaths that a poet must undergo in order to become, in Mallarme's words, 'Tel qu'en lui-meme enfin l'éternité le change' (such that at last eternity transforms him into himself). Second, the theme of inspiration: 'It is when Orphée renounces his own themes, and accepts messages from the outside, that everything is spoiled.' The third theme is that of free-will. 'Heurtebise,' writes Cocteau, 'is not at all an angel as he was in the play and as he is often said to be. He is a young dead soul, in the service of one of the innumerable satellites of death. He is as yet scarcely tainted by death. On several occasions, he tries to forewarn people, for example, Orphée of the worthlessness of the radio messages, and Eurydice of the accident which will happen on the road. But the destiny which he attempts to frustrate by an act of free will is a destiny initiated by the Princess. Hence the Superior Tribunal has no accusation to make against him. . . .

'At their trial . . . the Princess and Heurtebise are forced to avow the shadow of a shadow of the sentiment they feel, for the human kingdom to which they have belonged still has some power over them.' (A power corresponding perhaps to the 'ace of hearts' in *Le Sang d'un Poète.*)

The Princess and Heurtebise are not simply 'Death'; they are further advanced in death than the living. Throughout the film, Heurtebise *opposes* the Princess. There is a continuity between the dead and the living—the glazier in the Zone believes he is still alive, his habits persist. The hotel of *Marienbad* is situated in a posh suburb of the Zone. The state of total death towards which we are all slowly drifting is inconceivable, perhaps it does not exist, perhaps there is always the shadow of a shadow of a shadow, recurring like decimals.

In a general way, death is the opposite of love; maybe it is the ultimate bureaucracy, a concentrationary universe, fate. In so far as the Princess rebels against it, we can call the film *Countess Dracula Versus the Gestapo.*

The characters are divided within themselves. Love and death are inextricably intertwined. Orphée, who is alive, loves his death; his death, because she loves him, kills his wife, and later, when he is killed, undoes his death. Orphée's death keeps him alive, against his own wishes. If Heurtebise tries to thwart her, it is perhaps less for the sake of Orphée, than of Eurydice. In a way, he is the 'negative' of

Orphée—he adores Eurydice hopelessly, as Orphée adores the Princess. Life in each of the worlds is reaching out for the other. Cégèste, too, is a paradoxical figure; the darling of the *avant-garde*, yet shy and clumsy and soon poetically bankrupt. Although the one line is Apollinaire's, he may also recall Cocteau's friend Radiguet, author of *Le Diable Au Corps*, who died young; he may even represent Cocteau himself, as a young poet, accepted by the *avant-garde* but basically uncertain of everything. . . . The Princess cannot be labelled either a true or a false muse; she is a patroness of the arts, yet some of her actions menace Orphée's inspiration, while others renew it. Eurydice, who, if anyone, represents Life and happiness (she is pregnant, loyal, sentimental) at one point tries to commit suicide, and so is on the 'side' of Death as well. The living are morally no superior to the dead—Orphée is killed by the living, the Bacchantes, whom Eurydice trusts. Death is the work of the living, as well as of the dead.

As in all the best dramas, the principal characters are constantly being forced into reversals of their positions, and a cut-and-dried interpretation is likely to miss all the tragic force of these contradictions.

Perhaps the moral of the film is that poetic inspiration comes from the poet's inability to be either alive or dead. In whichever world he finds himself, he feels driven to break through into, or to get himself hounded by, the other. Orphée follows Eurydice to the underworld, for contradictory reasons, one an affirmation of life (to bring back Eurydice), the other a longing to embrace Death. The poet's inspiration is A.C. flashing to and fro between opposite poles. It is an everlasting contradiction, so close and intimate as to leave him perpetually confused. Cégèste's broadcasts are both pearls of poetry—and rubbish. In this 'union of contradictions', which is also an emotional ambivalence, we can perhaps glimpse, obscurely, why Heurtebise in the play and the film of *Orphée* is so different from Heurtebise in the poem and in *Le Sang d'un Poète*. In the poetry he is a sensual, kindly-brutal angel, here, on the contrary, he is lightly, politely and genuinely in love with Eurydice, but always impotent—in the warnings he gives, in his attempted intervention with the revolver, as a lover. However, the final strangling of Orphée on the orders of the Princess recalls the brutal assault which Cocteau's poem seems to crave.

The poet's task is to master—by remaining ever-obedient to—the 'union of contradictions'. He must become 'such that at last eternity transforms him into himself'; but he must also renounce, in the words of *Le Sang d'un Poète*, the fatal boredom of immortality (*l'ennui mortel de l'immortalité*). It is no easy task to distinguish the two; the poet is a lonely wanderer, a man without passports, the Garry Davis of all possible worlds—a fate worse than—yet eerily immune from—and also perhaps a result of—some death of the heart.

But *Orphée* could never be reduced to this meaning. The feelings suggested by the other interpretations are still valid. We can all recognize the Princess as a despot, a vampire, and the idea of women as danger is asserted again in the person of Aglaonice and her 'monstrous regiment of women'. Like Plyne in *Tirez Sur le Pianiste*, Cocteau says: 'La femme est magique . . .'—indeed, the episode of the Bacchantes' intervention might be called *Tirez Sur le Poète*. It is the simultaneous validity of so many emotional strands that gives the film the richness and the mystery of feelings far more real than those we can label with ease.

The film would be much less gripping if it were less convincing on its most superficial level; a spy story, gaining added tension from its supernatural overtones. Although its setting is post-war, it is packed with occupation memories; midnight arrests, power cuts, a Fascist militia who train guns on the ordinary police, spies and counter-spies, collaborationists and Gestapo tortures. Cocteau beat the ton-up boys to the draw in exploiting the Fascist virility of black-clad and be-goggled motor-cyclists, centaurs of a mechanical age.

Orphée is *also* one of the best films about the Occupation, because of its vivid atmosphere of an arbitrary, rapacious despotism.

The people aren't allegorical absolutes, symbols of philosophical principles. They are all what we have called 'wobblers', torn between opposing principles. Only by resisting 'allegory' can we reveal the film's richness, and obviate the short-circuiting effect of premature interpretation. All interpretations are bad in so far as their secret, but real, purpose is to simplify, to explain subordinate themes away, to replace all the uncertainties of dramatic struggle by a definite meaning.

The divergence of 'high culture' criteria from the 'popular' tradition of poetry not only renders many admirable works of art in the former illegible to the masses, but many admirable works of art in the latter illegible to *aficionados* of the former. It induces a naïvely rationalist approach to popular poetry which, if applied to other media, would annihilate poetry as a method of communication altogether. If we use as text J. G. Weightman's remarks on Ingmar Bergman's *The Seventh Seal* (1956) it is precisely because this writer, so careful and thoughtful when he writes about literary culture, often approaches films with expectations pitched so low that no artist could conceivably make himself understood. The reproach is hardly directed at Weightman himself, nor, for that matter, at the other 'visiting firemen' who drop nonchalantly into film criticism from their great cultural heights. As we have seen, those who should have been championing the film medium were contentedly using it to titillate their own complacency.

Bergman's film has a medieval setting. Death, a stern monk-like figure 'comes for' a Knight who, once idealistic, now disillusioned, is returning from the Crusades. The Knight challenges death to a chess game, so earning a brief respite, which he uses to search for someone or something which will checkmate Death. But by the end of the film, all the characters are whisked off in the Dance of Death—except for a family of travelling mountebanks—a young clown, who has visions of the Holy Family; his beautiful but more earthy wife; and their baby. The search for a 'checkmate' is, clearly, not so much a search for immortality, as for a meaning which will 'outlast' Death-as-nihilism—though the 'confusion' between the two senses is itself a meaning: a 'value' with which one can identify is, in a sense, oneself. . . .

Mr. Weightman, identifying Death with evil, comments, 'It is true that, in ordinary living, most people, after failing to cope with evil (which in fact cannot be coped with and merely has to be endured) start on a new phase. The trouble with *The Seventh Seal* is that it is trying to say much more than this, but only offers very confused symbolism. Why should Joseph, Mary and the babe be saved when the knight perishes? What is the connection with the Holy Family? Why should Death appear as a person, who admits that he knows nothing about the mystery of creation? Why should the knight play chess with Death? Psychologically he is not struggling against Death, he is worried about evil, which is rather a different problem . . . why should there be a tremendously impressive return to the knight's castle in a storm, only to be followed by resignation and extinction? Then, having accepted death with dignity, why should the seven victims be made to dance in anguish along the horizon? . . .

To have Death laboriously sawing down a tree to kill a minor character is grotesque. . . .'

But the answers to these questions are, surely, not Bergman's confusions, but his most elementary meanings, which he could hardly make clearer, except by inserting little subtitles which explain, 'I am not confused about this scene, the meaning of it is. . . .'

Very curtly and schematically, then, the answers are:

The clown, his wife and their baby are not Joseph, Mary and the Babe, but a low, earthly, earthy, comic, loving human family. The clown has visions, of Mary and her Babe, i.e. of all he loves, his wife and child, on the plane of ideal immortality. His wife does not have visions, she has womanly wisdom and motherhood instead.

They escape death for a little while because (*a*) he has Visions, which is like immortality-in-a-split-second, and (*b*) one-family-after-another, fertility and love, is as immortal as Death, for a little while, though perhaps one day the human race will die out, and because (*c*) Clown and Woman are the 'lowest common denominator' of humanity (like Picasso's clowns, say). The contrast-identity of clowning and the sacred is used in the anecdote about the Jester who turned somersaults to honour the statue of Our Lady, who kissed him when the monks objected. The durability of 'low' human nature appears in Louis MacNiece's lines:

> *. . . the whore and the buffoon,*
> *Will come off best: no dreamers, they cannot lose*
> *Their dream. . . .*

Only this clown is a dreamer, even if he pretty quickly loses his dignity in reality (when bullied into dancing on the tavern table). The young couple's profession (travelling showmen) has a nomadism like 'one's journey through life, man has no home' and a quality of illusion like, 'All the world's a stage.' Illusions, visions. . . .

Death appears as a person for the same reason that he appears as a person in medieval imagery. Given the human tendency to anthropomorphism, what form could be more easily understood? Analogous examples: Old Father Time, the Four Horsemen of the Apocalypse, Satan. In the language which myth-makers and poets have long permitted themselves, death is not only an inescapable event, it, or rather He, is also the ultimate persecutor. He dresses like a Monk because he does in folklore and because a monk's dress is a way of saying that he has renounced this world, which is what Death is making you do. It is also a mysterious, sinister kind of dress (like Dracula's black cloak). Death is ignorant of everything because he, or it, is the ultimate and total negation. A theological equivalent: the proposition that evil is both a positive force and a non-created Nothing.

The chess-match is a well-known symbol for cerebration and the processes of the intellect. The Knight, Crusader and idealist, represents the human attempt to affirm, or to search for, a 'good meaning'. Like that attempt, he's considerably weary and disillusioned. He is now looking for an answer more sophisticated than that of the sword, for a winning move, some value, which will negate Nothingness. It's not his own skin he wants to save, particularly; as a fighting man he has faced death without complaint before. It's absolute death, the death to man's values posed by The Absolute, that he's facing now, and this isn't quite the same thing as evil, although, of course, it's associated with it, traditionally, as in 'The Wages of sin is death.' The Bible often equates evil with Death, good with immortality. It's not a 'confusion' of Bergman's, but a venerable cultural association, and presumably has its origins in the inability of the unconscious mind to come to grips with reality and its nuances. The only punishments it knows are violent ones (castration, abandonment, approximity to 'death'), while on the other hand, the feeling of virtue catapults into omnipotent fantasies ('I'm going to live forever'). It would seem to be all but ineradicable from human thought.

The Knight's return to his castle is his reunion with his faithful Lady, the feminine equivalent of himself. His idealism has drained her life of happiness, but he hoped to find in her patience, faith and approval a value, a communion, so impervious to the chances and hazards of this world that she would, so to speak, 'check-mate' Death. He was attacking Death with his Queen, the most powerful fighting piece on the board, and his Queen is taken, by her unhappiness. The 'return home' is a dramatic symbol for the 'self-confrontation', the 'moment of truth', the 'summing-up', the 'home-stretch', the 'driving things home', the climactic point of the knight's return from the disastrous Crusade. I'm quite unable to understand why an impressive storm scene shouldn't be followed by resignation and extinction. It's common enough, surely, for storms, in literary convention, to precede disastrous events.

We may think we accept death with dignity, we may put a brave and philosophical face on it, but nature screams out against it and tugs away but gets tugged on, and that's the dance, which isn't a dance at all. We are all conscripts, members of a chain-gang, hold hands in a compulsory 'solidarity' which we may hate; we like it or we lump it, but we all go off into the dark.

The character in a tree is an actor-seducer, and the slick scintillating illusions of his profession and his hobby contrasts with the gross and cogent materialism of Death as a slow but sure old manual labourer. The scene's 'laboriousness' is presumably Swedish humour. It also relates to a general tradition, like the antiquated old car driven by Death in Dreyer's *They Met at the Ferry* (1948).

If modern rationalism can no longer follow the poetic language of a film so clearly in the folklore idiom, so much the worse for modern rationalism; one doubts whether it's even rational, except in trivial mannerisms.

It's not as if a film had to be particularly sophisticated to blend dramatic, poetic and philosophic meanings as Bergman's does, and our last chapter will, provocatively, concern itself with their confluence in the screen equivalent of 'pulp' idioms.

24 · The Wedding of Poetry and Pulp—Can They Live Happily Ever After and Have Many Beautiful Children?

Much science fiction is in the tradition of *Paradise Lost*, in that it relates the human condition to the basic physical and mental structures of the cosmos. Its explorations of 'other worlds' are akin to metaphysics. Usually, it 'decapitates' metaphysics, for, instead of leading up to the crowning-and-unifying notion of God (or a hierarchy of Gods) it often hints that all our acting, and even thinking, assumptions will be further undermined from outside our present 'unity'. From this point of view, science-fiction whose intention is to satirize our society is less science-fiction than satire; or at least is, poetically speaking, best read in reverse, ignoring the author's satirical purpose and dwelling on his other world. In either event, of course, no *s.f.* story entirely escapes the gravitational pull of society today—if only because its readers are formed by that society, and must refer everything to its terms.

Yet little of this aspect of *s.f.* has penetrated to the screen. For in the cinema, with its mass public, prevalent professional theories, whereby the public seeks above all familiar reality either ameliorated, melodramatized or 'comicalized', are compounded by the prevalence of critical theories determined to prove that the cinema medium is essentially realistic, sociological and psychological. As precious as rare therefore are those films which, developing within the tradition of childhood like Flash Gordon, not only lead us on an odyssey through space-time, but into the terms of interplanetary ethics. One thinks avidly of what might have been done with the ideas behind a few turnips, notably Sid Pink's *Journey to the Seventh Planet* (1961), where an extrastellar creature, defending its terrain, weaves destructive mirages out of the spacemen's own minds. . . .

Yet, whether a film whisks us to the twenty-first century, or to

Atlantis in its prime (*circa* 10,000 B.C., according to Umberto Scarpelli) the spectators remain, alas, in the pedestrian here and now. As bizarre as the robes, the décor, the technological contraptions, may be, they must refer back to the structures of our *musée imaginaire*, our lives, our unconscious, our society. It would be oddly hard for most of us to adjust to the sight of a space-hero dressed according to a time when narrow, drooping shoulders were considered smart (though they were, less than a hundred years ago). It's hard enough to understand certain assumptions of the Samoans, the Balinese or the Americans, and all but impossible to empathize into the perceptions and drives of, say, a boa constrictor. How much more difficult then to identify with the notions of, say, the immortal twelve-sensed telepathic polymorphoids whose natural habitat is the ammonia clouds of Galaxy X7?

As with sensations, so with ethics, philosophies, emotions. Flash *v.* Ming is the cowboy against the Yellow Peril (from Ming to Mao . . .), is James Bond against the intergalactic No.

If here we endeavour to focus on the pedestrian 'resonance' of five 'assonant' fantasies, it is in no way to deny to the fantastic cinema that beauty which is all the more disturbing for being so radically anti-anthropomorphic, the beauty of its super-romanticism. On the contrary; we imply a plea for a greater audacity in extrapolation, as well as to pose a challenge to the alleged 'seriousness' of 'realism'. For the dream language of fantasy reflects reality, too; often, more clearly, for camouflaged undercurrents are allowed nearer the surface. Ming is Mao, before Mao.

These reflections were stimulated by Umberto Scarpelli's *The Giant of Metropolis* (1962) an Italian film which, involuntarily perhaps, is the reactionary retort to all that is democratic and happily pagan in Vittorio Cottafavi's *Hercules Conquers Atlantis* (1961). With Fred M. Wilcox's *Forbidden Planet* (U.S.A., 1956), Kurt Maetzig's *First Spaceship on Venus* (East Germany-Poland, 1959), and Joseph M. Newman's *This Island Earth* (U.S.A., 1955), the films of Scarpelli and Cottafavi form a quintet on the theme of: a 'modern' man discovering a dying, or only posthumously active, civilization. In Scarpelli's film—related to Lang's futuristic *Metropolis* only by cashing in on its name—Metropolis has become the city of Atlantis ten thousand years before Christ (it might as well exist in the twenty-first century). The name indeed suggests the futuristic, super-capitalist tyranny in Lang's vision, that of Marxism stood on its head (a universal change of heart solves all class tensions; its scriptwriter, Thea Von Harbou, became a passionate Nazi). In Scarpelli's film, the 'concentrationary' future is that of a scientific totalitarianism, even though it is in the past (Atlantis). For the scientific hubris which destroyed one civilization may destroy another. . . .

The two Italian epics have much in common. Both assent to the startling recent mythological *volte-face*, whereby the social basis of Atlantis is not, as the novelist Pierre Benoit, in his *L'Atlantide* and his screen adaptors, Jacques Feyder (1921) and G. W. Pabst (1932) presumed, the erotic despotism of a Queen, but a system much nearer *s.f.*—the transmogrification of man into Superman.[1]

Both films locate Atlantis on a mist-shrouded, rocky island, which is sunk by a cataclysmic atomic explosion. But if the new generation of historians have certain points in common, so far as the general geo-political picture is concerned, their interpretations of the decline and fall of Atlantis are more diverse than ever. For Cottafavi, Atlantis was, morally, doomed because the do-or-die experiments perpetrated on an expropriated peasantry in order to make of them fanatical warriors were part of a totalitarian system inimical to democracy and the dignity of the individual. But for Scarpelli, the corresponding scientific experiments are seen as sins against Nature, whom man was not meant to master. Again, whereas Hercules (Reg Park) smilingly tolerates the effeminate dancers temptingly paraded before him by the high priest of Antinea, Scarpelli is indignant that a young dancing lady should be sandwiched in a *pas de trois* between two muscly youths, one of whom, moreover, is black. It's true that the trio's intensely lascivious motions suggest a yet more closely integrated activity, and it's also true that the girl in the middle has been hypnotized into it, that is to say, that her liberty has been infringed. But the affiliation of these factors characterizes puritan classifications; libertarianism is associated with all possible vices, all the

[1] The nineteenth-century realms of the 'eternal feminine' *à la She* seem, like the vamps of the time, to have been the day dream of a paternalist and puritan ethos. In our hedonistic and feminist ethos, the realms of fantasy and fear are macabre, or harbour our male ideal. For the same reason, the Western, hitherto a hick's or kid's genre, flourishes among more sophisticated audiences than ever before in its history. Conversely, Robert Day's recent version of *She* (1964) stresses less the female's enormity than political upheavals (the slave tribe seeking freedom) and desert adventure. The originator of the 'transmogrificatory' Atlantis is George Pal, in his *Atlantis the Lost Continent* (U.S.A., 1961); Edgar Ulmer's *The Lost Kingdom* (1961) is a none-too-convincing throwback in which Antinea plays second-fiddle to her Frenchman.

virtues being reserved for the other side, a division justifying the intolerance and vituperation specifically repudiated by the smile of Hercules. Nor is it accidental that Scarpelli's film speaks less of 'liberty' than of 'freedom of the will and of the intelligence'. The Thomism of this last juxtaposition is quite evident. In this context, there is a special pointedness about the anti-scientific Jeremiads placed in the mouth of a very old, kind, good Sage, who, slain by the wicked Regent, returns as his own ghost—thus incarnating *both* 'tradition' and 'immortality'. All this has an odour of incense. Whether or not the film's producer is Roman Catholic I don't know; his film is.

In any event, the moral pattern of every film fantasy is as studied as that of any other type of film. The critical Round Table of *Motion No. 6* raised, in connection with Cottafavi's film, the question of whether Hercules and his friend the King of Thrace, in refusing to inform his ship's crew of their true destination, had, in effect 'conscripted' them, trampled on their rights. It was only on seeing the film a second time that I realized that Cottafavi had given the reply. The crew consists of convicted assassins and criminals; the trip is part of their jail sentence. And when they mutiny and attempt to assassinate Hercules, he makes no attempt to punish them further, simply marooning them, prophylactically, on an island. For they were now seeking to avoid the journey to Atlantis, and Hercules, having saved his life, respects their right to attempt to regain their liberty. The argument relates, of course, to those arguments of Hobbes which most clearly reveal that under his totalitarianism is a fierce anarchist undertow.

Easy to decode morally, too easy, even, are the events of *First Spaceship on Venus*, that semi-Ulbrichtian endeavour to renew the fantasy traditions of U.F.A. The only hypothesis I can advance to explain the general platitudinousness of post-war German films (and post-war is two decades, a very long time) is that those German film-makers who might have become leading artists hesitate between the 'respectable' dramatic emphases—modern, liberal, 'American' sentiments—and the retrospective guilts which they too readily arouse, if allowed to deviate from prim little dotted lines. There are also, perhaps, the sullen but powerful tendencies established by Siegfried Kracauer, that is to say, towards authority, hierarchy, submission, boundless desire, all neatly tucked away under a bland insensitivity towards, and unawareness of, the moral and emotional complexities of which German film production is almost uniquely devoid. One could hardly expect much better from an Ulbrichtian entertainment.

In any event, the dramatic interplay of Maetzig's film is of an astonishing incompetence. Apart from the agreeable Yoko Tani (whose presence is, of course, not only anti-racist and anti-patriarchalist but, then, pro-Mao), even the faces of the supposedly 'sympathetic' astronauts are set, brutal and cold. The first rocket to Venus finds the débris of a very advanced civilization which was preparing to destroy the earth by projecting on to it extremely powerful radiations. The radiations ran amok on the home planet. One thinks of *Forbidden Planet*, whose 'Robbie the Robot' (a benevolent pre-Dalek) si echoed in this little armoured tank which, uncharmingly, resembles nothing more than the teleguided mines developed by the Nazis towards the end of the war. Subtle laughter about the lack of gravity and the ineluctable meteor bombardment (scratches on film), decorate the film's morality: 'Let us have nuclear disarmament before we blow ourselves and our planet up,' a morality near in spirit to that of the American film. It would be fair to see it, not just as a parallel, but as a not unfriendly riposte to its American predecessor, shifting the latter's Freudian, non-political terms into the Kruschevite party-line.

The M.G.M. film's moral patterns are richer and more complex. The Forbidden Planet of the title is Altair–4, on which a U.S. Army spaceship lands, only to find, to its chagrin, that Professor Morbius (Walter Pidgeon) has got there first, by some sort of blend of scientific wizardry and private enterprise. As is well known by now, *Forbidden Planet* is, quite deliberately, a transposition of Shakespeare's *The Tempest*. Altair–4=Prospero's island, Morbius=Prospero, his daughter (Ann Francis)=Miranda (she has never seen a young man before), the spaceship commander=Ferdinand, Robbie the Robot=Ariel. But who is Caliban? Well, Morbius's scientific researches ('magic books') have led him to explore the city of the long-dead Krells, and he is hot in pursuit of their incredible power of converting mental energy into colossal physical forces.

Despite warnings, this scientific Prometheus refuses to draw back, and involuntarily unleashes, not only his own mental energy, but his own destructiveness—a King-Kong-shaped outline described as The Monster from the Id. When he calls on the daintily omnipotent Robbie the Robot to suppress it, Robbie, suddenly neurotic, refuses—for this hatred is Morbius himself, his 'Mr. Hyde'.

More complex still are the moral patterns of *This Island Earth*, one of whose merits is its resonance with certain psychopathological traits in American political thought.

The story develops very, indeed excessively, slowly (probably as a result of a rather pedantic thoroughness in establishing resonance with familiar reality). The producers have apparently convinced themselves that they must aim primarily to please the tastes of older male children, for the hero, Cal (Rex Reason) lives their day-dreams through. We discover this handsome young cadet-cum-tycoon, already President of his own electronics corporation, at the controls of his private executive jet. But a mysterious green light suddenly fills his cabin—green, once the colour of fairies, having retained its associations with the supernatural in popular art—accompanied by a mysterious force which takes control of his craft, forcing it down to an uncannily perfect three-point-landing. Clearly, this was only a demonstration—or a warning. . . .

As Cal returns to his office, he finds that a company, hitherto unknown to him, has sent him, as sample, an electronic item of an unprecedented, but clearly very advanced type. Cal writes off for their catalogue, receiving, by return of post, instructions to construct an enigmatic object described as an 'interociter'. (Thus the fantasy develops by 'resonance' with (*a*) mail order catalogues and (*b*) do-it-yourself constructors. I suspect that the original novel began here, but that the film opened on the premonitory green light to reassure a public less familiar with *s.f.* than its addicts that eerie marvels are to come.)

The interociter turns out to be nothing more than two-way TV, whose triangular screen is bathed in changing coloured lights (another of the film's more childish ideas). On the screen appears Mr. Exeter (Jeff Morrow), whose kindly expression does not suffice to reassure us, in view of the forces at his disposition, and who explains that the construction of this apparatus was only an 'entrance examination', which Cal has passed. He invites Cal to join an international team of idealistic scientists who are working together, in secret, to perfect a method of rendering war impossible. And then, from long-distance, he reduces the interociter to a heap of smoking junk.

Despite the misgivings of his buddy, Cal goes to the meeting, drawn more by scientific-intellectual curiosity than by idealist naïvety. At midnight he enters a Dakota whose interior and windows are completely white and in whose empty cabin the controls move as if of their own volition—a visually very beautiful mutation of the theme of the 'phantom carriage'.

Cal begins work on the project. Among his colleagues are Ruth Adams (Faith Domergue) and her fiancé (Russell Johnson). Around this trio the possibilities of an eternal triangle float without actually settling (a rather weak solution to another problem—reconciling children's impatience with romance with adults' liking of it). The likeable Exeter has a more disturbing associate, Brack (Lance Fuller), younger, stronger, fiercer. Both have very high, bulbous foreheads, and the stiffness of their hair faintly suggests the wig of English judges. Thus we know they come from another planet long before the script officially informs us of the fact. And from the conversations between Exeter, Brack, and, on the screen of their own interociter, The Monitor (Douglas Spencer), an elderly man with a noble but sharp face, we gather that their world, Metaluna, is at war with Zahgon, beneath whose attack the hitherto impregnable 'ionization barrier' is at last giving way. Exeter and Brack have been 'kidnapping' the researches of the world's scientists, to find a substitute for the failing barrier. Brack wishes to hurry progress by brainwashing their guests, a procedure forbidden by Exeter as utterly repugnant to the decent Metalunar ethos.

Meanwhile Cal, Ruth and Steve have come to the conclusion that they must escape. But before they can do so, the Monitor orders Exeter to destroy the terrestrial plant and return at once, so that the spaceship's energy can reinforce the pulverized barrier. Guiltily conscious that his scruples have brought Metaluna to this plight, Exeter equally guiltily gives the order to assassinate the scientists. Steve sacrifices himself for Cal and Ruth, whose escape attempt in a propeller-driven light plane, fails when what they thought was a green hill 'erupts', and from beneath its grass crust arises a gigantic flying saucer. Its green rays draw the light aircraft steadily up towards, and into, its ventral hatch.

Against all 'waking' logic, but following a sort of dream-reasoning, the appearance of the flying saucer helps to guarantee the story, to add to its plausibility. For we have all considered the possibility of such machines; the U.S. air force has reported sighting them; they are mentally familiar to us all; and here, at a crucial moment, we see something we *know*. . . .

To survive the various pressures of the voyage, the humans and their humanoid hosts alike are obliged to stay in a transparent tube and to undergo what Michel Laclos has called 'the integral striptease' —their clothes, skins, muscles, veins and bones successively dissolve as their molecular structure is dissolved and held in 'protective suspension' in the tube.

Thus the 'indefinite duration' of interstellar travel (and all the problems it poses for the scenarist) is 'paraphrazed', in an intimate and unexpected manner. Outer Space becomes Inner Space. Two disturbing notions are fused into a vivid, yet exceptionally economical, image. This kind of reinforcement-by-contradiction, as audacious poetically as it is opaque to Cartesian analysis, is a transposition of mental sensation immediately comprehensible in terms of the 'dreamwork'. And its 'anatomical' key sets the key for some dream overtones of subsequent passages.

Approaching Metaluna, the ship must volatilize the incandescent meteors which Zahgonian bombers hurl, like guided missiles, against it. Finally the ship lands, and not just on the surface of the planet, but *into* its crust, which, ravaged by the Zahgonian bombardment, is by now little more than a spider's web of stone holding together a network of craters (this 'insubstantiality' is not unfitting for a meta-moon). After gliding across an impressive panorama of the riddled planet, the ship slips itself into a crater to glide further underneath its surface and finally rests in the wreckage of the once proud civilization of Metaluna.

The Monitor, barbarically stern and desperate, orders Exeter to transform his captives into mere automata. And they see another, less benevolent, aspect of Metalunar science, a guard-slave, human in form, except for an insect-like hand, with huge eyes and a mass of exposed brains bubbling up out of sutures like gaping fontanelles. This grotesque achievement of Metalunar science permits us to watch, without unbearably sharp regrets, a high civilization crumble beneath the hammerblows of the barbarians.

The moment the Monitor is killed and the too-loyal Exeter is freed from his pledge, he helps his human friends fight off the guard, and restores them to their native planet. Then, despite their invitation to stay with them, he maintains that he must set off in search of other worlds on which Metalunar knowledge can be a power for good. But Cal and Ruth suspect that his ship has no more energy, and it is with a heavy heart that they watch his craft rise, and then plunge, like a shooting-star, into the ocean.

The construction of the story is extremely disciplined, in a characteristic Hollywood manner, metamorphosing a few basic themes in a quasi-musical manner.

Theme A; Brains. 1. Emphasis on know-how. 2. Brainwashing. 3. Exeter's and Brack's noble brows. 4. The Guard-slave's ignoble brow, whose extruding brains are an 'excess' of Exeter's bulbousness. (Excess becomes contradiction—a characteristic of the folk aesthetic.) Exeter is Metaluna's Jekyll, the slave, his Mr. Hyde.

Theme B; Remote Control. 1. Of Cal's jet. 2. Of (by destruction) the Interociter. 3. Of the Dakota. 4. Of (by surveillance) scientists in the laboratories. 5. Of the light aircraft. 6. Control of the meteors by Zahgonian bombers.

Theme C; Penetration. 1. Gruyerization of Metaluna by meteors. 2. Transmolecularization of the human body, with 3–4. Associated theme of being sheltered and passive: the ionization barrier complements the glass tubes. 5. Transparence of the insect skull. 6. See theme E.

Theme D; Crescendo of voyages. 1. Personal jet. 2. Funerary Dakota. 3. Escape attempt by automobile and then light plane, climaxing in their converse. 4. Flying Saucer. (Measured against the private plane, the saucer is about the size of an ocean liner. In turn, it appears tiny against the sloping flank of Metaluna—illogically, since the fact that it's visible at all against the planet's globularity should prove that Metaluna's very small. But, by onirist logic, the curve tells us that Metaluna is 'an entire planet', a boundless immensity, a whole world.)

Theme E; Unusual landings. 1. Cal's, under remote control. 2. The Dakota's. 3. The private plane 'lands' in the saucer, *upwards*, and *into* it. 4. The saucer lands into Metaluna, flies along under the muddy, sulphurous, desert-like surface of the planet. 6. The saucer lands *into* the ocean (giving the contrasting series: green valley—desert—ocean). 7. Impact of meteors.

Theme F; Crescendo of altruistic suicides. 1. Cal risks himself for his scientific curiosity. 2. Steve risks himself for Cal and Ruth, and is killed. 3. Exeter sacrifices himself to die with his race (death-wish?).

Theme G; Tension of malevolence. 1. Exeter (sinister but reassuring). 2. Brack (more sinister). 3. Monitor (ascetic, dictatorial). 4. The guard-slave, like a giant insect.

Theme H; The film's basic opposition is between (1) Metaluna, which kidnaps (*a*) research, (*b*) scientists and (*c*) brains, that is, mental things; whereas (2) Zahgon kidnaps matter—meteors. These resemble little suns; incandescent, they are the most terrible of deserts. Finally, under their blows, the desert of Metaluna explodes 'like a sun', says Exeter. There is a crescendo from the green hills of earth to the desert craters of Metaluna to—a sun. Parallel: from the intellectual curiosity of Cal through Exeter's brow-and-wig to the insect's 'exploding' grey matter. *Metaluna, planet of scientists, is also a gigantic brain*, visually; we have returned to Theme A.[1]

But these threads interweave with a much tougher and stronger thread, of *moral* suspense. Is Metaluna, an advanced, largely humane civilization with its back to the wall against a more barbaric foe, justified in kidnapping a handful of Earth scientists? Exeter is pretty sympathetic, which helps us to see things from the Metalunar viewpoint, so we want to reply, Yes. But we have a still closer identification with our co-terrestrials, so we also want to reply, No. Instead of looking for a compromise between our two attitudes, the film maintains both simultaneously, creating a moral suspense which is completely unstated but none the less intense. We can't decide without pain. An associated paradox: it's Exeter's moral scruples which lead him to fail Metaluna, just as his lofty loyalty leads him to menace our heroes. Clearly, overall, in all interplanetary clashes, the earth is our

[1] Although of course the film has a pleasing variety of event and mood, it is, as this analysis suggests, very 'ordered' in construction, and also respects a relatively tight thematic unity.

Apologists sometimes try to defend the cinema by saying that Shakespeare, were he living in the twentieth century, would have been a Hollywood scriptwriter. This is true enough in so far as both Hollywood and the Elizabethan theatre are popular media (though modern audiences don't have the same tastes as groundlings), but it is also interesting to query whether his genius would have flourished in view of the screen's special requirements, and whether, in fact, he would have been a very good scriptwriter, so important in films are such qualities as terseness, crispness, and precision in the construction and inflection of situations and reactions. Screen dialogue is telegrammatic. Indeed if Shakespeare weren't a great poet he would be one of the worst scenarists in literary history. His situations are fuzzy, messy and uncertain, the narrative movement of his plays fitful, his characters speak at great length because their creator isn't too sure what his own themes are, nor which of their sentiments are relevant to the story, which indeed appears to change in his mind as he goes along.

On the other hand, Racine would have been an excellent scriptwriter (and said that a play was virtually finished once he had constructed the 'scenario' in prose). From the point of view of a film script, many a novel is full of 'false starts', gropings, repetitions, etc., and is virtually its own rough draft, or rather, all its own rough drafts jumbled up. A really good scriptwriter can establish with one short line of dialogue what many a novelist chooses to spin out into a chapter of rumination, trivia, noodling notation, and so on.

In other words, the film has its own skills, its own qualities of genius, just as novels have—though many novels would benefit from scriptwriters' economy.

motherland, and we're all patriots. But we're distinctly worried patriots. Finally, as between Zahgon and Metaluna, the film's attitude is a tragic acceptance of amorality, that is, of force.

But this Mother Earth of ours is also 'the free world'. Let us put ourselves in the place of the average American spectator. Which country is always kidnapping and/or deluding scientists and egg-heads? Russia. Which country organizes so-called 'peace' congresses? Russia. Which country specializes in brainwashing? Russia. At the laboratories the screens reveal to Brack (Big Brother) and Exeter (Little Father) all the scientists are doing—this is the Stalinist *1984*. Exeter's disobedience to dictatorial orders that pain him is all that is best in Russia, no doubt.

But the film's political moral isn't at all an equation of Russia and Metaluna. The conversations between Metalunans lead us to accept their thesis that Metaluna has so far been too scrupulous, too peace-loving, too cultured, too passive, too complacent behind its 'Maginot Line', too slow to mobilize. Though, at the beginning of the film, we fear that Exeter is a Communist undercover agent, towards the end Metaluna is not at all Communism. It is: 'What will happen to us if we're sluggish and passive towards an unscrupulous enemy.' And from this point on it is Zahgon which is Russia—Communism battering at the gentle, defensive Free World.

One can follow this symbolism in another direction. The wigs, the very English name, 'Exeter', his expression, his scruples, suggest a certain gentlemanliness. His situation of a weak Father, too obedient to hierarchic loyalties is England's (historically, as Gorer points out, the 'weak father' of America, and ever since, her alter ego—a surprisingly strong and courageous land, considering how effete it seems, and with a perfidious streak, but none the less, too weak to 'hold' America). The implication is that *because* Exeter and Metaluna were weak before, now they must kidnap and brainwash. It repeats the switch from Jekyll to Hyde, but in a more realistic way. Exeter represents 'England and our other pretty-soft-on-communism' allies. But above all, he incarnates the last stage of the temptation against which the U.S.A. must be on guard—confidence-in-advanced-technology, and isolationalism, without an aggressive counter-initiative, a warlike readiness.

The ionization barrier recalls, perhaps, the 'early warning' systems. They are only a Maginot Line. The Zahgonians' technique is relatively crude, but, given their obsessional persistence, effective. Instead of hithering and dithering about scientists' work and brains, they scoop up huge lumps of incandescent matter and hurl it with neither scruple nor subtlety. It's Russia's technological 'crudity', the mass attacks of the Chinese in Korea. And it can succeed.

If we go so far as to see in the 'International Congress of Scientists for Peace' a reference to the United Nations we can see that in the course of the film Metaluna becomes, successively, the U.N., Russia, Britain and a too-liberal U.S.A. The symbolism depends on associations, not on a consistent code. This 'sliding symbolism' isn't at all unique in movies. We can find an analogy in *Henry V*, where the English are the English but Agincourt is D-Day, where the French are the Germans, until Henry courts Katherine, whereupon the French are probably the French. Such 'contradictions' are typical, also, of Freudian dreamwork, where symbolism is dominated less by the 'objective' correlative of each mental entity than by polarities in an emotional situation.

The McArthur-like morality of the American film is fundamentally mitigated by our sympathy for Exeter, a sympathy due to his 'liberal' scruples, and it is this ambivalance which creates a great part of the film's emotional excitation. In a sense, it is only 'accidentally' a committed film. It exploits the current international situations to insert a 'plausibility', an 'everyday correlative', to its own story. Left-wing critics can enjoy it with a clear conscience. Many, perhaps most, American spectators will see in it only a philosophical meditation, a reflection of violence and idealism, in the 'abstract' of Outer Space, so to speak. If they have hitherto taken aggressiveness as axiomatic, they may be surprised to find themselves feeling so concerned for the alien Exeter—and in this case the film's 'meaning' ('effect') would be anti-racist, anti-xenophobe, pro-liberal. The effect and meaning of a film is rarely provable by however meticulous a textual analysis; one must also know what assumptions, in the mind of its spectators, it is coming up against.

But *This Island Earth* probes more deeply still into American attitudes. Exeter with his 'binary' Brack, the Monitor with his 'binary' the Insect, are paternal symbols (Exeter and the Monitor via their age, their superiority and their control over the hero's destiny). The Metalunar civilization is, in short, a weak father. (But let us beware of a cruelty hidden in this benevolence. . . .) Yet, Metaluna, the moon, round, like a dry breast, devastated—is the dead mother. The association is underlined: Metaluna and the saucer are both globes, the light plane enters the saucer's belly (birth in reverse), as the saucer enters Metaluna's pores (birth in reverse), before plunging into the sea (birth in reverse). The Metalunans are not exactly feminoid men, but passive—and feminoid in the sense that, for Americans, passivity, pacifism, moral scrupulosity, gentleness, altruism, and preoccupation with education and culture are associated with the 'schoolmarm ethos' (cf. Hofstadter), with the 'cissy'. The Zahgonian bombers are dart-shaped (as opposed to globes) and throw little suns (phallic-sadistic) against the moon which at last becomes the sun—the female, tormented, ravaged, by the sadism of the nightmare father (opposed to the reasonable, weak father) becomes male, explosive. Femininity disappears. In fantasy, even the women are masculine. 'Vienna', that feminine name, all waltzes and romance, has 'caught fire' and become a black-booted gunslinger. Indeed, Faith Domergue wears black slacks and boots throughout. Fathers are passive, women no more so. . . .

Thus Metaluna is simultaneously breast and brain. Both are attached simultaneously. We knew that Americans fear that to be intellectual is to be cissy, and we may suspect that their obsession with mammary hypertrophy conceals a certain fear of the castrating female—just as their anti-intellectuality goes with an obsession with dangerous Masterminds (mad scientists, Mr. Bigs, and so on).

If we indicate these Freudian categories, it is only to underline that the film is founded on the *confusion* of sexual qualities, a confusion arising from the presence of an uncontrolled, scarcely sublimated sadism. The meteors (which we have characterized as 'phallic-sadistic') are also globes (feminine); Metaluna (the body of the dead mother) is inhabited by a hierarchy of Fathers (with Brack as 'elder sibling'—i.e. both brother as competitor and threat, and 'Father as pal'). The Insect signals the undertow of Zahgonianism in Metalunar culture. Between Zahgon and Metaluna the 'sympathetic self-preservation' of Cal, Steve and Ruth is the best compromise (and a heterosexual *camaraderie*).

The Metalunans are more sympathetic than the Zahgonians, but they lost. Thus a 'puritan' morality of liberal scruple is contrasted with the cynical 'morality' of success. . . .

If we assume that the film responds to authentic currents of American thought, we could have deduced from it how deeply rooted in the American psyche were attitudes which would naturally try to emerge, on the political plane, as McCarthyism, McArthurism, or

Goldwaterism. The old 'isolationism' turns into bellicosity. There is a haunting fear that a 'liberal' policy towards Communism is the policy of men who are, not exactly feminized, but neutered, castrated, by their scruples. Similarly, Margaret Mead and Geoffrey Gorer tell us that in America the woman rather than the man tends to possess the moral ascendancy within the family; and it may be that this ascendancy is subtly reinforced by the masculinization of woman imposed by an individualistic, and therefore competitive, society. Thus, femininity disappears on Metaluna, and Faith Domergue, the woman dressed like a man, has undergone a transmogrification analagous to the insect-slave's.

Exeter, the gentle father, is vowed to autodestruction by observing the 'severely obeyed gentleness'. The paradox of the American soul is that a strongly competitive, puritan ethic, whose principles, for all the mitigating effects of a subsequent 'fun morality' are, in their stern, simple imperatives, 'masculine'. Yet they are imposed by women, who thus become not so much the indulgent member of the family, as the taskmaster. Within the family, 'Pop' is Exeter. But, outside the family, in the jungle of 'rugged individualism' (the ratrace), father's ideals are (or are supposed to be) more Zahgonian. Simultaneously, in the very bosom of the family, Oedipal rivalry creates 'monsters'—the insect-warrior-slave, malicious and ugly, being the symbol of the jealousy faintly suggested by, but never crystallized, between, Cal, Ruth and Steve. And so the middle-class 'quiet American', with his picture of himself as gentle, reasonable, liberal, conscientiously represses his Zahgonian undertow until he finds an enemy on whom he can project it—which justifies a Zahgonian brutality in his own reaction. How often have we not seen, in American war films, the American forces napalm and pulverize the enemy with a Zahgonian mindlessness?[1]

[1] There is a similar opposition in Byron Haskin's *From the Earth to the Moon* (1958), adapted from Jules Verne's novel. On the one hand, Stuyvesant (George Sanders), a scientist with Confederate loyalties (gentlemanly, 'olde-worlde', doomed to defeat) invents an impregnable armour (passive defence) which he idealistically hopes will render war impossible. On the other, Barbicane (Joseph Cotton), an ambitious Yankee capitalist, invents an atomic shell which volatilizes that armour. Stuyvesant ≏ Metaluna, Barbicane ≏ Zahgon. The President of the U.S. appeals to Barbicane to turn aside from warlike applications of his hideous power; Barbicane consents, but, rebelliously, refuses to destroy it, turning it, by way of compromise between his egoistic will to power and the President's will to peace, to peaceful purposes: a moon rocket. Stuyvesant pretends to generously forgive him, and they pool atomic power and armour. But once in Outer Space, Stuyvesant reveals that he has sabotaged the rocket, to doom them

The general polarity can be seen in other American films. Thus in Kazan's *On the Waterfront* the hero's apparently friendly elder brother (Rod Steiger) and 'meta-father', Johnny Friendly (Lee J. Cobb), have 'sold him down the river'. Thus 'Metaluna' is rapidly revealed as 'Zahgon'. There is a basic conflict between Brando's 'Zahgonian' ideas of revenge (guns, fists) and the softening influence of the fatherly priest (Karl Malden)—a 'Metalunar castrate'—and a schoolmarm (Eva-Marie Saint). This 'Metalunar' approach to racket-busting, however, accommodates his virility: first, the schoolmarm enjoys being raped by him, and second, he asserts himself *vis-à-vis*, the dockers as one of them by a fist-fight with Friendly's men (which he loses). Again, in Zinnemann's *High Noon* there is a clash between Gary Cooper's aggressive ideas of self-defence and his Quaker wife's 'treacherous' passivity. Clearest of all is the overt propaganda of Tay Garnett's Korean war film *One Minute to Zero*, which contrasts Robert Mitchum as a tough U.S. Army Colonel and Ann Blyth as a 'schoolmarm' U.N. worker who isn't at all sure that North Korea is really the aggressor. After he's slapped her and saved her she finally sees his point, and even acquieses in his final 'Zahgonian' ruthlessness; he orders his artillery to blast a column of South Korean refugees which include women, children and Commie infiltrators. In King Vidor's *Duel in the Sun*, the kind, reasonable, liberal son Jess (Joseph Cotton), with his woman's name, is his mother's favourite and is pacifistic about gunslinging, preferring the (intellectual-moral) law, is the 'Metalunan' son. He loses the passionate girl to his brother Lewt (Gregory Peck), the egoist-assassin,

all, himself included. His pretext is outraged idealism (rockets are sinful), although it's plain enough to Barbicane and ourselves, whose viewpoint we have by now adopted, that his motive is repressed hatred of Barbicane. Thus, again, the apparent, and no doubt, sincere 'weak idealist' reveals a hidden brutality; again he is associated with altruistic suicide; and he has a female association; where Barbicane has a son, the only thing Stuyvesant loves more than his principles is his daughter (Debra Paget). Again the two young people re-establish the heterosexual ideal in a film that might be called *From the Earth to the Meta-Moon.*

It's arguable that Haskin's film is a deliberate copy of Newman's (rather than an independent confirmation of it, except in so far as imitation can be a valid index of relevance), which is one reason why I relegate it to a footnote; and certainly it *advocates* a turning-away from the arms-race, a channelling of energies into peaceful competition, which itself is felt to be sufficiently aggressive, rebellious and not devoid of risk. It maintains the aggressiveness of 'rugged individualism' as, on the whole, better and more decent than Stuyvesant's love of 'peace'.

There is a scarcely different permutation of the same conflicts in Delbert Mann's *Our Man Flint*, 1966.

the father's son, who dies, in the desert, under the sun, together with a shotgun-carrying (masculinoid) girl. . . .

Universal as is the resonance of these films, can we not recognize in them a preoccupation, an atmosphere, a tonus which are specifically American? After all, the Wild West, with its deserts, its killings, its men-without-women, is—Metaluna. It would be easy to translate Newman's film into a Western—*Duel Under the Moon*—although its tragic breakdown of a social order might well be resented, as a criticism of the American way of life. . . .

Revealing as it is, the film is not a masterpiece; its style is rather plodding, it respects too many American sentimentalities. Notably, Cal and Ruth are 'pure', they are implicated, a very little, but too little, in the emotional paradoxes. Despite the title (which is ironical: No Planet is an Island) the film doesn't complete the spiritual voyage whereby Zahgon is also in the hero's heart. It's still, perhaps, interesting to see how many moral complexities an 'ordinary' film can bear. What lifts this out of the ordinary is that, to a sufficient complexity of moral sympathy, is added a certain fantastic poetry.

Morally, one may prefer it to *Forbidden Planet*. Not that this doesn't maintain some of the main points. For Morbius is Metaluna and his Mr. Hyde is Zahgon. Once again, the intellectual with the daughter reveals a hidden destructiveness, remains passive under the attack of active evil, and commits suicide, though retaining, like Exeter, our respect and love; while the 'honest militancy' of the U.S. Army is the really peaceful force. But the film goes further than either Newman's or Haskin's in imputing Morbius's hidden aggression to all of us. The phrase, The Monster from the Id, imputes such a creature to every man jack of us.

The visuals of all these films play the same 'parodic' game with reality. Even Scarpelli's film whirls up its potpourri of clichés in such a way as to attain a certain charm—thus we find characters in pharaoh-shaped blue helmets peering through tele-periscopes, brain-transplanting operations determined by astrological conjunctions, an operating-table whose form recalls an anvil, circular arches over triangular doors (the triangle is quite a 'supernatural' shape, what with interocitors too), hairpin-shaped doors cheek by jowl with octagonal windows and Gothic ogives, and pagodesque structures hobnobbing with aerodynamic edifices in the style of William Cameron Menzies' *Things to Come* (1936).

Far more Corneillian is the décor of Cottafavi's film. As Jean-

Louis Barrault remarked, the true colour of classicism is not ivory-white but blood-red; and Cottafavi has given us such a classicism, the only genre possible in an epoque as profoundly marked as ours by psychoanalysis. The film's soul is not only in the physique of the amiable Hercules (Reg Park), whose muscles stand out like bunches of grapes, purple in Technicolor, but in the contrast between this benign strength of flesh and the temples of Atlantis—with their scarlet columns and heavily barbaric decorations; with its chariot, drawn by flowing-maned white horses, bounding through flames between the massive pillars of hillocky-floored catacombs whose roof slopes steadily, oppressively down; with the buildings jumbled among yellow rocks, like Monkey Hill; with the simple but striking off-key harmonies between the black, gold and electric-blue colours of Queen Antinea (Fay Spain) and the yellow and coral green of her apartments. Hercules himself is a kindly soul who smiles and sleeps until the very last moment, not only preferring *la Dolce far niente* to *la Dolce Vita*, but as far removed as possible from 'Zahgonism'.

The merits of *Forbidden Planet* are more literary and moral than architectural, and the furnishing of Prospero's planet isn't without a certain flowers-and-leopard sentimentality. By contrast, *First Spaceship on Venus* more than compensates for its moral poverty by the work of art designers, Anatol Radzinowicz and Alfred Kirschmeier, and its team of special effects designers, who, very cleverly indeed, transpose pictorial motifs from, among others, Dali and Tanguy, and find in the junk forms of a derelict planet, an opportunity not only to match, but to go beyond, the old expressionist delirium Ever since 1945, Polish films have been notable for the tragic virulence of their sense of devestation. . . . What atrocious beauty invests these ruined and incomprehensible installations! Bunches of steel plates are warped into arcs recalling the wind-bellied sails of tea-clippers; huge, half-molten domes evoke white skulls from whose eye-sockets drip dissolute forms like white worms; from a bird's-eye-view a reactivated 'energy complex' suggests Broadway Boogie-Woogie as it might have been rendered into a grotesque contraption by Jean Tinguely. And the inconstant winds of Venus are evoked by white and oxblood washes drifting across the images.

Less rich in ideas, perhaps, but convulsive, too, are the Metalunar desertscapes, whose craters recall the pores in the giantesses' breasts to which Gulliver clung in Brobdingnag. . . .

Note: Depth Psychology and Popular Cinema

In discussing *This Island Earth*, and the uneasy link which it establishes between an unconscious conflict, certain cultural stereotypes, a philosophy of violence, and Cold War attitudes, we are in no sense offering any summary of American thinking on any of these levels. We are discussing one 'myth' (or configuration of archetypal images) among many myths. This is not at all to suggest that this myth is 'the key' to American attitudes. A myth, like a dream, is only a partial picture of the unconscious processes; and even within its field it is distorted and disguised. And of course the primitive quality of the attitudes is refined, restrained by and overladen with the more obvious considerations of rational political thought. It's just because they are held in check that they appear more clearly on the level of film entertainment than anywhere else.

Hence entertainment, like dreams, makes its own contribution to our general self-awareness. To say there is a joker in the pack is not to reduce the pack to its joker. Insofar as this exegesis of *This Island Earth* refers to actual political attitudes, it is no more than a study in one particular aspect of the 'hidden persuasion' to which respectable political rhetoric never dares make open appeal but which, if 'Dichterism' has any validity at all, must influence political feeling, to, no doubt, a limited extent. All the same, our intention is not to throw light on American politics, simply to underline the fact that the emotional and moral 'catchment-area' of an apparently 'escapist' film may be far more extensive, and realistic, than its overt content. The political link-up (which the film itself suggests) is a way of stressing that these emotions can't be dismissed as 'mere triviality'. Thus poetry is indissolubly blended with philosophy. To indicate a paranoiad streak in American political thinking is not to indulge in that favourite pastime of European intellectuals—scoring off American 'vulgarity'. That that is in no way the burden of these remarks, the tone of earlier chapters should make clear. Indeed, of all the movies examined in this chapter, it is the two American movies which show the most sophisticated and self-critical awareness of inner tensions.

This Island Earth has everything against it. It's a fantasy, it's science-fiction, it's slanted at adolescents, it's a routine product from a studio with no intellectual pretentions, it has no *auteurs*, its artistic 'texture' is largely mediocre—and for all that, it has a genuine charge of poetry and of significant social feeling. It's not cliché; with its sense of inner tensions, of moral tragedy, it's myth.

Our suggestion is that academic criticism is condemned to misunderstand the film, to dismiss it as routine trash, because its psychology is straightforward, its terms melodramatic, and so on. 'High culture' is preoccupied with what Henry James called 'density of specification' and what F. R. Leavis calls 'texture', with the question: 'Does it work on my level?' But such criteria are irrelevant to this as to most movies. The question must be, rather, 'Does it work on its level?' (for people who freely respond to simpler textures).

The temptation then is to swing to the other extreme, and fall into the studiedly uncritical acceptance of any and every form of popular art as 'myth' and 'folklore of the twentieth century'; or, at a slightly more aware level, to abandon oneself to the ironic relish of 'camp'. Too often this is both a studied falsity and a (completely unnecessary) surrender to the (supposed) naïvety of popular thought. Our implication is that some pulp-movies are very much more considerable than others, that the mythic can be distinguished from the cliché, that, through the myth, movies communicate with people's *real* doubt and feelings, that such movies are in a very real sense 'good' art as opposed to others which are in a very real sense 'bad' art. This isn't to elevate the subversive possibilities of entertainment above its reinforcing of social attitudes; *This Island Earth* isn't subversive, for most of its spectators. But its tragic sense of moral tensions is very different from the comic-strip images which many 'pop-artists' prefer to plunder.

If stated baldly, the moral of *This Island Earth* would make it an expression of American right-wing extremism (obviously, it is not suggested that right-wing extremism is confined to American thought; it's obviously virulent in European politics too). It would mean: 'Look out for aliens! rearm!' And 'aliens' would be definable as 'intellectuals' (high foreheads), 'idealists' and 'internationalists' (UNO, pseudo-allies). By the vast majority of spectators, its moral won't be stated baldly, or even seen clearly, because of its mythic quality and its ambivalence. But, as Richard Hofstadter remarks, 'It is the use of paranoiad modes of expression by more or less normal people that makes the phenomenon significant.' It's probably no coincidence that the themes emerging from *This Island Earth* exactly fit the titles of Richard Hofstadter's books: his (Pulitzer Prize-winning) *Anti-Intellectualism In American Life* and his *The Paranoiad Style In American Politics*.

Certainly, Hofstadter relates these themes to socio-cultural 'images', and doesn't go on to make, as we have done, a further link with themes culled from depth-psychology. The (necessarily summary) sketch of family tensions which, though not unique, seem in America to be a conspicuous or prevalent variety of universal conflicts, is congruent with that offered by Nathan Leites and Martha Wolfenstein (in, particularly, Chapter Two of *Movies: A Psychological Study*) and by Geoffrey Gorer in *The Americans* (especially his opening chapters). This is not to imply that the family situation is the simple cause of which socio-political thinking is the simple effect. The total social situation also influences the family situation. In no way are we hinting at a 'simplistic' reduction of politics and art alike to infantile conflicts.

Nor is our exegesis meant to suggest that 'the' American character is fixed, once and for all, in the conflicts we have described. Obviously the film's relevance to individual Americans is as 'artificial' as all cultural myths about character—(though a myth is not a cliché, and may be as false, yet as significant, as the statistic that the average adult has 1.1 children). For these characteristic myths evolve as fast as the culture evolves. Wolfenstein and Leites point to the fact that in American movies of the late '40's two situations predominate. In films which are overtly about family relationships, fathers and sons are usually presented as being on idyllic terms, whereas melodramas abound in situations in which apparently benevolent father-figures turn out to be treacherous and ruthless. The emphasis was significantly different, or, indeed, reversed, in French and English films (which also differed from each other). *This Island Earth* is an example of this genre.

Nonetheless, during the '50's, father-son conflicts, which had hitherto been idealized away (and only paraphrased in melodrama) now began to appear overtly; notable examples included Nicholas Ray's *Rebel Without a Cause*, and John Frankenheimer's *The Young Stranger*. One reason for the immense prestige of Arthur Miller's plays *All My Sons* and *Death of a Salesman* is that they were among the first plays to combine overt father-son conflicts with other central, and rarely acknowledged, conflicts in the American conscience. During the '50's, too, many films which weren't overtly about father-son conflicts made references suggesting an awareness, at least by the makers, and certainly by many spectators, of the underlying 'Freudian' pattern. Thus Marlon Brando in *The*

Wild One, while being beaten up by the head of the lynch-mob, mumbles, 'My old man could whup me harder'n that', and Brando, again, in *One Eyed Jacks*, is pitted against the apparently benevolent, actually evil 'Dad' Longworth. Westerns abound in stories about ambivalent love-hate relationships between young men and older men who father them (*Tribute To a Bad Man*, *The Tin Star*). It's fair to say that American movies of the' 50's are preoccupied with parent-child and sibling realtionships, while adult sexual conflicts are treated with vastly less sophistication and intensity. By the '60's the situation seems to have been stabilised, or, at least, little further development is suggested from American movies.

It's clearly an advance in self-consciousness if covert conflicts can be made overt (and a regression of overt conflicts become covert).

In a parallel way, the paranoiad undertow in *This Island Earth* becomes the subject of Stanley Kubrick's *Dr. Strangelove or How I Learned to Stop Worrying and Love the Bomb*. The connections between Kubrick's film and Hofstadter's remarks on 'the paranoiad style' are very clear; General Jack D. Ripper, with his fear of fluoridation is a pantechnicon of political paranoias, and, for that matter, of related sexual ones.

But the philosophical and psychoanalytical catchment-areas of *This Island Earth* are not its whole story. It is, also, a story about these people, these worlds, in outer space.

Citations and References

AGATE, James, *Around Cinemas*, Home & Van Thal Ltd., 1946.

AGATE, James, *Around Cinemas, Second Series*, Home & Van Thal Ltd., 1948.

AGEE, James, *Agee on Films: Vol. I, Reviews and Comments*, Beacon Press, 1964.

AGEL, Henri, *Miroirs de l'Insolite dans le Cinéma Français*, Editions du Cerf, 1958.

AGEL, Henri, *Les Grands Cinéastes*, Editions Universitaires, 1961.

AGER, Cecilia, *Camille*, in COOKE, Alastair, ed., *Garbo and the Nightwatchman.*

ALWYN, Sir William, in Interview, *The Sunday Times*, 1962.

ANDERSON, Lindsay, *The Last Sequence of On The Waterfront*, in *Sight and Sound*, Jan.–March 1955.

ANON, *Run of the Arrow*, in *Monthly Film Bulletin*, No. 282, July 1957.

ARISTOTLE, *On the Art of Fiction*, ed. Potts, L. J., Cambridge University Press, 1953.

ARTAUD, Antonin, *The Theatre and its Double*, Grove Press, 1958.

AYRTON, Michael, *Golden Sections*, Methuen, 1957.

BARDECHE, Maurice and BRASILLACH, Robert, *Histoire du Cinema*, André Martel, 1948.

BARRAULT, Jean-Louis, *Jean Racine: Phèdre*, Editions du Seuil, 1946.

BAZIN, André, *Qu'est-ce Que le Cinema?, Vols. 1–4*, Editions du Cerf, 1958–62.

BEAUVOIR, Simone de, *Brigitte Bardot and the Lolita Syndrome*, Andre Deutsch and Weidenfeld and Nicolson, 1960.

BELL, Daniel, *The End of Ideology*, The Free Press, 1960.

BENTON, Robert and NEWMAN, David, *The New Sentimentality*, in *Esquire*, July 1964.

BERGER, John, *Clouzot as Delilah* in *Sight and Sound*, Spring 1958.

BERGLER, Edmund, *Counterfeit-Sex*, Evergreen Press, 1961.

BERNHARDT, Sarah, cited in VAN THAL, Herbert, *James Agate: An Anthology*, Rupert Hart-Davis, 1961.

BRUNIUS, Jacques, *Experimental Film in France*, in MANVELL, Roger, ed., *Experiment in the Film*, Grey Walls Press, 1949.

CAEN, Michael, *A Stake is a Stake* (unpublished).
CAMERON, Ian and JARVIE, Ian, *Attack on Film Criticism* in *Film*, No. 25, Oct. 1960.
CARNÉ, Marcel, cited in QUÉVAL, Jean, *Marcel Carné*, British Film Institute, 1950.
CHABROL, Claude and ROHMER, Eric, Hitchcock, Editions Universitaires, 1957.
COCTEAU, Jean, *Opium*, Peter Owen, 1957.
COCTEAU, Jean, *Orphée* (screenplay), La Parade, 1950.
COCTEAU, Jean, *Orphée* (play), in COCTEAU, Jean, *Le Grand Ecart+ Orphée*, Librairie Arthème Fayard, 1954.
COCTEAU, Jean, in FRAIGNEAU, André, *Cocteau on the Film*, Dobson, 1954.
COCTEAU, Jean, *L'Ange Heurtebise*, in LANNES, Roger, *Jean Cocteau*, Pierre Seghers, 1945.
COMFORT, Alex, *Darwin and the Naked Lady*, Routledge & Kegan Paul, 1961.
COOKE, Alastair, see under AGER.
DONIOL-VALCROZE, Jacques, *Histoire de Femmes: Gilda, Love Letters, The Razor's Edge*, in *La Revue du Cinema No. 7*, Summer 1947.
DREYER, Carl, *Reflexions sur mon Métier*, in *Cahiers du Cinema*, No. 65, Dec. 1956.
DUCA, Lo, *L'Erotisme au Cinema, Vol. I*, Jean-Jacques Pauvert, 1958.
DURGNAT, Raymond, *Eros in the Cinema*, Calder and Boyars, 1966.
DURGNAT, Raymond, *Nouvelle Vague—The First Decade*, Motion Publications, 1962.
DURGNAT, Raymond, *Standing Up for Jesus*, in *Motion*, No. 6, 1963.
DYER, Peter John, *London Festival*, in *Sight and Sound*, Winter 1960–1.
DYER, Peter John, *Evil Eden* (*La Mort dans ce Jardin*), in *Monthly Film Bulletin*, No. 298, Nov. 1958.
EISNER, Lotte, *L'Ecran Demoniaque*, Le Terrain Vague, 1966.
FIENBURGH, Wilfrid, *No Love for Johnnie*, Hutchinson, 1959.
FONDA, Jane and KAST, Pierre, *Jane*, in *Cahiers du Cinema*, No. 150/151, Dec. 1963/Jan. 1964.
FOREMAN, Carl, cited in *Carl Foreman on 'Snob' Reviewers*, in *Variety* 10th May 1963.
FOWLER, H. W. & F. G. and MCINTOSH, E., *Concise Oxford Dictionary*, Oxford University Press.
GORER, Geoffrey, *The Americans*, Grey Arrow Books, 1959.
GOZLAN, Gerard, *Les Délices de l'Ambiguité* (*Eloge d'André Bazin*), in *Positif* 46, June 1962, and *Positif* 47, July 1962.
GRIERSON, John, *Review of Reviews*, in *Sight and Sound*, July–Sept. 1954.
GRIERSON, John, in HARDY, Forsyth: *Grierson on Documentary*, Faber, 1966.
H., P., *The Big Heat*, in *Monthly Film Bulletin*, No. 243, April 1954.
HARCOURT, Peter, *German Expressionism in the Cinema* (unpublished lecture).
HEPBURN, Katharine, cited in interview in London *Evening Standard*, 1956.

HEPWORTH, Cecil M., *Those Were the Days*, in *Penguin Film Review*, No. 6, 1948.

HOBBES, Thomas, *Leviathan* (1651), Dent-Dutton Everyman's Library.

HOFSTADTER, Richard, *Anti-Intellectualism in American Life*, Jonathan Cape, 1961

HOFSTADTER, Richard, *The Paranoiad Style in American Politics*, Jonathan Cape, 1966

HOUSTON, Penelope, *The Critical Question*, in *Sight and Sound*, Autumn, 1960.

HOUSTON, Penelope, *Critics' Notebook*, in *Sight and Sound*, Spring 1961.

HOUSTON, Penelope, *L'Avventura*, in *Sight and Sound*, Winter 1960.

HOVALD, Patrice G., cited in TRUFFAUT, François, ed., *Le Courrier des Lecteurs*, in *Cahiers du Cinema*, No. 52, Nov. 1955.

HUYGHE, René, *Discovery of Art*, Thames & Hudson, 1959.

JAMES, Louis, *Fiction for the Working Man, 1830–1850*, Oxford University Press, 1963.

KAEL, Pauline, *Fantasies of the Art-House Audience*, in *Sight and Sound*, Winter 1961–2, and in *I Lost it at the Movies*, Jonathan Cape, 1966.

KAST, Pierre, *Une Production de Moebius*, in *Cahiers du Cinema*, No. 127, Jan. 1962.

KHIM, Jean-Jacques, *Orphée et le Livre des Morts Tibetain*, in *Cahiers du Cinema*, No. 106, April 1960.

KITCHIN, Lawrence, *The Drifters*, BBC Third Programme, 25th May 1964.

KRACAUER, Siegfried, *From Caligari to Hitler*, Dennis Dobson, 1947.

KYROU, Ado, *L'Amour-Erotisme au Cinéma*, Le Terrain Vague, 1958.

KYROU, Ado, *Le Surréalisme au Cinéma*, Le Terrain Vague, 1963.

KYROU, Ado, BEDOUIN, Jean-Louis, BENAYOUN, Robert, GOLDFAYN, Georges, LEGRAND, Gerard, PERET, Benjamin, ROGER, Bernard, SCHUSTER, Jean, SEGHERS, Anne, TOYEN, ZIMBACCA, Michael, *Éléments Pour l'Élargissement Irrationel d'un Film: 'Shanghai Gesture'*, in *L'Age du Cinema*, No. 4/5, Aug.–Nov. 1951.

LA CARRIERE, Joseph, *The God-Possessed*, Allen & Unwin, 1963.

LACLOS, Michel, *Le Fantastique Au Cinema*, Jean-Jacques Pauvert, 1958.

LANG, Fritz, cited in BARTLETT, Nicholas, *The Dark Struggle*, in *Film*, No. 32, Summer 1962.

LEITES, Nathan and WOLFENSTEIN, Martha, *Movies: A Psychological Study*, Free Press, 1950.

M., T., *The Face of Fu-Manchu*, in *Monthly Film Bulletin*, No. 382, Nov. 1965.

MCMULLEN, Roy, *Will The Human Face Come Back Into the Picture?* in *Realités*, January 1965.

MACNEICE, Louis, in *Collected Poems, 1925–1958*, 1959.

MACNEICE, Louis, *An Eclogue for Christmas*, in *Collected Poems, 1925–1958*, Faber, 1959.

MANVELL, Roger, *Film*, Penguin Books, 1944.

MASON, James, cited in ROUD, Richard, *An Index: Max Ophuls*, British Film Institute, 1958.

MAYER, Arthur and GRIFFITHS, Richard, *The Movies*, Paul Hamlyn, 1965.

MAYER, J. P., *British Cinemas and Their Audiences*, Dobson, 1948.
MEAD, Margaret, *The American Character*, Penguin Books, 1944.
MINCHINTON, John and LAMBERT, Gavin, *Lambert and Cocteau*, in *Sequence*, No. 13.
MORIN, Edgar, *The Stars*, Grove Press, 1960.
MOURLET, Michel, *Sur un Art Ignoré*, La Table Ronde, 1964.
MURRAY, Peter and Linda, *Dictionary of Art and Artists*, Penguin Books, 1959.
NEWTON, Eric, in *The Critics*, BBC Home Service, 1962.
OMS, Marcel, *Mon Cher, Mon Tres Cher Tourment*, in *Positif* 50/51/52, March 1963.
PABST, G. W., in DESTERNES, Jean, *Débat sur le Réalisme: Quatre Premiers Entretiens*, in *La Revue du Cinema*, No. 18, Oct. 1948.
PALINURUS, (CONNOLLY, Cyril), *The Unquiet Grave* (1943), Grey Arrow, 1963.
POWELL, Dilys, in *The Critics*, BBC Home Service, 1962.
PUDOVKIN, V. I., *Film Technique* (1929), and *Film Acting* (1933), Vision Press, 1954.
RAFT, George, *You've Got to be Tough With Hollywood*, in *Films and Filming*, July 1962.
READ, John, *L. S. Lowry*, in *Ark* 23.
REISMAN, David, GLAZER, Nathan and DENNEY, Reuel, *The Lonely Crowd*, Yale University Press, 1950.
REISZ, Karel, *Ophuls and La Ronde*, in *Sequence*, 14, 1952.
RENOIR, Jean, cited in LENNON, Peter, *Behind the Screen: An Interview With Jean Renoir*, in *The Guardian*, Nov. 9th 1961.
RENOIR, Jean, cited by VARGAS, Alain, *Tirez sur le Pianiste*, in *Cinema 60*, No. 44, March 1960.
RHODE, Eric, *Why Neo-Realism Failed*, in *Sight and Sound*, Winter 1960–1.
RHODE, Eric, *La Dolce Vita*, in *Sight and Sound*, Winter 1960–1.
RICHARDSON, Tony, *The Metteur-en-Scene*, in *Sight and Sound*, Oct.–Dec. 1954.
RIVA, Emanuelle, cited in STRICK, Philip, *Emanuelle Riva*, in *Film*, No. 33, Autumn 1962.
ROTHA, Paul and GRIFFITHS, Richard, *The Film Till Now*, Vision Press, 1949.
ROUD, Richard, *Five Films*, in *Sight and Sound*, Winter 1960–1.
ROUD, Richard, *The French Line*, in *Sight and Sound*, Autumn, 1960.
SADOUL, Georges, *Dictionnaire des Cinéastes*, Pierre Seghers, 1965.
SARRIS, Andrew, *The American Cinema*, in *Film Culture*, No. 28, Spring 1963.
SARRIS, Andrew, *Luis Bunuel, The Devil and the Nun, Viridiana*, in *Movie*, No. 1, June 1962.
SARRIS, Andrew, *Dialogue of a Schizo-Critic*, in *New York Film Bulletin*, No. 45, 1961.
SEGUIN, Louis and TAILLEUR, Roger, *Venice 60, de A à V*, in *Positif*, No. 36, Nov. 1960.

STERNBERG, Joseph Von, *Fun in a Chinese Laundry*, Macmillan, New York, 1965.
TERRY, Ellen, in VAN THAL, Herbert, ed., *James Agate: An Anthology*, Rupert Hart-Davis, 1961.
THOMPSON, Denys, cited in *The Times Educational Supplement*, 1960.
TOROK, J.-P., *Le Cadavre Exquis*, in *Positif*, No. 40, July 1961.
USTINOV, Peter, cited in BACHMANN, Gideon, Ustinov, *Interview* in *Film*, No. 30, Winter 1961.
VIDOR, King, *A Tree is a Tree*, Longmans, Green, 1954.
VISCONTI, Luchino, *Visconti Talks About Rocco*, in *Continental Film Review*, Sept. 1961.
WEIGHTMAN, J. G., *An Uncertain Talent*, in *The Twentieth Century*, Dec. 1958.
WINNINGTON, Richard, *Drawn and Quartered*, Saturn Press, 1948.
WOOD, Robin, *Hitchcock's Films*, Tantivy Press-Zwemmer, 1965.

Index

This index follows strict alphabetical order, but otherwise respects custom rather than logic, giving the title by which the film is usually referred to in serious English film criticism (with other useful titles in brackets). Thus French titles are usually given in French, with an English title where that departs from the French sense. English titles are given for all foreign languages other than French, except where the film never acquired an English title, or is usually referred to by its foreign title (e.g. Antonioni's *Cronaca di un Amore* and *L'Avventura*).